AUTHOR'S GUIDE TO JOURNALS
IN SOCIOLOGY & RELATED FIELDS

Author's Guide to Journals Series

Author's Guide to Journals in the Health Field
Edited by Donald Ardell and John James

Author's Guide to Journals in Law, Criminal Justice & Criminology
Edited by Roy Mersky, Robert Berring, and James McCue

Author's Guide to Journals in Psychology, Psychiatry & Social Work
Edited by Allan Markle and Roger C. Rinn

Author's Guide to Journals in Sociology & Related Fields
Edited by Marvin B. Sussman, Ph.D.

AUTHOR'S GUIDE TO JOURNALS
in sociology &
related fields

Edited by

Marvin B. Sussman, Ph.D.

THE HAWORTH PRESS, NEW YORK

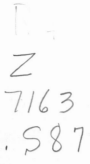

Z
7163
.S87

The Haworth Press, 149 Fifth Avenue, New York, New York 10010

Library of Congress Cataloging in Publication Data

Sussman, Marvin B
    Author's guide to journals in sociology & related fields.

    (Author's guide to journals series)
    Includes index.
    1. Social sciences--Periodicals--Directories. 2. Psychology--Periodicals--Directories. 3. Sociology--Periodicals--Directories. 4. Social science literature--Publishing--United States--Directories. 5. American periodicals--Directories.
I. Title. II. Series.
Z7163.S87 [H1]   016.3'005   78-1952
ISBN 0-917724-03-8

Printed in the United States of America

CONTENTS

ACKNOWLEDGMENTS

Special appreciation and thanks are due to Judy MacKintosh, Marcia Periman, and Pam Poolos, staff members in the Department of Medical Social Sciences, who worked as a team in preparing the materials for publication. They did the job with humor, exactitude, patience, and understanding.

INTRODUCTION

Today the "Publish or Perish" decree is alive and controlling.

Outstanding teachers are not receiving tenure. A typical message given to the academic is: "Your teaching is outstanding and, we might say, even brilliant, but we are sorely disappointed that your contribution in terms of publications has not come up to the expectations we had for you."

And so it goes. The script is played over and over again, until how to publish more and where to publish it now becomes the primary concern of otherwise dedicated teachers.

This volume is designed to provide sociologists and social scientists in related fields with a wider variety of publishing opportunities. The notion behind this compendium is that scholars can successfully increase their number of publications if they pay more attention to the "fit" or "match" between the subject of their research and writing to the current interests and scope of specialized sets of individual scholarly journals.

The *Author's Guide* provides over 350 profiles of scholarly journals in sociology and related fields. Each profile includes detailed information for the publishing scholar in order that he or she might judge in finer detail the suitability of his or her manuscript for submission, and to estimate with more accuracy the probability of acceptance and/or speed of publication.

Almost all of the information obtained came from direct questionnairing of the journal editors themselves. Occasionally, no response was returned from a few editors despite repeated attempts (the usual problem in compendiums of this type), so as much information as possible was gleaned from recent samples of the journals themselves. Table I describes the areas covered in our questionnaire.

Selection of journals was determined mainly by contacting editors of those English-language journals included in *Sociological Abstracts,* and journals listed under the heading of "Sociology" in the 1976 Edition of *Ulrich's International Periodicals Directory.* Naturally, new periodicals appear all the time, but an effort was made to keep as much up to date as possible at press time.

The *Author's Guide* is not intended to endorse or otherwise support the "Publish or Perish" stance. It is, however, intended to support the view that scholarly publication is not out of harmony with top flight, classroom performance. The process of professional writing and the organization of research can and does enhance teaching effectiveness on many levels. Thus, this volume is for the beginning as well as the seasoned researcher and practitioner—a cookbook of publishing options, as well as an aid to avoid perishing.

—Marvin B. Sussman, Ph.D.

TABLE 1
Information Included for Each Journal

JOURNAL TITLE: The correct, current title of the journal.

MANUSCRIPT ADDRESS: The correct address for submitting manuscripts.

TYPE OF ARTICLES: The type of articles (research, review, theoretical, etc.) which the present editor indicates he or she will usually accept for publication.

MAJOR CONTENT AREAS: The broad topics which are of prime interest to the journal, as indicated by the journal's present editor.

TOPICS PREFERRED: A list of topics which the present editor indicates he or she currently prefers to publish.

INAPPROPRIATE TOPICS: Types of topics identified by the editor as frequently received but "wish I hadn't." Inappropriate topics usually deal with content, but other reasons may be explained in this entry.

NUMBER OF MANUSCRIPT COPIES: The number of copies of a manuscript required of the editor for review purposes.

REVIEW PERIOD: The editor's estimate of the average time interval between the time a manuscript is received and the time the author is notified whether it has been accepted or rejected. It must be noted that these are averages, and any given paper may require more or less review time.

PUBLICATION LAG TIME: The editor's estimate of the usual interval between the time an article is accepted for publication and the actual time it is published.

EARLY PUBLICATION OPTION: Whether the journal will publish an article sooner than its normal lag time. There is normally an early publication charge for this service, and the advantages gained fluctuate considerably from year to year. The editor should be contacted if additional and current information on this option is desired.

ACCEPTANCE RATE: The editor's estimate of the approximate percentage of manuscripts accepted for publication.

AUTHORSHIP RESTRICTIONS: If the editor has any restrictions as to who may publish in the journal (e.g., sociologists only, society members only, etc.)

PAGE CHARGES: If the journal has any page charges.

STYLE REQUIREMENTS: The style requirements followed by the journal.

STYLE SHEET: Whether the editor will send a copy of the journal's complete style requirements to prospective authors.

REVISED THESES: Whether M.A./Ph.D. graduates are encouraged to submit revised theses for publication.

STUDENT PAPERS: Whether "student papers" are encouraged by the editor of the journal.

REPRINT POLICY: The policy of the journal regarding the purchase of reprints. If the journal provides a quantity of free reprints, the number provided is indicated. Additional ones may usually be purchased for an extra fee. Certain journals provide copies of the journal in which the article is published instead of reprints. Where this is applicable, the notation is made "_____ journals."

SUBSCRIPTION ADDRESS: Correct address for ordering subscriptions.

ANNUAL SUBSCRIPTION RATE: Cost of individual and institutional subscriptions. It should be noted that some journals also have special rates for students, association members, etc. Since complete information on special financial arrangements could not be included for each journal, it would be advisable before ordering to check recent issues or to write to the subscription address for complete information on frequency, special supplements, availability of an annual index, etc.

INDEXED/ABSTRACTED IN: A comprehensive listing of where the journal is indexed or abstracted.

CIRCULATION: The size of the journal's circulation.

FREQUENCY: The number of times per year the journal is published.

ABBREVIATIONS USED
Abstracting and Indexing Services

A	America	CAA	Current Anthropology Abstracts
A	Ayers		
AA	Abstracts in Anthropology	CAS	Council of Abstracting Services
ABCPS	Advance Bibliography of Contents, Political Science and Government	CC	Current Contents
		CC/BSES	Current Contents/Behavioral, Social and Educational Sciences
ACA	Automatic Citation Alert		
ACP	Abstracts in Criminology and Penology	CC/BSMS	Current Contents/Behavioral, Social and Management Sciences
AEP	America's Education Press		
AES	Abstracts in English Studies	CCLP	Contents of Current Legal Periodicals
AHL	American History and Life		
AHMS	Abstracts of Hospital Management Studies	CDA	Child Development Abstracts
		CDL	Crime and Delinquency Literature
AI	Anthropological Index		
AMP	American Management Publications	CGCI	Chronicle Guidance Career Index
AMB	Abstract of Military Bibliography	CICNRD	Committee for International Coordination of National Research and Demography
APC	Abstracts of Popular Culture		
API	Alternative Press Index	CIJE	Current Index to Journals in Education
ASW	Abstracts for Social Workers		
		CINAHL	Cumulative Index to Nursing and Allied Health Literature
BA	Biological Abstracts		
BAMS	British Abstracts of Medical Sciences	CINL	Cumulative Index to Nursing Literature
BAS	Bibliography of Asian Studies	CIS	Computer and Information Systems
B-D	Biz—Dex		
BEI	British Education Index	CJA	Criminal Justice Abstracts
BI	Bibliographic Index	CJPI	Criminal Justice Periodicals Index
BIAU	Bulletin of the International Association of Universities	CLS:SWHC	Current Literature Service: Social Work in Health Care
BII	Black Information Index		
BIS	Biosciences Information Service	CMHR	Community Mental Health Review
BPAIS	Bulletin of the Public Affairs Information Service	CNRS	Centre National de Recherche Scientifique
BRD	Book Review Digest	CPLI	Chicago Psychoanalytic Literature Index
BRI	Book Review Index		
BRSSP	Book Review to Social Science Periodicals	CRIS	Combined Retrospective Index Sets
BSD	Bowker Serial Directories	CSPA	College Student Personnel Abstracts
BSSH	Bulletin Signaletique Sciences Humaines	CUND	Consumers Union News Digest
C	Cicred	DA	Dissertation Abstracts
CA	Chemical Abstracts	DPD	Data Processing Digest

DSHA	Deafness, Speech and Hearing Abstracts	ISI	Institute for Scientific Information
DW	Development and Welfare		
		JA	Johnson Associates
E	Education	JAMA	Journal of the American Medical Association
EA	Economic Abstracts		
EAA	Education Administration Abstracts	JASA	Journal of Alcoholism Studies Abstracts
ECEA	Exceptional Child Education Abstracts	JEL	Journal of Economic Literature
ED	Education Digest	JPC	Journal of Popular Culture
EI	Education Index		
EIA	Environmental Information Access	KRC	Kraus Reprint Company
EM	Excerpta Medica	KSTIC	Korea Science and Technical Information Center
EMY	Educational Media Yearbook		
EP	Environment Periodicals		
EPB	Environmental Periodicals Bibliography	LH	Librarian's Handbook
		LLA	Language and Language Abstracts
EY	Europa Yearbook		
		LLBA	Language and Language Behavior Abstracts
G	Grinstein		
GA	Geographical Abstracts	LMP	Literary Market Place
GB	Grantsman's Bibliography		
GPE	Guide to Periodicals in Education	M	Medfact
		MC	Management Contents
GPPS	Government and Public Policy Series	MCR	Medical Care Review
		MIG	Marketing Information Guide
GRBHH	Guide to Reviews of Books From and About Hispanic America	MLA	Modern Language Association
		MMRI	Multi-Media Reviews Index
		MR	Management Research
		MRA	Mental Retardation Abstracts
HA	Historical Abstracts	MRSTMA	Mathematical Reviews and Statistical Theory and Method Abstracts
HWW	H. W. Wilson		
HLI	Hospital Literature Index		
HPG	Helping Person in Group	MSRS	Medical Socioeconomic Research Studies
HRA	Human Resources Abstracts		
HS	Historical Studies		
HSSI	Humanities and Social Science Index	N	Nexus
		OR/MS	Operations Research/ Management Science
IAB	International African Bibliography		
IBS	International Bibliography of Sociology	PA	Psychiatric Abstracts
		PA	Psychological Abstracts
IBSS	International Bibliography of Social Science	PAIS	Public Affairs Information Service
IDL	Index to Dental Literature	PHR	Public Health Review
IEJ	Index of Economic Journals	PHRA	Poverty and Human Resources Abstracts
II	International Index		
ILP	Index to Legal Periodicals	PI	Philosophers Index
IM	Index Medicus	PMA	Personnel Management Abstracts
IN	Index to Nursing		
INI	International Nursing Index	PRG	Psychological Readers Guide
IPSA	International Political Science Abstracts	PRR	Peace Research Reviews
		PS	Policy Sciences
IRPL	Index to Religious Periodical Literature	PS	Political Science
		PSG	Political Science & Government
ISA	Information Science Abstracts		

PTA	Personnel and Training Abstracts	SUSA	Sage Urban Studies Abstracts
		SWA	Social Work Abstracts
RA	Reading Abstracts	T-A	Trans-Action
RBP	Repertoire Bibliographique de la Philosophie	TL	Theologische Literaturzeitung
		TMA	Top Management Abstracts
RG	Reader's Guide		
RGPL	Readers Guide to Periodical Literature	UAA	Urban Affairs Abstracts
		UB	UNESCO Bibliography
RIBA/ARPA	RIBA/Annual Review of Periodical Articles	UCIS	University Center for International Studies
RL	Rehabilitation Literature	UIPD	Ulrich's International Periodicals Directory
RRBC	R. R. Bowker Co.		
RTA	Religious and Theological Abstracts	UIS	Ulrich's Irregular Serials
		UM	University Microfilms
		UNESCOSA	UNESCO Sociological Abstracts
S	Strasburg		
SA	Sociological Abstracts	URS	Universal References System
SCI	Science Citation Index	USPD	U.S. Political Documents
SEA	Social Education Abstracts	USPSD	U.S. Political Science Documents
SES	Social and Educational Sciences		
SPAA	Sage Public Administration Abstracts	WAERSA	World Agricultural Economics and Rural Sociology Abstracts
SPD	Standard Periodicals Directory		
SS	Social Science	WCIS	Wilson Company Indexing Service
SSCA	Sutomatic Subject Citation Alert	WFSD	World Future Society Directory
SSCI	Social Sciences Citation Index		
SSCR	Social Science Citation Review	WRA	Work Related Abstracts
SSHI	Social Sciences and Humanities Index	WSA	Women Studies Abstracts
SSI	Social Sciences Index	XMS	Xerox Microfilm Series

ABBREVIATIONS USED
Style Manuals

AAA	American Anthropological Association	Chicago	A Manual of Style, University of Chicago Press
APA	American Psychological Association	HLRA	Harvard Law Review Association
		IM	Index Medicus
		JAMA	Journal of the American Medical Association
ASA	American Sociological Association	MLA	Modern Language Association

*

STYLE MANUAL PUBLISHERS

If authors cannot locate certain style manuals in their libraries or through university bookstores, inquire at these publishers' addresses.

AAA   American Anthropological Association
Publications Department
1703 New Hampshire Avenue, N.W.
Washington, DC 20009

APA   American Psychological Association
Publications Department
Publication Manual of the APA, 2nd Ed., 1974
1200 Seventeenth Street, N.W.
Washington, DC 20036

ASA   American Sociological Association
Publications Department
1722 North Street N.W.
Washington, DC 20036

Chicago   University of Chicago Press
A Manual of Style
5801 Ellis Avenue
Chicago, IL 60637

Ind Med   *Index Medicus*
U.S. Government Printing Office
Washington, DC 20402

JAMA   American Medical Association
JAMA Style Book and Editorial Manual
535 North Dearborn Street
Chicago, IL 60610

JOURNAL TITLE: ACADEMY OF MANAGEMENT JOURNAL

MANUSCRIPT ADDRESS: Dr. L.L. Cummings, Editor
Graduate School of Business
University of Wisconsin
Madison, WI 53706
TYPE OF ARTICLES: Research articles

MAJOR CONTENT AREAS: Administrative behavior, bureaucracy, groups,
sociology of work, professions, leadership,
human organizations, industrial sociology,
economy and society
TOPICS PREFERRED: Management

INAPPROPRIATE TOPICS: Not given

NUMBER OF MANUSCRIPT COPIES:	3	PAGE CHARGES:	No
REVIEW PERIOD:	1-2 months	STYLE REQUIREMENTS:	Not given
PUBLICATION LAG TIME:	12 months	STYLE SHEET:	Yes
EARLY PUBLICATION OPTION:	No	REVISED THESES:	No
ACCEPTANCE RATE:	12%	STUDENT PAPERS:	No
AUTHORSHIP RESTRICTIONS:	No	REPRINT POLICY:	0

SUBSCRIPTION ADDRESS: Dr. Dennis F. Ray, Business Manager
Graduate School of Business
University of Wisconsin-Madison
Madison, WI 53706
ANNUAL SUBSCRIPTION RATE: $20 individual, Not given institutional
INDEXED/ABSTRACTED IN: BPA, APA, PMA

CIRCULATION: 5300   FREQUENCY: Quarterly

JOURNAL TITLE: ACTA CRIMINOLOGICA

MANUSCRIPT ADDRESS: Centre International de Criminologie
Comparée, 3150, Jean-Brillant
Université de Montréal
Montréal, Canada
TYPE OF ARTICLES: Research articles, case studies

MAJOR CONTENT AREAS: Administrative behavior, adolescence, alcoholism & drug abuse, criminology, delinquency
& crime, deviant behavior, law, poverty,
inequality, and policy, rehabilitation
TOPICS PREFERRED: Every criminological topic

INAPPROPRIATE TOPICS: Not given

NUMBER OF MANUSCRIPT COPIES:	1	PAGE CHARGES:	No
REVIEW PERIOD:	10 days	STYLE REQUIREMENTS:	ASA
PUBLICATION LAG TIME:	Variable	STYLE SHEET:	Yes
EARLY PUBLICATION OPTION:	Yes	REVISED THESES:	Yes
ACCEPTANCE RATE:	Not given	STUDENT PAPERS:	Yes
AUTHORSHIP RESTRICTIONS:	No	REPRINT POLICY:	Not given

SUBSCRIPTION ADDRESS: Presses de l'Université de Montréal
2910, Edouard-Montpetit
Montréal, Canada

ANNUAL SUBSCRIPTION RATE: $5 individual, $5 institutional
INDEXED/ABSTRACTED IN: PL, USR

CIRCULATION: 1000   FREQUENCY: Semiannually

JOURNAL TITLE: ACTA SOCIOLOGICA

MANUSCRIPT ADDRESS: Department of Social Policy
University of Helsinki, Franzeninkatu 13
SF-00500, Helsinki 50, Finland

TYPE OF ARTICLES: Theoretical articles, review articles, research
articles, commentaries, unsolicited book reviews,
case studies

MAJOR CONTENT AREAS: Anthropology, bureaucracy, collective behavior,
communes, economy and society, general sociology,
modernization, social conflict, social ideology,
social issues, social policy

TOPICS PREFERRED: Scandinavian research topics

INAPPROPRIATE TOPICS: Not given

NUMBER OF MANUSCRIPT COPIES: 2   PAGE CHARGES: No
REVIEW PERIOD: 1-3 monthsSTYLE REQUIREMENTS: ASA
PUBLICATION LAG TIME: 4-8 months   STYLE SHEET: Yes
EARLY PUBLICATION OPTION: Yes   REVISED THESES: No
ACCEPTANCE RATE: 50%   STUDENT PAPERS: No
AUTHORSHIP RESTRICTIONS: No   REPRINT POLICY: 50

SUBSCRIPTION ADDRESS: Universitetsfurlaget
PO Box 7508 Skillebekk
Oslo 2 Norway

ANNUAL SUBSCRIPTION RATE: $32 individual , $32 institutional
INDEXED/ABSTRACTED IN: SA

CIRCULATION: 2500   FREQUENCY: Quarterly

JOURNAL TITLE: ADMINISTRATION AND SOCIETY

MANUSCRIPT ADDRESS: William Eddy, Gary Wamsley
School of Administration
University of Missouri
Kansas City, MO 64110

TYPE OF ARTICLES: Research articles, theoretical articles, review
articles, case studies, commentaries

MAJOR CONTENT AREAS: Administrative behavior, bureaucracy, human
organizations, organizations, social policy,
systems analysis

TOPICS PREFERRED: Not given

INAPPROPRIATE TOPICS: Not given

NUMBER OF MANUSCRIPT COPIES: 3   PAGE CHARGES: No
REVIEW PERIOD: Not given STYLE REQUIREMENTS: Not given
PUBLICATION LAG TIME: Not given   STYLE SHEET: Yes
EARLY PUBLICATION OPTION: No   REVISED THESES: Not given
ACCEPTANCE RATE: Not given   STUDENT PAPERS: No
AUTHORSHIP RESTRICTIONS: No   REPRINT POLICY: 24

SUBSCRIPTION ADDRESS: Sage Publications, Inc.
275 S Beverly Drive
Beverly Hills, CA 90212

ANNUAL SUBSCRIPTION RATE: $13.50 individual, $22.50 institutional
INDEXED/ABSTRACTED IN: IPSA, ABC PS, HRA, SPAA, SUSA

CIRCULATION: Not given   FREQUENCY: Quarterly

JOURNAL TITLE: ADMINISTRATION IN MENTAL HEALTH

MANUSCRIPT ADDRESS: PO Box 2088
Rockville, MD 20852

TYPE OF ARTICLES: Theoretical articles, case studies, research articles, commentaries, review articles

MAJOR CONTENT AREAS: Administrative behavior, alcoholism & drug abuse, bureaucracy, epidemiology, human organizations, leadership, mental health & illness, organizations, public health

TOPICS PREFERRED: The organization and administration of mental health services

INAPPROPRIATE TOPICS: Not given

NUMBER OF MANUSCRIPT COPIES:	3	PAGE CHARGES:	No
REVIEW PERIOD:	4 months	STYLE REQUIREMENTS:	Not given
PUBLICATION LAG TIME:	6 months	STYLE SHEET:	Yes
EARLY PUBLICATION OPTION:	No	REVISED THESES:	No
ACCEPTANCE RATE:	15%	STUDENT PAPERS:	No
AUTHORSHIP RESTRICTIONS:	No	REPRINT POLICY:	1 journal

SUBSCRIPTION ADDRESS: PO Box 2088
Rockville, MD 20852

ANNUAL SUBSCRIPTION RATE: $14 individual, $19 institutional
INDEXED/ABSTRACTED IN: SWA, IM

CIRCULATION: 2000   FREQUENCY: Semiannually

JOURNAL TITLE: ADMINISTRATIVE SCIENCE QUARTERLY

MANUSCRIPT ADDRESS: Professor Thomas M. Lodahl, Editor
314 Malott Hall
Cornell University
Ithaca, NY 14853

TYPE OF ARTICLES: Research articles, theoretical articles, case studies, commentaries, unsolicited book reviews, review articles

MAJOR CONTENT AREAS: Administrative behavior, social theory, educational sociology, groups, human organizations, industrial sociology, occupations & careers, social institutions

TOPICS PREFERRED: Organizational behavior, book review essays

INAPPROPRIATE TOPICS: Not given

NUMBER OF MANUSCRIPT COPIES:	4	PAGE CHARGES:	No
REVIEW PERIOD:	3 weeks	STYLE REQUIREMENTS:	Chicago Manuscript
PUBLICATION LAG TIME:	Not given	STYLE SHEET:	Yes
EARLY PUBLICATION OPTION:	Yes	REVISED THESES:	Yes
ACCEPTANCE RATE:	10%	STUDENT PAPERS:	No
AUTHORSHIP RESTRICTIONS:	No	REPRINT POLICY:	Not given

SUBSCRIPTION ADDRESS: Business Manager
314 Malott Hall
Cornell University
Ithaca, NY 14853

ANNUAL SUBSCRIPTION RATE: $14 individual, $22 institutional
INDEXED/ABSTRACTED IN: MR, PAIS, WCIS, PA, PS, SA, T-A, AMAP, PMA, EAA, IPSA

CIRCULATION: 4800   FREQUENCY: Quarterly

JOURNAL TITLE: ADOLESCENCE

MANUSCRIPT ADDRESS: Libra Publishers, Inc.
PO Box 165
391 Willets Road
Roslyn Heights, L.I., NY 11577

TYPE OF ARTICLES: Research articles, case studies, theoretical
articles, commentaries

MAJOR CONTENT AREAS: Adolescence, aging and aged, alcoholism & drug
abuse, counseling, criminology, delinquency &
crime, deviant behavior, educational sociology

TOPICS PREFERRED: Not given

INAPPROPRIATE TOPICS: Not given

NUMBER OF MANUSCRIPT COPIES:	2	PAGE CHARGES:	No
REVIEW PERIOD:	2-3 weeks	STYLE REQUIREMENTS:	Chicago Manuscript
PUBLICATION LAG TIME:	2 years	STYLE SHEET:	Yes
EARLY PUBLICATION OPTION:	Yes	REVISED THESES:	No
ACCEPTANCE RATE:	40%	STUDENT PAPERS:	No
AUTHORSHIP RESTRICTIONS:	No	REPRINT POLICY:	Not given

SUBSCRIPTION ADDRESS: Libra Publishers, Inc.
PO Box 165
391 Willets Road
Roslyn Heights, L.I., NY 11577

ANNUAL SUBSCRIPTION RATE: $16 individual, $20 institutional
INDEXED/ABSTRACTED IN: Not given

CIRCULATION: 3000   FREQUENCY: Quarterly

JOURNAL TITLE: AFRICA TODAY

MANUSCRIPT ADDRESS: Mr. Edward A. Hawley, Executive Editor
Africa Today, c/o GSIS
University of Denver
Denver, CO 80208

TYPE OF ARTICLES: Research articles, case studies, theoretical
articles, review articles, commentaries,
unsolicited book reviews

MAJOR CONTENT AREAS: Anthropology, economy and society, human
organizations, political sociology, race
relations, rural sociology, social change, social
conflict, social issues, social movements

TOPICS PREFERRED: Articles on contemporary Africa. Sociological
articles with political or economic implications

INAPPROPRIATE TOPICS: Not given

NUMBER OF MANUSCRIPT COPIES:	2	PAGE CHARGES:	No
REVIEW PERIOD:	3-9 mos.	STYLE REQUIREMENTS:	Chicago Manuscript
PUBLICATION LAG TIME:	3-9 months	STYLE SHEET:	Yes
EARLY PUBLICATION OPTION:	No	REVISED THESES:	Acceptable
ACCEPTANCE RATE:	30-35%	STUDENT PAPERS:	No
AUTHORSHIP RESTRICTIONS:	No	REPRINT POLICY:	5 journals

SUBSCRIPTION ADDRESS: Graduate School of International Studies
University of Denver
Denver, CO 80208

ANNUAL SUBSCRIPTION RATE: $8 individual, $12 institutional
INDEXED/ABSTRACTED IN: PAIS, SSCI, SSI, IAB, HA, AHL

CIRCULATION: 2000   FREQUENCY: Quarterly

JOURNAL TITLE: ALTERED STATES OF CONSCIOUSNESS

MANUSCRIPT ADDRESS: Dr. Colin Martindale, Editor
Department of Psychology
University of Maine
Orono, ME   04473

TYPE OF ARTICLES: Research articles, theoretical articles, review
articles, commentaries, case studies

MAJOR CONTENT AREAS: Alcoholism and drug abuse, anthropology, evolution,
human development, sociology of knowledge, mental
health and illness, religion, sociobiology

TOPICS PREFERRED: States of consciousness

INAPPROPRIATE TOPICS: Not given

NUMBER OF MANUSCRIPT COPIES: 3   PAGE CHARGES: No
REVIEW PERIOD: 2 months STYLE REQUIREMENTS: Not given
PUBLICATION LAG TIME: 6 months   STYLE SHEET: Yes
EARLY PUBLICATION OPTION: No   REVISED THESES: Yes
ACCEPTANCE RATE: 50%   STUDENT PAPERS: No
AUTHORSHIP RESTRICTIONS: No   REPRINT POLICY: 20

SUBSCRIPTION ADDRESS: Baywood Publishing Company, Inc.
120 Marine Street
Farmingdale, NY 11735

ANNUAL SUBSCRIPTION RATE: $35 individual, $35 institutional
INDEXED/ABSTRACTED IN: Not given

CIRCULATION: 300   FREQUENCY: Quarterly

JOURNAL TITLE: AMERICAN ANTHROPOLOGIST

MANUSCRIPT ADDRESS: Richard B. Woodbury, Editor-in-Chief
Machmer Hall, University of Massachusetts
Amherst, MA 01003

TYPE OF ARTICLES: Theoretical articles, review articles, research
articles, surveys, syntheses, commentaries

MAJOR CONTENT AREAS: Anthropology, demography, ecology, ethnic groups,
evolution, human organizations, social change,
social structure, sociobiology, values, economy
and society

TOPICS PREFERRED: Not given

INAPPROPRIATE TOPICS: Not given

NUMBER OF MANUSCRIPT COPIES: 4   PAGE CHARGES: No
REVIEW PERIOD: 4 months STYLE REQUIREMENTS: AAA
PUBLICATION LAG TIME: 8 months   STYLE SHEET: Yes
EARLY PUBLICATION OPTION: No   REVISED THESES: No
ACCEPTANCE RATE: 15%   STUDENT PAPERS: No
AUTHORSHIP RESTRICTIONS: No   REPRINT POLICY: Not given

SUBSCRIPTION ADDRESS: 1703 New Hampshire Avenue, NW
Washington, DC 20009

ANNUAL SUBSCRIPTION RATE: $30 individual, $40 institutional
INDEXED/ABSTRACTED IN: EM, HA, A, AA, SSHI, CA, ABC PS, CC: BH&MS

CIRCULATION: Not given   FREQUENCY: Quarterly

JOURNAL TITLE: AMERICAN EDUCATIONAL RESEARCH JOURNAL

MANUSCRIPT ADDRESS: Dr. Maryellen McSweeney, Editor
College of Education
Michigan State University
East Lansing, MI 48823

TYPE OF ARTICLES: Research articles, case studies, theoretical
articles

MAJOR CONTENT AREAS: Topics relating to sociology of education:
collective behavior, economy and society,
political sociology, social conflict, social
ideology, social issues, social policy

TOPICS PREFERRED: Educational research

INAPPROPRIATE TOPICS: Not given

NUMBER OF MANUSCRIPT COPIES: 3   PAGE CHARGES: No
REVIEW PERIOD: 9 months   STYLE REQUIREMENTS: APA
PUBLICATION LAG TIME: 6 months   STYLE SHEET: Yes
EARLY PUBLICATION OPTION: No   REVISED THESES: No
ACCEPTANCE RATE: 20%   STUDENT PAPERS: No
AUTHORSHIP RESTRICTIONS: No   REPRINT POLICY: 50

SUBSCRIPTION ADDRESS: Publications
American Educational Research Association
1126 16th Street NW
Washington, DC 20036

ANNUAL SUBSCRIPTION RATE: $12 individual, $14 institutional
INDEXED/ABSTRACTED IN: SPD, LMP, EY, CGCI, LH, PA, EMY, EAA

CIRCULATION: 14,000   FREQUENCY: Quarterly

JOURNAL TITLE: AMERICAN BEHAVIORAL SCIENTIST

MANUSCRIPT ADDRESS: Sage Publications
275 S Beverly Drive
Beverly Hills, CA 90212

TYPE OF ARTICLES: Research articles, theoretical articles

MAJOR CONTENT AREAS: Each issue is devoted to a topic in interdisciplinary social science

TOPICS PREFERRED: Not given

INAPPROPRIATE TOPICS: Not given

NUMBER OF MANUSCRIPT COPIES: Not given   PAGE CHARGES: No
REVIEW PERIOD: Not given STYLE REQUIREMENTS: Not given
PUBLICATION LAG TIME: Not given   STYLE SHEET: Yes
EARLY PUBLICATION OPTION: No   REVISED THESES: Not given
ACCEPTANCE RATE: Not given   STUDENT PAPERS: No
AUTHORSHIP RESTRICTIONS: Yes   REPRINT POLICY: 24

SUBSCRIPTION ADDRESS: Sage Publications
275 S Beverly Drive
Beverly Hills, CA 90212

ANNUAL SUBSCRIPTION RATE: $16.80 individual, $28 institutional
INDEXED/ABSTRACTED IN: PAIS, SSA, SSCI, CC, SSI, SPAA, HRA, SA, PA,
SUSA, USPSD, UAA, EAA, ACP
CIRCULATION: Not given   FREQUENCY: Bimonthly

JOURNAL TITLE: AMERICAN JOURNAL OF COMMUNITY PSYCHOLOGY

MANUSCRIPT ADDRESS: Charles D. Spielberger, Univ. of South Florida
Department of Psychology
Tampa, FL 33620

TYPE OF ARTICLES: Research articles, theoretical articles, review articles

MAJOR CONTENT AREAS: Community, applied social, community mental health

TOPICS PREFERRED: Empirical research on community psychology

INAPPROPRIATE TOPICS: Clinical psychology, abnormal psychology, descriptions of clinical services

NUMBER OF MANUSCRIPT COPIES: Not given   PAGE CHARGES: Not given
REVIEW PERIOD: 2-4 mos. STYLE REQUIREMENTS: APA
PUBLICATION LAG TIME: 10-14 months   STYLE SHEET: Yes
EARLY PUBLICATION OPTION: No   REVISED THESES: Not given
ACCEPTANCE RATE: 35-40%   STUDENT PAPERS: Not given
AUTHORSHIP RESTRICTIONS: Not given   REPRINT POLICY: Not given

SUBSCRIPTION ADDRESS: Plenum Publishing Corp.
227 West 17th Street
New York, NY 10011

ANNUAL SUBSCRIPTION RATE: $16 individual, $32 institutional
INDEXED/ABSTRACTED IN: PA, CCSBS

CIRCULATION: 800   FREQUENCY: Not given

JOURNAL TITLE: AMERICAN JOURNAL OF ECONOMICS & SOCIOLOGY

MANUSCRIPT ADDRESS: 50 East 69th Street
New York, NY 10021

TYPE OF ARTICLES: Research articles, case studies, theoretical articles

MAJOR CONTENT AREAS: Anthropology, economy and society, general sociology, industrial sociology, rural sociology, social change, social conflict, social ideology, social institutions
TOPICS PREFERRED: Not given

INAPPROPRIATE TOPICS: Not given

NUMBER OF MANUSCRIPT COPIES: 3   PAGE CHARGES: No
REVIEW PERIOD: 3 months STYLE REQUIREMENTS: MLA
PUBLICATION LAG TIME: 12 months   STYLE SHEET: Yes
EARLY PUBLICATION OPTION: No   REVISED THESES: Yes
ACCEPTANCE RATE: 25%   STUDENT PAPERS: No
AUTHORSHIP RESTRICTIONS: Yes   REPRINT POLICY: 100

SUBSCRIPTION ADDRESS: 50 East 69th Street
New York, NY 10021

ANNUAL SUBSCRIPTION RATE: $10 individual, $10 institutional
INDEXED/ABSTRACTED IN: Not given

CIRCULATION: 10,000   FREQUENCY: Quarterly

JOURNAL TITLE: AMERICAN JOURNAL OF MENTAL DEFICIENCY

MANUSCRIPT ADDRESS: Dr. H. Carl Haywood
George Peabody College
Box 503
Nashville, TN 37203

TYPE OF ARTICLES: Research articles, case studies, unsolicited book reviews

MAJOR CONTENT AREAS: Not given

TOPICS PREFERRED: Not given

INAPPROPRIATE TOPICS: Not given

NUMBER OF MANUSCRIPT COPIES:	3	PAGE CHARGES:	No
REVIEW PERIOD:	3 months	STYLE REQUIREMENTS:	APA
PUBLICATION LAG TIME:	3 months	STYLE SHEET:	Yes
EARLY PUBLICATION OPTION:	Not given	REVISED THESES:	Yes
ACCEPTANCE RATE:	Not given	STUDENT PAPERS:	Yes
AUTHORSHIP RESTRICTIONS:	No	REPRINT POLICY:	None

SUBSCRIPTION ADDRESS: Not given

ANNUAL SUBSCRIPTION RATE: $20 individual, $40 institutional
INDEXED/ABSTRACTED IN: ECEA

CIRCULATION: 12,000   FREQUENCY: Bimonthly

JOURNAL TITLE: AMERICAN JOURNAL OF ORTHOPSYCHIATRY

MANUSCRIPT ADDRESS: 1775 Broadway
New York, NY 10019

TYPE OF ARTICLES: Research articles, theoretical articles, review articles

MAJOR CONTENT AREAS: Adolescence, aging and aged, communes, epidemiology, human development, marriage and divorce, minorities, sex roles, sexual behavior, social psychology, alcoholism & drug abuse, mental health & illness

TOPICS PREFERRED: Prevention of mental illness, articles that synthesize knowledge from the various disciplines

INAPPROPRIATE TOPICS: Not given

NUMBER OF MANUSCRIPT COPIES:	3	PAGE CHARGES:	No
REVIEW PERIOD:	3-4 mos.	STYLE REQUIREMENTS:	Not given
PUBLICATION LAG TIME:	6-8 months	STYLE SHEET:	No
EARLY PUBLICATION OPTION:	No	REVISED THESES:	No
ACCEPTANCE RATE:	15%	STUDENT PAPERS:	No
AUTHORSHIP RESTRICTIONS:	No	REPRINT POLICY:	1 journal

SUBSCRIPTION ADDRESS: 49 Sheridan Avenue
Albany, NY 12210

ANNUAL SUBSCRIPTION RATE: $16 individual, $16 institutional
INDEXED/ABSTRACTED IN: Not given

CIRCULATION: 9500   FREQUENCY: Quarterly

JOURNAL TITLE: AMERICAN JOURNAL OF PHYSICAL MEDICINE

MANUSCRIPT ADDRESS: H.D. Bowman, M.D.
Box 617
Downtown Station
Phoenix, AZ 85001

TYPE OF ARTICLES: Research articles, case studies, theoretical articles

MAJOR CONTENT AREAS: Rehabilitation

TOPICS PREFERRED: Physical medicine and rehabilitation

INAPPROPRIATE TOPICS: Not given

NUMBER OF MANUSCRIPT COPIES:	3	PAGE CHARGES:	No
REVIEW PERIOD:	6-8 weeks	STYLE REQUIREMENTS:	Not given
PUBLICATION LAG TIME:	6-8 months	STYLE SHEET:	Yes
EARLY PUBLICATION OPTION:	No	REVISED THESES:	Not given
ACCEPTANCE RATE:	50%	STUDENT PAPERS:	No
AUTHORSHIP RESTRICTIONS:	No	REPRINT POLICY:	None

SUBSCRIPTION ADDRESS: The Williams and Wilkins Company
42nd East Preston Street
Baltimore, MD 21202

ANNUAL SUBSCRIPTION RATE: $16 individual, $20 institutional

INDEXED/ABSTRACTED IN: Not given

CIRCULATION: 2000   FREQUENCY: Bimonthly

JOURNAL TITLE: AMERICAN JOURNAL OF POLITICAL SCIENCE

MANUSCRIPT ADDRESS: W. Phillips Shively, Editor
Political Science Department
University of Minnesota
Minneapolis, MN 55455

TYPE OF ARTICLES: Research articles, theoretical articles, review articles, case studies

MAJOR CONTENT AREAS: Administrative behavior, mass communication, epidemiology, human organizations, law, mass media, migration, social planning, public opinion, race relations, sex roles, social ideology, values

TOPICS PREFERRED: Not given

INAPPROPRIATE TOPICS: Not given

NUMBER OF MANUSCRIPT COPIES:	4	PAGE CHARGES:	No
REVIEW PERIOD:	12 weeks	STYLE REQUIREMENTS:	Chicago Manuscript
PUBLICATION LAG TIME:	10 months	STYLE SHEET:	No
EARLY PUBLICATION OPTION:	No	REVISED THESES:	Yes
ACCEPTANCE RATE:	10%	STUDENT PAPERS:	No
AUTHORSHIP RESTRICTIONS:	No	REPRINT POLICY:	None

SUBSCRIPTION ADDRESS: Ellis Perlman, Secretary/Treasurer
Political Science Department
University of Michigan at Flint
Flint, MI 48503

ANNUAL SUBSCRIPTION RATE: $15 individual, $22 institutional

INDEXED/ABSTRACTED IN: Not given

CIRCULATION: 3000   FREQUENCY: Quarterly

JOURNAL TITLE: THE AMERICAN JOURNAL OF PSYCHIATRY

MANUSCRIPT ADDRESS: 1700 18th Street NW
Washington, DC 20009

TYPE OF ARTICLES: Research articles, clinical articles, review
articles, theoretical articles, case studies

MAJOR CONTENT AREAS: Adolescence, aging and aged, alcoholism & drug
abuse, death & dying, delinquency & crime, groups,
health and illness, human development, minorities,
suicide, social conflict, social change

TOPICS PREFERRED: Psychiatry

INAPPROPRIATE TOPICS: Drug abuse

NUMBER OF MANUSCRIPT COPIES:	3	PAGE CHARGES:	No
REVIEW PERIOD:	4-6 mos.	STYLE REQUIREMENTS:	Not given
PUBLICATION LAG TIME:	4-6 months	STYLE SHEET:	Yes
EARLY PUBLICATION OPTION:	Yes	REVISED THESES:	No
ACCEPTANCE RATE:	20%	STUDENT PAPERS:	No
AUTHORSHIP RESTRICTIONS:	No	REPRINT POLICY:	None

SUBSCRIPTION ADDRESS: 1700 18th Street NW
Washington, DC 20009

ANNUAL SUBSCRIPTION RATE: $18 individual, $18 institutional
INDEXED/ABSTRACTED IN: ASW, BA, CA,   CINL, EM, HLI, IM, INI, NA, PA,
SSI
CIRCULATION: 30,500   FREQUENCY: Monthly

JOURNAL TITLE: AMERICAN JOURNAL OF PSYCHOLOGY

MANUSCRIPT ADDRESS: 425 Psychology Building
University of Illinois
Champaign, IL 61820

TYPE OF ARTICLES: Research articles, book reviews, theoretical
articles, review articles

MAJOR CONTENT AREAS: Clinical, developmental, all experimental
areas, industrial/organizational, social

TOPICS PREFERRED: General experimental psychology

INAPPROPRIATE TOPICS: Original "fiction"

NUMBER OF MANUSCRIPT COPIES:	Not given	PAGE CHARGES:	Not given
REVIEW PERIOD:	3-6 mos.	STYLE REQUIREMENTS:	APA
PUBLICATION LAG TIME:	6 months	STYLE SHEET:	No
EARLY PUBLICATION OPTION:	No	REVISED THESES:	Not given
ACCEPTANCE RATE:	33%	STUDENT PAPERS:	Not given
AUTHORSHIP RESTRICTIONS:	Not given	REPRINT POLICY:	Not given

SUBSCRIPTION ADDRESS: Marilyn Morey
University of Illinois Press
Champaign, IL 61820

ANNUAL SUBSCRIPTION RATE: $15 individual, Not given institutional
INDEXED/ABSTRACTED IN: PA, IM, BA, BS, CA, CCSBS, CIJE, DSHA,
JHE, LLBA, RHEA
CIRCULATION: 3500   FREQUENCY: Not given

JOURNAL TITLE: AMERICAN JOURNAL OF PSYCHOTHERAPY

MANUSCRIPT ADDRESS: 114 East 78th Street
New York, NY 10021

TYPE OF ARTICLES: Research articles

MAJOR CONTENT AREAS: All clinical areas

TOPICS PREFERRED: Psychotherapy

INAPPROPRIATE TOPICS: Not given

NUMBER OF MANUSCRIPT COPIES: Not given   PAGE CHARGES: Not given
REVIEW PERIOD: 3 months   STYLE REQUIREMENTS: Index Medicus
PUBLICATION LAG TIME: 9-12 months   STYLE SHEET: No
EARLY PUBLICATION OPTION: Yes   REVISED THESES: Not given
ACCEPTANCE RATE: 25%   STUDENT PAPERS: Not given
AUTHORSHIP RESTRICTIONS: Not given   REPRINT POLICY: Not given

SUBSCRIPTION ADDRESS: Mrs. E. Hyde, Business Manager
119-21 Metropolitan Avenue
Jamaica, NY 11415

ANNUAL SUBSCRIPTION RATE: $16 individual, Not given institutional
INDEXED/ABSTRACTED IN: PA, IM, ASW, BI, CCBS, LLBA

CIRCULATION: 4500   FREQUENCY: Not given

JOURNAL TITLE: AMERICAN JOURNAL OF SOCIOLOGY

MANUSCRIPT ADDRESS: 1130 E 59th Street
Chicago, IL 60637

TYPE OF ARTICLES: Research articles, theoretical articles

MAJOR CONTENT AREAS: Bureaucracy, demography, deviant behavior,
ethnic groups, groups, human organizations,
mental health & illness, minorities, political
sociology, population, sex roles
TOPICS PREFERRED: General theoretical and methodological issues
in sociology

INAPPROPRIATE TOPICS: Apocalyptic and panacean studies

NUMBER OF MANUSCRIPT COPIES: 3   PAGE CHARGES: No
REVIEW PERIOD: 2 months   STYLE REQUIREMENTS: Chicago Manuscript
PUBLICATION LAG TIME: 7-9 months   STYLE SHEET: Yes
EARLY PUBLICATION OPTION: No   REVISED THESES: No
ACCEPTANCE RATE: 8%   STUDENT PAPERS: No
AUTHORSHIP RESTRICTIONS: No   REPRINT POLICY: 25

SUBSCRIPTION ADDRESS: University of Chicago Press
5801 S Ellis Avenue
Chicago, IL 60637

ANNUAL SUBSCRIPTION RATE: $15 individual, $20 institutional
INDEXED/ABSTRACTED IN: SCI, SA, BRI

CIRCULATION: 11,000   FREQUENCY: Bimonthly

JOURNAL TITLE: AMERICAN POLITICAL SCIENCE REVIEW

MANUSCRIPT ADDRESS: Professor Charles O. Jones
Department of Political Science
University of Pittsburgh
Pittsburgh, PA 15260

TYPE OF ARTICLES: Research articles, theoretical articles, case
studies, review articles

MAJOR CONTENT AREAS: Administrative behavior, bureaucracy, collective
behavior, ethnic groups, groups, leadership,
migration, minorities, political sociology, social
theory, socialization, social conflict

TOPICS PREFERRED: Political science

INAPPROPRIATE TOPICS: Political commentary, personal reflections on
current events

NUMBER OF MANUSCRIPT COPIES: 4	PAGE CHARGES:	No
REVIEW PERIOD: 2 months	STYLE REQUIREMENTS:	Not given
PUBLICATION LAG TIME: 1 year	STYLE SHEET:	Yes
EARLY PUBLICATION OPTION: No	REVISED THESES:	No
ACCEPTANCE RATE: 10%	STUDENT PAPERS:	No
AUTHORSHIP RESTRICTIONS: No	REPRINT POLICY:	None

SUBSCRIPTION ADDRESS: APSA
1527 New Hampshire Avenue NW
Washington, DC 20036

ANNUAL SUBSCRIPTION RATE: Not given - individual, $50 institutional
INDEXED/ABSTRACTED IN: RGPL, IPSA, SSHI, CC:BSMS, BRI, ABC PS

CIRCULATION: 15,000   FREQUENCY: Quarterly

JOURNAL TITLE: AMERICAN POLITICS QUARTERLY

MANUSCRIPT ADDRESS: Harlan Hahn
Department of Political Science
University of Southern California
Los Angeles, CA 90007

TYPE OF ARTICLES: Research articles, theoretical articles, review
articles, case studies, commentaries

MAJOR CONTENT AREAS: Political sociology

TOPICS PREFERRED: Not given

INAPPROPRIATE TOPICS: Not given

NUMBER OF MANUSCRIPT COPIES: 3	PAGE CHARGES:	No
REVIEW PERIOD: Not given	STYLE REQUIREMENTS:	Not given
PUBLICATION LAG TIME: Not given	STYLE SHEET:	Yes
EARLY PUBLICATION OPTION: No	REVISED THESES:	Not given
ACCEPTANCE RATE: Not given	STUDENT PAPERS:	No
AUTHORSHIP RESTRICTIONS: No	REPRINT POLICY:	24

SUBSCRIPTION ADDRESS: Sage Publications
275 S Beverly Drive
Beverly Hills, CA 90212

ANNUAL SUBSCRIPTION RATE: $13.50 individual, $22.50 institutional
INDEXED/ABSTRACTED IN: SUSA, SPAA, HRA, PAIS, SSCI, CC, ABC PS,
IPSA

CIRCULATION: Not given   FREQUENCY: Quarterly

JOURNAL TITLE: AMERICAN PSYCHOLOGIST

MANUSCRIPT ADDRESS: Charles A. Kiesler, Editor
1200 17th Street, NW
Washington, DC 20036

TYPE OF ARTICLES: Archival documents, current issues in psychology
as well as empirical, theoretical, and practical
articles on broad aspects of psychology

MAJOR CONTENT AREAS: Not given

TOPICS PREFERRED: Not given

INAPPROPRIATE TOPICS: Not given

NUMBER OF MANUSCRIPT COPIES:	3	PAGE CHARGES:	No
REVIEW PERIOD:	3 months	STYLE REQUIREMENTS:	APA
PUBLICATION LAG TIME:	11 months	STYLE SHEET:	Yes
EARLY PUBLICATION OPTION:	No	REVISED THESES:	No
ACCEPTANCE RATE:	15%	STUDENT PAPERS:	No
AUTHORSHIP RESTRICTIONS:	No	REPRINT POLICY:	20

SUBSCRIPTION ADDRESS: APA
Subscription Section
1200 17th Street, NW
Washington, DC 20036

ANNUAL SUBSCRIPTION RATE: Free with membership, $18 nonmember

INDEXED/ABSTRACTED IN: PA

CIRCULATION: 51,650   FREQUENCY: Monthly

JOURNAL TITLE: THE AMERICAN SCHOLAR

MANUSCRIPT ADDRESS: 1811 Q Street, NW
Washington, DC 20009

TYPE OF ARTICLES: Commentaries, review articles, unsolicited
book reviews

MAJOR CONTENT AREAS: Not given

TOPICS PREFERRED: General

INAPPROPRIATE TOPICS: Literary

NUMBER OF MANUSCRIPT COPIES:	1	PAGE CHARGES:	No
REVIEW PERIOD:	2 weeks	STYLE REQUIREMENTS:	Chicago Manuscript
PUBLICATION LAG TIME:	3-12 months	STYLE SHEET:	No
EARLY PUBLICATION OPTION:	No	REVISED THESES:	No
ACCEPTANCE RATE:	Not given	STUDENT PAPERS:	No
AUTHORSHIP RESTRICTIONS:	No	REPRINT POLICY:	None

SUBSCRIPTION ADDRESS: 1811 Q Street, NW
Washington, DC 20009

ANNUAL SUBSCRIPTION RATE: $8 individual, $8 institutional

INDEXED/ABSTRACTED IN: Not given

CIRCULATION: 40,000   FREQUENCY: Quarterly

JOURNAL TITLE: AMERICAN SOCIETY FOR PUBLIC ADMINISTRATION (JOURNAL OF)

MANUSCRIPT ADDRESS: 1225 Connecticut Avenue, NW, Suite 300
Washington, DC 20036

TYPE OF ARTICLES: Research articles, theoretical articles, review articles

MAJOR CONTENT AREAS: Administrative behavior, anthropology, human development, leadership, organizations, social planning, society and institutions, bureaucracy, community development

TOPICS PREFERRED: Administration of government at all levels

INAPPROPRIATE TOPICS: Not given

NUMBER OF MANUSCRIPT COPIES:	3	PAGE CHARGES:	No
REVIEW PERIOD:	2 months	STYLE REQUIREMENTS:	Turabian
PUBLICATION LAG TIME:	6-12 months	STYLE SHEET:	Yes
EARLY PUBLICATION OPTION:	Yes	REVISED THESES:	No
ACCEPTANCE RATE:	10%	STUDENT PAPERS:	Yes
AUTHORSHIP RESTRICTIONS:	No	REPRINT POLICY:	3 journals

SUBSCRIPTION ADDRESS: 1225 Connecticut Avenue, NW, Suite 300
Washington, DC 20036

ANNUAL SUBSCRIPTION RATE: $25 individual, $25 institutional
INDEXED/ABSTRACTED IN: PAIS, SSI, BRI

CIRCULATION: 19,000   FREQUENCY: Bimonthly

JOURNAL TITLE: AMERICAN SOCIOLOGICAL REVIEW

MANUSCRIPT ADDRESS: Department of Sociology
University of Illinois
Urbana, IL 61801

TYPE OF ARTICLES: Research articles, theoretical articles, recent advances in methods, commentaries, case studies

MAJOR CONTENT AREAS: Administrative behavior, adolescence, aging and aged, migration, minorities, reference groups, sex roles, social change, social conflict, social interaction, urban sociology, sociometry

TOPICS PREFERRED: Anything that advances general knowledge of social behavior

INAPPROPRIATE TOPICS: Highly specialized topics

NUMBER OF MANUSCRIPT COPIES:	4	PAGE CHARGES:	No
REVIEW PERIOD:	3 months	STYLE REQUIREMENTS:	ASA
PUBLICATION LAG TIME:	6-8 months	STYLE SHEET:	Yes
EARLY PUBLICATION OPTION:	No	REVISED THESES:	No
ACCEPTANCE RATE:	10%	STUDENT PAPERS:	No
AUTHORSHIP RESTRICTIONS:	No	REPRINT POLICY:	None

SUBSCRIPTION ADDRESS: American Sociological Association
1722 N Street, N W
Washington, D C   20036

ANNUAL SUBSCRIPTION RATE: $15 individual, $30 institutional
INDEXED/ABSTRACTED IN: SA

CIRCULATION: 15,000   FREQUENCY: Bimonthly

JOURNAL TITLE: AMERICAN SOCIOLOGIST

MANUSCRIPT ADDRESS: Allen D. Grimshaw, Editor
Institute for Social Research
1022 East Third Street
Bloomington,IN 47401

TYPE OF ARTICLES: Not given

MAJOR CONTENT AREAS: Not given

TOPICS PREFERRED: Not given

INAPPROPRIATE TOPICS: Not given

NUMBER OF MANUSCRIPT COPIES:	5	PAGE CHARGES:	No
REVIEW PERIOD:	6 weeks	STYLE REQUIREMENTS:	ASA
PUBLICATION LAG TIME:	5 months	STYLE SHEET:	Yes
EARLY PUBLICATION OPTION:	No	REVISED THESES:	No
ACCEPTANCE RATE:	5%	STUDENT PAPERS:	No
AUTHORSHIP RESTRICTIONS:	No	REPRINT POLICY:	None

SUBSCRIPTION ADDRESS: American Sociological Association
1722 N Street, NW
Washington, DC 20036

ANNUAL SUBSCRIPTION RATE: $12 individual, $16 institutional
INDEXED/ABSTRACTED IN: Not given

CIRCULATION: 6000   FREQUENCY: Quarterly

JOURNAL TITLE: THE ANTIOCH REVIEW

MANUSCRIPT ADDRESS: PO Box 148
Yellow Springs, OH 45387

TYPE OF ARTICLES: Theoretical articles, commentaries, case studies, research articles, review articles, unsolicited book reviews, essays

MAJOR CONTENT AREAS: Bureaucracy, demography, economy and society, educational sociology, law, mass media, popular culture, public opinion, rehabilitation, social change, social issues, social policy

TOPICS PREFERRED: Social and cultural problems, current affairs

INAPPROPRIATE TOPICS: Pornography

NUMBER OF MANUSCRIPT COPIES:	1	PAGE CHARGES:	No
REVIEW PERIOD:	2-8 weeks	STYLE REQUIREMENTS:	Chicago Manuscript
PUBLICATION LAG TIME:	2-4 months	STYLE SHEET:	No
EARLY PUBLICATION OPTION:	No	REVISED THESES:	No
ACCEPTANCE RATE:	5%	STUDENT PAPERS:	No
AUTHORSHIP RESTRICTIONS:	No	REPRINT POLICY:	None

SUBSCRIPTION ADDRESS: PO Box 148
Yellow Springs, OH 45387

ANNUAL SUBSCRIPTION RATE: $8 individual, $8 institutional
INDEXED/ABSTRACTED IN: SSHI, PAIS, HA SA, AES, BRI, PI

CIRCULATION: 4000   FREQUENCY: Quarterly

JOURNAL TITLE: ARCHIVES EUROPÉENNES DE SOCIOLOGIE

MANUSCRIPT ADDRESS: Editor
Musée de l'Homme
F 75116 Paris
France

TYPE OF ARTICLES: Research articles, theoretical articles, commentaries, review articles

MAJOR CONTENT AREAS: Anthropology, bureaucracy, collective behavior,
death & dying, demography, deviant behavior,
minorities, human development, human organizations, social change, social conflict

TOPICS PREFERRED: Not given

INAPPROPRIATE TOPICS: Not given

NUMBER OF MANUSCRIPT COPIES:	5	PAGE CHARGES:	No
REVIEW PERIOD:	1-5 mos.	STYLE REQUIREMENTS:	Not given
PUBLICATION LAG TIME:	2-6 months	STYLE SHEET:	Yes
EARLY PUBLICATION OPTION:	No	REVISED THESES:	No
ACCEPTANCE RATE:	10%	STUDENT PAPERS:	Yes
AUTHORSHIP RESTRICTIONS:	No	REPRINT POLICY:	50

SUBSCRIPTION ADDRESS: Cambridge University Press
32 East 57th Street
New York, NY 10022

ANNUAL SUBSCRIPTION RATE: $7.50 individual, $11 institutional
INDEXED/ABSTRACTED IN: SA

CIRCULATION: 1800   FREQUENCY: Semiannually

JOURNAL TITLE: ARCHIVES OF SEXUAL BEHAVIOR

MANUSCRIPT ADDRESS: Dept.of Psychiatry and Behavioral Sciences,
Health Sciences Center, State University of
New York, Stony Brook, NY 11794

TYPE OF ARTICLES: Research articles, review articles

MAJOR CONTENT AREAS: Most areas as related to sexual behavior

TOPICS PREFERRED: Sex research, primarily human, but may
include non-human primates

INAPPROPRIATE TOPICS: Not given

NUMBER OF MANUSCRIPT COPIES:	Not given	PAGE CHARGES:	Not given
REVIEW PERIOD:	2 months	STYLE REQUIREMENTS:	Not given
PUBLICATION LAG TIME:	10-13 months	STYLE SHEET:	No
EARLY PUBLICATION OPTION:	Yes	REVISED THESES:	Not given
ACCEPTANCE RATE:	33%	STUDENT PAPERS:	Not given
AUTHORSHIP RESTRICTIONS:	Not given	REPRINT POLICY:	Not given

SUBSCRIPTION ADDRESS: Plenum Publishing Corp.
227 W 17th Street
New York, NY 10011

ANNUAL SUBSCRIPTION RATE: $19 individual, $54 institutional
INDEXED/ABSTRACTED IN: PA, IM, EM, BA, CCBS, WSA

CIRCULATION: 1000   FREQUENCY: Not given

JOURNAL TITLE: ARMED FORCES AND SOCIETY

MANUSCRIPT ADDRESS: Social Science Building
University of Chicago
1126 East 59th Street
Chicago, IL 60637

TYPE OF ARTICLES: Research articles, analytic, descriptive
articles, theoretical articles

MAJOR CONTENT AREAS: Alcoholism & drug abuse, demography, deviant
behavior, occupations & careers, organizations,
social conflict, social ideology, social
institutions, social interaction, military affairs

TOPICS PREFERRED: Military politics internationally, military
organization in society

INAPPROPRIATE TOPICS: Not given

NUMBER OF MANUSCRIPT COPIES: 3	PAGE CHARGES: No	
REVIEW PERIOD: 2 months	STYLE REQUIREMENTS: Chicago Manuscript	
PUBLICATION LAG TIME: 6-10 months	STYLE SHEET: Yes	
EARLY PUBLICATION OPTION: Not given	REVISED THESES: Yes	
ACCEPTANCE RATE: 20%	STUDENT PAPERS: No	
AUTHORSHIP RESTRICTIONS: No	REPRINT POLICY: 24	

SUBSCRIPTION ADDRESS: Social Science Building
University of Chicago
1126 East 59th Street
Chicago, IL 60637

ANNUAL SUBSCRIPTION RATE: $12 individual, $18 institutional
INDEXED/ABSTRACTED IN: SA, CLIO, CC, AMB

CIRCULATION: 2000   FREQUENCY: Quarterly

JOURNAL TITLE: ASIAN SURVEY

MANUSCRIPT ADDRESS: Mr. Leo E. Rose, Editor
University of California Press
Berkeley, CA 94720

TYPE OF ARTICLES: Research articles

MAJOR CONTENT AREAS: Administrative behavior, rural sociology, social
conflict, stratification

TOPICS PREFERRED: Asian political, social and economic developments

INAPPROPRIATE TOPICS: Not given

NUMBER OF MANUSCRIPT COPIES: 2	PAGE CHARGES: No	
REVIEW PERIOD: 2-3 mos.	STYLE REQUIREMENTS: Chicago Manuscript	
PUBLICATION LAG TIME: 6 months	STYLE SHEET: Yes	
EARLY PUBLICATION OPTION: No	REVISED THESES: Yes	
ACCEPTANCE RATE: 50%	STUDENT PAPERS: No	
AUTHORSHIP RESTRICTIONS: No	REPRINT POLICY: 25	

SUBSCRIPTION ADDRESS: University of California Press
Berkeley, CA 94720

ANNUAL SUBSCRIPTION RATE: $15 individual, $21 institutional
INDEXED/ABSTRACTED IN: PAIS, HSSI, ABC/CPS

CIRCULATION: 3500   FREQUENCY: Monthly

JOURNAL TITLE: AUSTRALIAN & NEW ZEALAND JOURNAL OF SOCIOLOGY

MANUSCRIPT ADDRESS: The Editors
Psychology & Sociology Department
University of Canterbury, Christchurch 1
New Zealand

TYPE OF ARTICLES: Research articles, theoretical articles, case studies, commentaries, review articles, research on Australia, New Zealand and the South Pacific

MAJOR CONTENT AREAS: Bureaucracy, collective behavior, demography, general sociology, human development, human organizations, industrial sociology, migration, modernization, political sociology, population

TOPICS PREFERRED: Research on Australian and New Zealand society, social class/inequality, development in the South Pacific, New Guinea, and Southeast Asia

INAPPROPRIATE TOPICS: Not given

NUMBER OF MANUSCRIPT COPIES:	3	PAGE CHARGES:	No
REVIEW PERIOD:	3 months	STYLE REQUIREMENTS:	Chicago Manuscript
PUBLICATION LAG TIME:	3 months	STYLE SHEET:	Yes
EARLY PUBLICATION OPTION:	No	REVISED THESES:	Yes
ACCEPTANCE RATE:	30%	STUDENT PAPERS:	Yes
AUTHORSHIP RESTRICTIONS:	No	REPRINT POLICY:	20

SUBSCRIPTION ADDRESS: Psychology & Sociology Department
University of Canterbury, Christchurch 1
New Zealand

ANNUAL SUBSCRIPTION RATE: $7.50 individual, $15 institutional
INDEXED/ABSTRACTED IN: SA, CC:BSES

CIRCULATION: 2000   FREQUENCY: Tri-yearly

JOURNAL TITLE: AUSTRALIAN JOURNAL OF SOCIAL ISSUES

MANUSCRIPT ADDRESS: Ronald B. Burnheim, Editor
PO Box 388
Haymarket 2000
Sydney, Australia

TYPE OF ARTICLES: Not given

MAJOR CONTENT AREAS: Not given

TOPICS PREFERRED: Social welfare, public interest, social change

INAPPROPRIATE TOPICS: Not given

NUMBER OF MANUSCRIPT COPIES:	Not given	PAGE CHARGES:	Not given
REVIEW PERIOD:	1-2 months	STYLE REQUIREMENTS:	Not given
PUBLICATION LAG TIME:	6-15 months	STYLE SHEET:	Not given
EARLY PUBLICATION OPTION:	Not given	REVISED THESES:	Not given
ACCEPTANCE RATE:	80%	STUDENT PAPERS:	Not given
AUTHORSHIP RESTRICTIONS:	Not given	REPRINT POLICY:	10

SUBSCRIPTION ADDRESS: Ronald B. Burnheim, Editor
PO Box 388
Haymarket 2000
Sydney, Australia

ANNUAL SUBSCRIPTION RATE: Not given
INDEXED/ABSTRACTED IN: Not given

CIRCULATION: 1000   FREQUENCY: Quarterly

JOURNAL TITLE: BEHAVIORAL & SOCIAL SCIENCE TEACHER

MANUSCRIPT ADDRESS: Dr. Robert Mendelsohn
Institute of Advanced Psychological Studies
Adelphi University
Garden City, NY 11530

TYPE OF ARTICLES: Research articles, theoretical articles, review
articles, commentaries, case studies, unsolicited
book reviews

MAJOR CONTENT AREAS: Adolescence, anthropology, educational sociology,
occupations & careers, social psychology,
sociology of science

TOPICS PREFERRED: Articles related to teaching strategies,
curriculum ideas for high school behavioral
sciences courses

INAPPROPRIATE TOPICS: Papers on topics in no way related to pre-college
studies

NUMBER OF MANUSCRIPT COPIES: 3	PAGE CHARGES:	No
REVIEW PERIOD: 2 months	STYLE REQUIREMENTS:	APA
PUBLICATION LAG TIME: 16 months	STYLE SHEET:	Yes
EARLY PUBLICATION OPTION: No	REVISED THESES:	Yes
ACCEPTANCE RATE: 65%	STUDENT PAPERS:	No
AUTHORSHIP RESTRICTIONS: No	REPRINT POLICY:	3

SUBSCRIPTION ADDRESS: Human Sciences Press
72 Fifth Avenue
New York , NY 10011

ANNUAL SUBSCRIPTION RATE: $6.95 individual, $15 institutional
INDEXED/ABSTRACTED IN: PA, CIJE

CIRCULATION: 1020   FREQUENCY: Semiannually

JOURNAL TITLE: BEHAVIORAL SCIENCE

MANUSCRIPT ADDRESS: University of Louisville
PO Box 35260
Louisville, KY 40232

TYPE OF ARTICLES: Research articles, theoretical articles,
and applications

MAJOR CONTENT AREAS: Anthropology, bureaucracy, collective behavior,
mass communication, mental health and illness,
deviant behavior, ecology, groups, human development, human organizations, industrial sociology

TOPICS PREFERRED: General systems research. Articles which generalize
across types and levels of systems, living, and
non-living; especially quantitative articles

INAPPROPRIATE TOPICS: Dissertations, review articles, opinion pieces

NUMBER OF MANUSCRIPT COPIES: 3	PAGE CHARGES:	No
REVIEW PERIOD: 2-6 mos.	STYLE REQUIREMENTS:	APA
PUBLICATION LAG TIME: 2-4 months	STYLE SHEET:	Yes
EARLY PUBLICATION OPTION: Yes	REVISED THESES:	Acceptable
ACCEPTANCE RATE: 15%	STUDENT PAPERS:	Acceptable
AUTHORSHIP RESTRICTIONS: No	REPRINT POLICY:	None

SUBSCRIPTION ADDRESS: University of Louisville
PO Box 35260
Louisville, KY 40232

ANNUAL SUBSCRIPTION RATE: $21 individual, $35 institutional
INDEXED/ABSTRACTED IN: PA, SC, CAS, ABC, BA, USPSIS

CIRCULATION: 4000   FREQUENCY: Bimonthly

JOURNAL TITLE: BEHAVIOR RESEARCH METHODS & INSTRUMENTATION

MANUSCRIPT ADDRESS: Dr. Joseph B. Sidowski
Department of Psychology
University of South Florida
Tampa, FL 33620

TYPE OF ARTICLES: Descriptions of instruments, systems, computer
hardware and/or software, research methodology
and experimental designs, unsolicited book reviews

MAJOR CONTENT AREAS: Psychology, behavioral social sciences, biology,
clinical sciences, engineering, zoology, computer
sciences, bioengineering, medical technology

TOPICS PREFERRED: Instrumentation; computer technology; computer
program abstracts and algorithms, research methods
& designs, laboratory and/or field study

INAPPROPRIATE TOPICS: Not given

NUMBER OF MANUSCRIPT COPIES: 4   PAGE CHARGES: No
REVIEW PERIOD: 1-5 weeks STYLE REQUIREMENTS: APA
PUBLICATION LAG TIME: 3-4 months   STYLE SHEET: Yes
EARLY PUBLICATION OPTION: Yes   REVISED THESES: No
ACCEPTANCE RATE: 45-50%   STUDENT PAPERS: No
AUTHORSHIP RESTRICTIONS: No   REPRINT POLICY: None

SUBSCRIPTION ADDRESS: Psychonomic Society, Inc.
1108 West 34th Street
Austin, TX 78705

ANNUAL SUBSCRIPTION RATE: $10 individual, $20 institutional
INDEXED/ABSTRACTED IN: PA

CIRCULATION: 1000   FREQUENCY: Bimonthly

JOURNAL TITLE: BEHAVIOR SCIENCE RESEARCH

MANUSCRIPT ADDRESS: Box 2015 Yale Station
New Haven, CT 06520

TYPE OF ARTICLES: Theoretical articles, research articles,
methodological studies, annotated bibliographies,
review articles

MAJOR CONTENT AREAS: Aging and aged, alcoholism & drug abuse, anthropology, ethnic groups, human organizations,
marriage & divorce, migration, population, sex
roles, social change, social institutions

TOPICS PREFERRED: Cross-cultural studies, annotated bibliographies,
ethnology

INAPPROPRIATE TOPICS: Education, behavioral psychology

NUMBER OF MANUSCRIPT COPIES: 3   PAGE CHARGES: No
REVIEW PERIOD: 3 months STYLE REQUIREMENTS: Chicago Manuscript
PUBLICATION LAG TIME: 6 months   STYLE SHEET: Yes
EARLY PUBLICATION OPTION: No   REVISED THESES: No
ACCEPTANCE RATE: 66%   STUDENT PAPERS: No
AUTHORSHIP RESTRICTIONS: Not given   REPRINT POLICY: 100

SUBSCRIPTION ADDRESS: Box 2015 Yale Station
New Haven, CT 06520

ANNUAL SUBSCRIPTION RATE: $5 individual, $10 institutional
INDEXED/ABSTRACTED IN: Not given

CIRCULATION: 1000   FREQUENCY: Quarterly

JOURNAL TITLE: BERKELEY JOURNAL OF SOCIOLOGY

MANUSCRIPT ADDRESS: 410 Barrows Hall
U.C.-Berkeley
Berkeley, CA 94720

TYPE OF ARTICLES: Theoretical articles, research articles, review
articles, case studies

MAJOR CONTENT AREAS: Bureaucracy, collective behavior, mass communication, community development, criminology, sex
roles, sexual behavior, social change, social
conflict, social ideology, social mobility

TOPICS PREFERRED: Sociology of women, third world, Marxism,
socialism

INAPPROPRIATE TOPICS: Not given

NUMBER OF MANUSCRIPT COPIES:	2	PAGE CHARGES:	No
REVIEW PERIOD:	6 weeks	STYLE REQUIREMENTS:	ASA
PUBLICATION LAG TIME:	4 months	STYLE SHEET:	Yes
EARLY PUBLICATION OPTION:	Not given	REVISED THESES:	Yes
ACCEPTANCE RATE:	8%	STUDENT PAPERS:	Yes
AUTHORSHIP RESTRICTIONS:	No	REPRINT POLICY:	25

SUBSCRIPTION ADDRESS: 410 Barrows Hall
U.C.-Berkeley
Berkeley, CA 94720

ANNUAL SUBSCRIPTION RATE: $2.50 individual, $5.50 institutional
INDEXED/ABSTRACTED IN: Not given

CIRCULATION: 2000   FREQUENCY: Annually

JOURNAL TITLE: BRITISH JOURNAL OF EDUCATIONAL PSYCHOLOGY

MANUSCRIPT ADDRESS: Professor N.J. Entwistle
Department of Educational Research
University of Lancaster
Lancaster, England

TYPE OF ARTICLES: Not given

MAJOR CONTENT AREAS: Not given

TOPICS PREFERRED: Not given

INAPPROPRIATE TOPICS: Not given

NUMBER OF MANUSCRIPT COPIES:	2	PAGE CHARGES:	Not given
REVIEW PERIOD:	Not given	STYLE REQUIREMENTS:	Not given
PUBLICATION LAG TIME:	Not given	STYLE SHEET:	Not given
EARLY PUBLICATION OPTION:	Not given	REVISED THESES:	Not given
ACCEPTANCE RATE:	Not given	STUDENT PAPERS:	Not given
AUTHORSHIP RESTRICTIONS:	Not given	REPRINT POLICY:	50

SUBSCRIPTION ADDRESS: Scottish Academic Press
33 Montgomery Street
Edinburgh EH7 5JX, Scotland

ANNUAL SUBSCRIPTION RATE: $22 individual, Not given- institutional
INDEXED/ABSTRACTED IN: Not given

CIRCULATION: Not given   FREQUENCY: Not given

JOURNAL TITLE: BRITISH JOURNAL OF MATHEMATICAL &
STATISTICAL PSYCHOLOGY

MANUSCRIPT ADDRESS: Professor P. Levy
Department of Psychology
University of Lancaster
Lancaster LA1 4YF, United Kingdom

TYPE OF ARTICLES: Mathematical or statistical psychology,
psychological processes

MAJOR CONTENT AREAS: Mathematical or statistical content

TOPICS PREFERRED: Not given

INAPPROPRIATE TOPICS: Not given

NUMBER OF MANUSCRIPT COPIES: 3   PAGE CHARGES: No
REVIEW PERIOD: Not given   STYLE REQUIREMENTS: Not given
PUBLICATION LAG TIME: 6-9 months   STYLE SHEET: No
EARLY PUBLICATION OPTION: No   REVISED THESES: No
ACCEPTANCE RATE: Not given   STUDENT PAPERS: No
AUTHORSHIP RESTRICTIONS: No   REPRINT POLICY: 50

SUBSCRIPTION ADDRESS: John Wright & Sons Ltd.
42-66 Triangle West
Bristol BS8 1EX United Kingdom

ANNUAL SUBSCRIPTION RATE: $20 individual, Not given - institutional
INDEXED/ABSTRACTED IN: SSCI, PA

CIRCULATION: 1200   FREQUENCY: Semiannually

JOURNAL TITLE: BRITISH JOURNAL OF MEDICAL PSYCHOLOGY

MANUSCRIPT ADDRESS: Professor J.P. Watson
Department of Psychiatry
Guys Hospital Medical School
London Bridge, London SE1 9RT, United Kingdom

TYPE OF ARTICLES: Case studies, research articles, theoretical
articles, review articles

MAJOR CONTENT AREAS: Aging and aged, alcoholism & drug abuse, groups,
health and illness, medical sociology, mental
health and illness, sexual behavior

TOPICS PREFERRED: Not given

INAPPROPRIATE TOPICS: Not given

NUMBER OF MANUSCRIPT COPIES: 2   PAGE CHARGES: No
REVIEW PERIOD: Not given   STYLE REQUIREMENTS: Not given
PUBLICATION LAG TIME: 12 months   STYLE SHEET: No
EARLY PUBLICATION OPTION: No   REVISED THESES: No
ACCEPTANCE RATE: Not given   STUDENT PAPERS: No
AUTHORSHIP RESTRICTIONS: No   REPRINT POLICY: 50

SUBSCRIPTION ADDRESS: Cambridge University Press
32 E 57th Street
New York, NY 10022

ANNUAL SUBSCRIPTION RATE: $39.50 individual, Not given - institutional
INDEXED/ABSTRACTED IN: PA, BA,IM

CIRCULATION: 2100   FREQUENCY: Quarterly

JOURNAL TITLE: BRITISH JOURNAL OF POLITICAL SCIENCE

MANUSCRIPT ADDRESS: The Editor
University of Essex
Wivenhoe Park, Colchester
Essex, England

TYPE OF ARTICLES: Research articles, theoretical articles,
review articles

MAJOR CONTENT AREAS: Bureaucracy, political sociology, social
ideology, social policy, socialization

TOPICS PREFERRED: General political science

INAPPROPRIATE TOPICS: Not given

NUMBER OF MANUSCRIPT COPIES:	3	PAGE CHARGES:	No
REVIEW PERIOD:	2-3 mos.	STYLE REQUIREMENTS:	Chicago Manuscript
PUBLICATION LAG TIME:	6-9 months	STYLE SHEET:	Yes
EARLY PUBLICATION OPTION:	Yes	REVISED THESES:	No
ACCEPTANCE RATE:	12%	STUDENT PAPERS:	No
AUTHORSHIP RESTRICTIONS:	No	REPRINT POLICY:	25

SUBSCRIPTION ADDRESS: Cambridge University Press
32 East 57th Street
New York, NY 10022

ANNUAL SUBSCRIPTION RATE: $32 individual, $49 institutional
INDEXED/ABSTRACTED IN: Not given

CIRCULATION: 1050   FREQUENCY: Quarterly

JOURNAL TITLE: BRITISH JOURNAL OF PSYCHIATRY

MANUSCRIPT ADDRESS: 17 Belgrave Square
London SW1X 8PG
England

TYPE OF ARTICLES: Research articles, case studies, theoretical
articles, review articles, commentaries,
unsolicited book reviews

MAJOR CONTENT AREAS: Adolescence, aging and aged, alcoholism & drug
abuse, criminology, deviant behavior, health
and illness, mental health & illness, sex roles,
suicide, epidemiology

TOPICS PREFERRED: Clinical psychiatry, psychiatric research

INAPPROPRIATE TOPICS: Not given

NUMBER OF MANUSCRIPT COPIES:	3	PAGE CHARGES:	No
REVIEW PERIOD:	4-5 weeks	STYLE REQUIREMENTS:	Not given
PUBLICATION LAG TIME:	8-10 months	STYLE SHEET:	Yes
EARLY PUBLICATION OPTION:	Yes	REVISED THESES:	No
ACCEPTANCE RATE:	45%	STUDENT PAPERS:	No
AUTHORSHIP RESTRICTIONS:	No	REPRINT POLICY:	None

SUBSCRIPTION ADDRESS: Headley Brothers Ltd.
Invicta Press,
Ashford, Kent TN24 8HH
England

ANNUAL SUBSCRIPTION RATE: $100 individual, $125 institutional
INDEXED/ABSTRACTED IN: Not given

CIRCULATION: 8650   FREQUENCY: Monthly

JOURNAL TITLE: BRITISH JOURNAL OF PSYCHOLOGY

MANUSCRIPT ADDRESS: Prof. A.D.B. Clarke, Dept. of Psychology
The University
Hull HU6 7RX, England

TYPE OF ARTICLES: Research articles, book reviews

MAJOR CONTENT AREAS: General, experimental, statistics/methodology

TOPICS PREFERRED: Not given

INAPPROPRIATE TOPICS: Not given

NUMBER OF MANUSCRIPT COPIES: Not given	PAGE CHARGES:	Not given
REVIEW PERIOD: Not given	STYLE REQUIREMENTS:	Not given
PUBLICATION LAG TIME: Not given	STYLE SHEET:	Yes
EARLY PUBLICATION OPTION: Not given	REVISED THESES:	Not given
ACCEPTANCE RATE: Not given	STUDENT PAPERS:	Not given
AUTHORSHIP RESTRICTIONS: Not given	REPRINT POLICY:	50

SUBSCRIPTION ADDRESS: Cambridge University Press
32 E 57th Street
New York, NY 10022

ANNUAL SUBSCRIPTION RATE: $48 individual, $60 institutional
INDEXED/ABSTRACTED IN: PA, IM, BI, BA, BEI, BHI, CCSBS, CIJE,
DSHA, ISA, JHE, LLBA, RHEA, SSCI

CIRCULATION: 3200   FREQUENCY: Not given

JOURNAL TITLE: BRITISH JOURNAL OF SOCIAL AND CLINICAL
PSYCHOLOGY
MANUSCRIPT ADDRESS: Dr. H. Beloff, Department of Psychology
University of Edinburgh
60 Pleasance
Edinburgh EH8 9TJ, Scotland
TYPE OF ARTICLES: Research articles, case studies, theoretical
articles, commentaries, review articles

MAJOR CONTENT AREAS: Adolescence, aging and aged, alcoholism & drug
abuse, death & dying, delinquency & crime,
deviant behavior, groups, rehabilitation, sexual
behavior, socialization, social psychology
TOPICS PREFERRED: Social psychology/psychotherapy

INAPPROPRIATE TOPICS: Not given

NUMBER OF MANUSCRIPT COPIES: 2	PAGE CHARGES:	No
REVIEW PERIOD: 3 months	STYLE REQUIREMENTS:	Not given
PUBLICATION LAG TIME: 12 months	STYLE SHEET:	No
EARLY PUBLICATION OPTION: Yes	REVISED THESES:	No
ACCEPTANCE RATE: Not given	STUDENT PAPERS:	No
AUTHORSHIP RESTRICTIONS: No	REPRINT POLICY:	50

SUBSCRIPTION ADDRESS: Cambridge University Press
32 East 57th Street
New York, NY 10022

ANNUAL SUBSCRIPTION RATE: $47.50 individual, Not given - institutional
INDEXED/ABSTRACTED IN: PA, BA, IM,SSCI

CIRCULATION: 3000   FREQUENCY: Quarterly

JOURNAL TITLE: BRITISH JOURNAL OF SOCIOLOGY

MANUSCRIPT ADDRESS: The Editor
London School of Economics
Houghton Street
London, WC2A, 2AE England

TYPE OF ARTICLES: Theoretical articles, research articles, case
studies, commentaries, review articles

MAJOR CONTENT AREAS: Criminology, delinquency & crime, deviant
behavior, economy and society, political
sociology, mental health & illness, sex roles,
sexual behavior, social change, social conflict

TOPICS PREFERRED: Social theory

INAPPROPRIATE TOPICS: Not given

NUMBER OF MANUSCRIPT COPIES:	3	PAGE CHARGES:	No
REVIEW PERIOD:	6-8 weeks	STYLE REQUIREMENTS:	Not given
PUBLICATION LAG TIME:	12-18 months	STYLE SHEET:	Yes
EARLY PUBLICATION OPTION:	Yes	REVISED THESES:	No
ACCEPTANCE RATE:	Not given	STUDENT PAPERS:	No
AUTHORSHIP RESTRICTIONS:	Yes	REPRINT POLICY:	25

SUBSCRIPTION ADDRESS: Routledge & Kegan Paul Ltd.
Broadway House, Newtown Road
Henley-on-Thames, Oxon, RG9 1EN
England

ANNUAL SUBSCRIPTION RATE: $22 individual, $22 institutional

INDEXED/ABSTRACTED IN: SA, CC

CIRCULATION: 4000   FREQUENCY: Quarterly

JOURNAL TITLE: CANADIAN JOURNAL OF BEHAVIORAL SCIENCE

MANUSCRIPT ADDRESS: Dr. P.O. Davidson, Editor
Department of Psychology
University of British Columbia
Vancouver, B.C.   V6T 1W5

TYPE OF ARTICLES: Research articles, case studies, theoretical
articles, program evaluation descriptions

MAJOR CONTENT AREAS: Administrative behavior, adolescence, aging and
aged, alcoholism & drug abuse, collective
behavior, community development, sex roles,
sexual behavior, social change, social conflict

TOPICS PREFERRED: Any applied areas of psychology

INAPPROPRIATE TOPICS: Not given

NUMBER OF MANUSCRIPT COPIES:	3	PAGE CHARGES:	Yes
REVIEW PERIOD:	3-6 mos.	STYLE REQUIREMENTS:	APA
PUBLICATION LAG TIME:	12 months	STYLE SHEET:	No
EARLY PUBLICATION OPTION:	Yes	REVISED THESES:	No
ACCEPTANCE RATE:	10%	STUDENT PAPERS:	No
AUTHORSHIP RESTRICTIONS:	No	REPRINT POLICY:	None

SUBSCRIPTION ADDRESS: Ms. J. McGlynn, Business Office
Canadian Psychological Association
1390 Sherbrooke Street, West
Montreal, Quebec, Canada

ANNUAL SUBSCRIPTION RATE: $25 individual, $25 institutional

INDEXED/ABSTRACTED IN: PA

CIRCULATION: 2000   FREQUENCY: Quarterly

JOURNAL TITLE: CANADIAN JOURNAL OF POLITICAL SCIENCE

MANUSCRIPT ADDRESS: Department of Political Economy
University of Toronto, 100 St. George Street
Toronto, Ontario M5S 1A1
Canada

TYPE OF ARTICLES: Theoretical articles, research articles, case
studies, review articles, international relations,
public policy, comparative politics

MAJOR CONTENT AREAS: Bureaucracy, collective behavior, community
development, economy and society, leadership,
mass media, political sociology, public opinion,
sexual behavior, social change, social conflict

TOPICS PREFERRED: Political theory, political analysis, comparative
politics, public policy, international relations

INAPPROPRIATE TOPICS: Not given

NUMBER OF MANUSCRIPT COPIES:	3	PAGE CHARGES:	No
REVIEW PERIOD:	10 weeks	STYLE REQUIREMENTS:	Chicago Manuscripts
PUBLICATION LAG TIME:	12 months	STYLE SHEET:	Yes
EARLY PUBLICATION OPTION:	No	REVISED THESES:	Acceptable
ACCEPTANCE RATE:	25%	STUDENT PAPERS:	No
AUTHORSHIP RESTRICTIONS:	No	REPRINT POLICY:	25

SUBSCRIPTION ADDRESS: Wilfrid Laurier Press
Wilfrid Laurier University
Waterloo, Ontario N2L 3C5
Canada

ANNUAL SUBSCRIPTION RATE: Not given - individual, $30 institutional

INDEXED/ABSTRACTED IN: IPSA, ABC PS, P, SA, USPSD

CIRCULATION: 2500   FREQUENCY: Quarterly

JOURNAL TITLE: CANADIAN JOURNAL OF PSYCHOLOGY

MANUSCRIPT ADDRESS: The Editor
Canadian Journal of Psychology
Department of Psychology, Queen's University
Kingston, Ontario, Canada

TYPE OF ARTICLES: Research articles, review articles, theoretical
articles

MAJOR CONTENT AREAS: Not given

TOPICS PREFERRED: General experimental psychology

INAPPROPRIATE TOPICS: Not given

NUMBER OF MANUSCRIPT COPIES:	3	PAGE CHARGES:	No
REVIEW PERIOD:	3-6 mos.	STYLE REQUIREMENTS:	APA
PUBLICATION LAG TIME:	8 months	STYLE SHEET:	Yes
EARLY PUBLICATION OPTION:	No	REVISED THESES:	Yes
ACCEPTANCE RATE:	25%	STUDENT PAPERS:	No
AUTHORSHIP RESTRICTIONS:	No	REPRINT POLICY:	None

SUBSCRIPTION ADDRESS: Canadian Psychological Association
1390 Sherbrooke Street, West
Montreal, Quebec
Canada

ANNUAL SUBSCRIPTION RATE: $25 individual, $25 institutional

INDEXED/ABSTRACTED IN: PA, CC

CIRCULATION: 1950   FREQUENCY: Quarterly

JOURNAL TITLE: CANADIAN JOURNAL OF SOCIOLOGY

MANUSCRIPT ADDRESS: Department of Sociology
University of Alberta
Edmonton, Alberta, Canada

TYPE OF ARTICLES: Research articles, theoretical articles, case
studies, review articles

MAJOR CONTENT AREAS: Aging and aged, alcoholism & drug abuse,
anthropology, bureaucracy, collective
behavior, communes, criminology, death & dying,
delinquency & crime, demography, ecology

TOPICS PREFERRED: Not given

INAPPROPRIATE TOPICS: Not given

NUMBER OF MANUSCRIPT COPIES: 2	PAGE CHARGES:	No
REVIEW PERIOD: 10 weeks	STYLE REQUIREMENTS:	ASA
PUBLICATION LAG TIME: 9 months	STYLE SHEET:	Yes
EARLY PUBLICATION OPTION: No	REVISED THESES:	Yes
ACCEPTANCE RATE: 15%	STUDENT PAPERS:	No
AUTHORSHIP RESTRICTIONS: No	REPRINT POLICY:	25

SUBSCRIPTION ADDRESS: Department of Sociology
University of Alberta
Edmonton, Alberta, Canada

ANNUAL SUBSCRIPTION RATE: $12.50 individual, $25 institutional
INDEXED/ABSTRACTED IN: SA

CIRCULATION: 800   FREQUENCY: Quarterly

JOURNAL TITLE: CANADIAN REVIEW OF SOCIOLOGY AND ANTHROPOLOGY

MANUSCRIPT ADDRESS: A/S Université Concordia
1455 Boul. de Maisonneuve
Montreal, Quebec, Canada H3G 1M8

TYPE OF ARTICLES: Canadian society studies, theoretical articles,
research articles, case studies, commentaries,
review articles, unsolicited book reviews

MAJOR CONTENT AREAS: Not given

TOPICS PREFERRED: Not given

INAPPROPRIATE TOPICS: Not given

NUMBER OF MANUSCRIPT COPIES: 2	PAGE CHARGES:	Yes
REVIEW PERIOD: 3-6 mos.	STYLE REQUIREMENTS:	Not given
PUBLICATION LAG TIME: 6-8 months	STYLE SHEET:	No
EARLY PUBLICATION OPTION: Not given	REVISED THESES:	Yes
ACCEPTANCE RATE: 25%	STUDENT PAPERS:	No
AUTHORSHIP RESTRICTIONS: No	REPRINT POLICY:	25

SUBSCRIPTION ADDRESS: A/S Université Concordia
1455 Boul. de Maisonneuve
Montreal, Quebec, Canada H3G 1M8

ANNUAL SUBSCRIPTION RATE: $32 individual, $37 institutional
INDEXED/ABSTRACTED IN: Not given

CIRCULATION: 2000   FREQUENCY: Quarterly

JOURNAL TITLE: CATALYST

MANUSCRIPT ADDRESS: Otonabee College
Trent University
Peterboro, Ontario, Canada
K9J 7B8

TYPE OF ARTICLES: Theoretical articles, commentaries, review
articles, research articles, case studies

MAJOR CONTENT AREAS: General social science

TOPICS PREFERRED: Not given

INAPPROPRIATE TOPICS: Not given

NUMBER OF MANUSCRIPT COPIES: 2
REVIEW PERIOD: Not given
PUBLICATION LAG TIME: Not given
EARLY PUBLICATION OPTION: No
ACCEPTANCE RATE: 20%
AUTHORSHIP RESTRICTIONS: No

PAGE CHARGES: No
STYLE REQUIREMENTS: Chicago Manuscript
STYLE SHEET: Yes
REVISED THESES: Yes
STUDENT PAPERS: No
REPRINT POLICY: 25 journals

SUBSCRIPTION ADDRESS: Otonabee College
Trent University
Peterboro, Ontario, Canada
K9J 7B8

ANNUAL SUBSCRIPTION RATE: $6 individual, $12 institutional
INDEXED/ABSTRACTED IN: Not given

CIRCULATION: 2000   FREQUENCY: Not given

JOURNAL TITLE: CHANGE MAGAZINE

MANUSCRIPT ADDRESS: NBW Tower
New Rochelle, NY 10801

TYPE OF ARTICLES: Not given

MAJOR CONTENT AREAS: Not given

TOPICS PREFERRED: The future of higher education

INAPPROPRIATE TOPICS: Not given

NUMBER OF MANUSCRIPT COPIES: 1
REVIEW PERIOD: 2-3 mos.
PUBLICATION LAG TIME: 2-6 months
EARLY PUBLICATION OPTION: No
ACCEPTANCE RATE: 1%
AUTHORSHIP RESTRICTIONS: No

PAGE CHARGES: No
STYLE REQUIREMENTS: Chicago Manuscript
STYLE SHEET: Yes
REVISED THESES: No
STUDENT PAPERS: No
REPRINT POLICY: 6

SUBSCRIPTION ADDRESS: NBW Tower
New Rochelle, NY 10801

ANNUAL SUBSCRIPTION RATE: $14 individual, $14 institutional
INDEXED/ABSTRACTED IN: Not given

CIRCULATION: 30,000   FREQUENCY: Monthly

JOURNAL TITLE: CHARACTER POTENTIAL: A RECORD OF RESEARCH

MANUSCRIPT ADDRESS: Editor
207 State Street
Schenectady, NY 12305

TYPE OF ARTICLES: Research articles, review articles, theoretical
articles, commentaries, case studies,
unsolicited book reviews

MAJOR CONTENT AREAS: Adolescence, human development, occupations &
careers, social psychology, values

TOPICS PREFERRED: Not given

INAPPROPRIATE TOPICS: Not given

NUMBER OF MANUSCRIPT COPIES:	1	PAGE CHARGES:	No
REVIEW PERIOD:	4-6 weeks	STYLE REQUIREMENTS:	AAAS
PUBLICATION LAG TIME:	6 months	STYLE SHEET:	Yes
EARLY PUBLICATION OPTION:	No	REVISED THESES:	No
ACCEPTANCE RATE:	30%	STUDENT PAPERS:	No
AUTHORSHIP RESTRICTIONS:	No	REPRINT POLICY:	5 journals

SUBSCRIPTION ADDRESS: Union College Character Research Project
207 State Street
Schenectady, NY 12305

ANNUAL SUBSCRIPTION RATE: $7 individual, $7 institutional
INDEXED/ABSTRACTED IN: PA, PRG

CIRCULATION: 1000   FREQUENCY: Semiannually

JOURNAL TITLE: CHILD CARE QUARTERLY

MANUSCRIPT ADDRESS: Dr. J. Beker, Editor
5 Cloverdale Lane
Monsey, NY 10952

TYPE OF ARTICLES: Research articles, theoretical articles, review
articles, case studies, commentaries

MAJOR CONTENT AREAS: Administrative behavior, adolescence, alcoholism
& drug abuse, counseling, delinquency & crime,
groups, leadership, occupations & careers, sexual
behavior, social institutions, social issues

TOPICS PREFERRED: Day and residential care for children, the
emerging child care profession, applied research,
training for child care work

INAPPROPRIATE TOPICS: Not given

NUMBER OF MANUSCRIPT COPIES:	3	PAGE CHARGES:	No
REVIEW PERIOD:	3 months	STYLE REQUIREMENTS:	APA
PUBLICATION LAG TIME:	1 year	STYLE SHEET:	Yes
EARLY PUBLICATION OPTION:	Yes	REVISED THESES:	Yes
ACCEPTANCE RATE:	35%	STUDENT PAPERS:	Acceptable
AUTHORSHIP RESTRICTIONS:	No	REPRINT POLICY:	1 journal

SUBSCRIPTION ADDRESS: Human Sciences Press
72 Fifth Avenue
New York, NY 10011

ANNUAL SUBSCRIPTION RATE: $12.95 individual, $35 institutional
INDEXED/ABSTRACTED IN: PA, ASW, ECEA, CC/BSES, SSCI, CIJA, ACA, CMHR,
CLSSWHC

CIRCULATION: 2000   FREQUENCY: Quarterly

JOURNAL TITLE: CHILD DEVELOPMENT

MANUSCRIPT ADDRESS: W.E. Jeffrey, Ph.D.,Editor
Dept. of Psychology, UCLA
Los Angeles, CA 90024

TYPE OF ARTICLES: Research articles, review articles, theoretical
articles

MAJOR CONTENT AREAS: Developmental

TOPICS PREFERRED: Not given

INAPPROPRIATE TOPICS: Not given

NUMBER OF MANUSCRIPT COPIES: Not given	PAGE CHARGES:	Not given
REVIEW PERIOD: 3 months	STYLE REQUIREMENTS:	APA
PUBLICATION LAG TIME: 1 year	STYLE SHEET:	Yes
EARLY PUBLICATION OPTION: No	REVISED THESES:	Not given
·ACCEPTANCE RATE: 16%	STUDENT PAPERS:	Not given
AUTHORSHIP RESTRICTIONS: Not given	REPRINT POLICY:	Not given

SUBSCRIPTION ADDRESS: The University of Chicago Press
5801 S Ellis Avenue
Chicago, IL 60637

ANNUAL SUBSCRIPTION RATE: $35 individual, Not given institutional
INDEXED/ABSTRACTED IN: PA, ASW, AA, BS, CDA, CCSBS, CIJE, DSHA, EI,
ECEA, JHE, LLBA, RHEA, SSCI, WSA
CIRCULATION: 7500   FREQUENCY: Not given

JOURNAL TITLE: CHILDHOOD EDUCATION

MANUSCRIPT ADDRESS: Dr. Monroe D. Cohen, Editor
3615 Wisconsin Avenue, NW
Washington, DC 20016

TYPE OF ARTICLES: Word & picture illustrations of acceptable
classroom practices, articles with a blend of
theory and practical application, commentaries
MAJOR CONTENT AREAS: Adolescence, counseling, ethnic groups,
minorities, sex roles, social change, social
issues, leadership, delinquency and crime,
values, death and dying
TOPICS PREFERRED: Material geared to teachers and parents of
children , specific illustrations of acceptable
classroom practices, accounts of educational events
INAPPROPRIATE TOPICS: Not given

NUMBER OF MANUSCRIPT COPIES: 2	PAGE CHARGES:	No
REVIEW PERIOD: 3-6 mos.	STYLE REQUIREMENTS:	Chicago Manuscript
PUBLICATION LAG TIME: 3-6 months	STYLE SHEET:	Yes
EARLY PUBLICATION OPTION: No	REVISED THESES:	No
ACCEPTANCE RATE: 5-10%	STUDENT PAPERS:	No
AUTHORSHIP RESTRICTIONS: No	REPRINT POLICY:	5 journals

SUBSCRIPTION ADDRESS: Association for Childhood Education International
3615 Wisconsin Avenue, NW
Washington, DC 20016

ANNUAL SUBSCRIPTION RATE: $18 individual, $18 institutional
INDEXED/ABSTRACTED IN: BRI, ECEA

CIRCULATION: 19,000   FREQUENCY: Bimonthly

JOURNAL TITLE: CHILD PSYCHIATRY & HUMAN DEVELOPMENT

MANUSCRIPT ADDRESS: 7111 44th Street
Chevy Chase, MD 20015

TYPE OF ARTICLES: Review articles, case studies, child mental
health

MAJOR CONTENT AREAS: Adolescence, health and illness, human development,
mental health & illness

TOPICS PREFERRED: Studies in the field of child psychology

INAPPROPRIATE TOPICS: Research papers by clinical psychologists

NUMBER OF MANUSCRIPT COPIES:	3	PAGE CHARGES:	Not given
REVIEW PERIOD:	6-12 mos.	STYLE REQUIREMENTS:	Index Medicus
PUBLICATION LAG TIME:	1 year	STYLE SHEET:	No
EARLY PUBLICATION OPTION:	Yes	REVISED THESES:	No
ACCEPTANCE RATE:	50%	STUDENT PAPERS:	No
AUTHORSHIP RESTRICTIONS:	No	REPRINT POLICY:	None

SUBSCRIPTION ADDRESS: Human Sciences Press
72 Fifth Avenue
New York, NY 10011

ANNUAL SUBSCRIPTION RATE: $17.50 individual, $40 institutional
INDEXED/ABSTRACTED IN: IM, EM

CIRCULATION: 800   FREQUENCY: Quarterly

JOURNAL TITLE: CHILD STUDY JOURNAL

MANUSCRIPT ADDRESS: State University of New York
College at Buffalo, 1300 Elmwood Avenue
Buffalo, NY 14222

TYPE OF ARTICLES: Research articles, review articles, theoretical
articles

MAJOR CONTENT AREAS: Behavior therapy, counseling, developmental,
educational, learning, mental retardation, social

TOPICS PREFERRED: Educational and psychological implications of
research in development

INAPPROPRIATE TOPICS: Individual case studies, curriculum studies

NUMBER OF MANUSCRIPT COPIES:	Not given	PAGE CHARGES:	Not given
REVIEW PERIOD:	6-8 mos.	STYLE REQUIREMENTS:	APA
PUBLICATION LAG TIME:	12-18 months	STYLE SHEET:	Yes
EARLY PUBLICATION OPTION:	Yes	REVISED THESES:	Not given
ACCEPTANCE RATE:	25-40%	STUDENT PAPERS:	Not given
AUTHORSHIP RESTRICTIONS:	Not given	REPRINT POLICY:	1

SUBSCRIPTION ADDRESS: State University of New York
College at Buffalo, 1300 Elmwood Avenue
Buffalo, NY 14222

ANNUAL SUBSCRIPTION RATE: $6 individual, $12 institutional
INDEXED/ABSTRACTED IN: PA, SA, BS, CDA, CCSBS, CIJE, EI, ECEA,
PRG, SSCI
CIRCULATION: 500   FREQUENCY: Not given

JOURNAL TITLE: CHILD WELFARE

MANUSCRIPT ADDRESS: 67 Irving Place
New York, NY 10003

TYPE OF ARTICLES: Practice, policy, programs

MAJOR CONTENT AREAS: Not given

TOPICS PREFERRED: Not given

INAPPROPRIATE TOPICS: Not given

NUMBER OF MANUSCRIPT COPIES:	2	PAGE CHARGES:	No
REVIEW PERIOD:	2-3 weeks	STYLE REQUIREMENTS:	Not given
PUBLICATION LAG TIME:	9-12 months	STYLE SHEET:	Yes
EARLY PUBLICATION OPTION:	Yes	REVISED THESES:	No
ACCEPTANCE RATE:	25%	STUDENT PAPERS:	Yes
AUTHORSHIP RESTRICTIONS:	No	REPRINT POLICY:	None

SUBSCRIPTION ADDRESS: 67 Irving Place
New York, NY 10003

ANNUAL SUBSCRIPTION RATE: $8 individual, Not given - institutional
INDEXED/ABSTRACTED IN: Not given

CIRCULATION: 10,000   FREQUENCY: 10 times per year

JOURNAL TITLE: CLINICAL SOCIAL WORK JOURNAL

MANUSCRIPT ADDRESS: Mary Gottesfeld, MSS
385 Westend Avenue
New York, NY 10023

TYPE OF ARTICLES: Case studies, theoretical articles, research
articles, review articles, commentaries,
unsolicited book reviews
MAJOR CONTENT AREAS: Adolescence, aging and aged, alcoholism & drug
abuse, counseling, human development, mental
health & illness, sexual behavior, deviant
behavior
TOPICS PREFERRED: Clinical case material

INAPPROPRIATE TOPICS: Pedagogical articles

NUMBER OF MANUSCRIPT COPIES:	3	PAGE CHARGES:	No
REVIEW PERIOD:	1 month	STYLE REQUIREMENTS:	APA
PUBLICATION LAG TIME:	1 year	STYLE SHEET:	Yes
EARLY PUBLICATION OPTION:	No	REVISED THESES:	No
ACCEPTANCE RATE:	15%	STUDENT PAPERS:	No
AUTHORSHIP RESTRICTIONS:	No	REPRINT POLICY:	None

SUBSCRIPTION ADDRESS: Human Sciences Press
72 Fifth Avenue
New York, NY 10011

ANNUAL SUBSCRIPTION RATE: $15 individual, $35 institutional
INDEXED/ABSTRACTED IN: ASW, PA, CDA, CC, SSCI, PHRA, SWHCCL, DW

CIRCULATION: 3720   FREQUENCY: Quarterly

JOURNAL TITLE: COGNITIVE PSYCHOLOGY

MANUSCRIPT ADDRESS: Dr. Earl Hunt, Editor
Department of Psychology, NI-25
University of Washington
Seattle, WA 98195

TYPE OF ARTICLES: Research articles, theoretical articles, review articles

MAJOR CONTENT AREAS: Experimental psychology

TOPICS PREFERRED: Organization of human information processing, linguistics, artificial intelligence, and neurophysiology

INAPPROPRIATE TOPICS: Not given

NUMBER OF MANUSCRIPT COPIES: 3	PAGE CHARGES:	Not given
REVIEW PERIOD: 3-4 mos.	STYLE REQUIREMENTS:	APA
PUBLICATION LAG TIME: 4 months	STYLE SHEET:	No
EARLY PUBLICATION OPTION: No	REVISED THESES:	Not given
ACCEPTANCE RATE: 14%	STUDENT PAPERS:	Not given
AUTHORSHIP RESTRICTIONS: Not given	REPRINT POLICY:	50

SUBSCRIPTION ADDRESS: Academic Press, Inc.
111 Fifth Avenue
New York, NY 10003

ANNUAL SUBSCRIPTION RATE: $24 individual, $48 institutional

INDEXED/ABSTRACTED IN: Not given

CIRCULATION: 1770   FREQUENCY: Quarterly

JOURNAL TITLE: COLORADO QUARTERLY

MANUSCRIPT ADDRESS: Hellems 134
University of Colorado
Boulder, CO 80309

TYPE OF ARTICLES: Theoretical articles, research articles, case studies

MAJOR CONTENT AREAS: Not given

TOPICS PREFERRED: Not given

INAPPROPRIATE TOPICS: Pedantic writing

NUMBER OF MANUSCRIPT COPIES: 1	PAGE CHARGES:	No
REVIEW PERIOD: 2-4 weeks	STYLE REQUIREMENTS:	Chicago Manuscript
PUBLICATION LAG TIME: 6-24 months	STYLE SHEET:	Not given
EARLY PUBLICATION OPTION: No	REVISED THESES:	No
ACCEPTANCE RATE: 5%	STUDENT PAPERS:	No
AUTHORSHIP RESTRICTIONS: No	REPRINT POLICY:	None

SUBSCRIPTION ADDRESS: Hellems 134
University of Colorado
Boulder, CO 80309

ANNUAL SUBSCRIPTION RATE: $6.50 individual, $6.50 institutional

INDEXED/ABSTRACTED IN: HA, A:HL

CIRCULATION: 1000   FREQUENCY: Quarterly

JOURNAL TITLE: COMMUNICATION RESEARCH

MANUSCRIPT ADDRESS: Mr. Gerald F. Kline
Department of Journalism
University of Michigan
Ann Arbor, MI 48104

TYPE OF ARTICLES: Research articles, theoretical articles, review
articles, case studies, commentaries

MAJOR CONTENT AREAS: Mass communication, mass media, social psychology

TOPICS PREFERRED: Not given

INAPPROPRIATE TOPICS: Not given

NUMBER OF MANUSCRIPT COPIES: 3	PAGE CHARGES: No	
REVIEW PERIOD: Not given	STYLE REQUIREMENTS: Not given	
PUBLICATION LAG TIME: Not given	STYLE SHEET: Yes	
EARLY PUBLICATION OPTION: No	REVISED THESES: Not given	
ACCEPTANCE RATE: Not given	STUDENT PAPERS: No	
AUTHORSHIP RESTRICTIONS: No	REPRINT POLICY: 24	

SUBSCRIPTION ADDRESS: Sage Publications
275 S Beverly Drive
Beverly Hills, CA 90212

ANNUAL SUBSCRIPTION RATE: $13.50 individual, $22.50 institutional
INDEXED/ABSTRACTED IN: CC, ERIC/RCS, HRA, PA, SPAA, SCA, APC

CIRCULATION: Not given   FREQUENCY: Quarterly

JOURNAL TITLE: COMMUNITY COLLEGE SOCIAL SCIENCE QUARTERLY

MANUSCRIPT ADDRESS: Gerald Bayou, Editor
Grossmont College
El Cajon, CA 92020

TYPE OF ARTICLES: Book and media reviews

MAJOR CONTENT AREAS: Not given

TOPICS PREFERRED: Not given

INAPPROPRIATE TOPICS: Not given

NUMBER OF MANUSCRIPT COPIES: Not given	PAGE CHARGES: Not given
REVIEW PERIOD: 1-2 months	STYLE REQUIREMENTS: Not given
PUBLICATION LAG TIME: 4-5 months	STYLE SHEET: Not given
EARLY PUBLICATION OPTION: Not given	REVISED THESES: Not given
ACCEPTANCE RATE: 20%	STUDENT PAPERS: Not given
AUTHORSHIP RESTRICTIONS: Not given	REPRINT POLICY: 0

SUBSCRIPTION ADDRESS: Gerald Bayou, Editor
Grossmont College
El Cajon, CA 92020

ANNUAL SUBSCRIPTION RATE: $8 individual, $12 institutional
INDEXED/ABSTRACTED IN: Not given

CIRCULATION: 2000   FREQUENCY: Quarterly

JOURNAL TITLE: COMMUNITY MENTAL HEALTH JOURNAL

MANUSCRIPT ADDRESS: Dr. Baler
University of Michigan School of Public Health
Community Mental Health Program, Room M5108SPH11
Ann Arbor, MI 48104

TYPE OF ARTICLES: Research articles, theoretical articles, review
articles, case studies

MAJOR CONTENT AREAS: Mental health and illness

TOPICS PREFERRED: Community mental health: theory, practice and
research

INAPPROPRIATE TOPICS: Speeches

NUMBER OF MANUSCRIPT COPIES: 3	PAGE CHARGES:	Yes
REVIEW PERIOD: 3-6 mos.	STYLE REQUIREMENTS:	APA
PUBLICATION LAG TIME: 1-2 years	STYLE SHEET:	Not given
EARLY PUBLICATION OPTION: Yes	REVISED THESES:	Acceptable
ACCEPTANCE RATE: 15%	STUDENT PAPERS:	No
AUTHORSHIP RESTRICTIONS: No	REPRINT POLICY:	None

SUBSCRIPTION ADDRESS: Human Sciences Press
72 5th Avenue
New York, NY 10012

ANNUAL SUBSCRIPTION RATE: $16 individual, $36 institutional
INDEXED/ABSTRACTED IN: PA

CIRCULATION: 3600   FREQUENCY: Quarterly

JOURNAL TITLE: COMPARATIVE POLITICAL STUDIES

MANUSCRIPT ADDRESS: James Caporaso
Department of Political Science
Northwestern University
Evanston, IL 60201

TYPE OF ARTICLES: Research articles, theoretical articles, review
articles, case studies, commentaries

MAJOR CONTENT AREAS: Political sociology, society & institutions

TOPICS PREFERRED: Not given

INAPPROPRIATE TOPICS: Not given

NUMBER OF MANUSCRIPT COPIES: 3	PAGE CHARGES:	No
REVIEW PERIOD: Not given	STYLE REQUIREMENTS:	Not given
PUBLICATION LAG TIME: Not given	STYLE SHEET:	Yes
EARLY PUBLICATION OPTION: No	REVISED THESES:	Not given
ACCEPTANCE RATE: Not given	STUDENT PAPERS:	No
AUTHORSHIP RESTRICTIONS: No	REPRINT POLICY:	24

SUBSCRIPTION ADDRESS: Sage Publications
275 Beverly Drive
Beverly Hills,CA 90212

ANNUAL SUBSCRIPTION RATE: $15.60 individual, $26 institutional
INDEXED/ABSTRACTED IN: IPSA, SA, SUSA, HRA, ABC PS, SSCI, SSI, CC, URS

CIRCULATION: Not given   FREQUENCY: Quarterly

JOURNAL TITLE: COMPARATIVE STUDIES IN SOCIETY AND HISTORY

MANUSCRIPT ADDRESS: Department of History
University of Michigan
Ann Arbor, MI   48109

TYPE OF ARTICLES: Not given

MAJOR CONTENT AREAS: Anthropology, bureaucracy, collective behavior,
communes, demography, economy and society, ethnic
groups, groups, law, leadership, migration,
minorities, political sociology, values
TOPICS PREFERRED: Sociology, history, anthropology, law, political
science

INAPPROPRIATE TOPICS: Not given

NUMBER OF MANUSCRIPT COPIES: 2
REVIEW PERIOD: 1-4 mos.
PUBLICATION LAG TIME: 1 year
EARLY PUBLICATION OPTION: No
ACCEPTANCE RATE: Not given
AUTHORSHIP RESTRICTIONS: No

PAGE CHARGES: No
STYLE REQUIREMENTS: Chicago Manuscript
STYLE SHEET: Yes
REVISED THESES: Acceptable
STUDENT PAPERS: No
REPRINT POLICY: 50

SUBSCRIPTION ADDRESS: H. Florentine
Journals Dept. Cambridge University Press
510 North Avenue
New Rochelle, NY
ANNUAL SUBSCRIPTION RATE: $18.50 individual, $32.50 institutional
INDEXED/ABSTRACTED IN: SA, HA

CIRCULATION: 2300

FREQUENCY: Quarterly

JOURNAL TITLE: COMPENSATION REVIEW

MANUSCRIPT ADDRESS: American Mgt. Associations
135 West 50th Street
New York, NY   10020

TYPE OF ARTICLES: Research articles, case studies

MAJOR CONTENT AREAS: Not given

TOPICS PREFERRED: Compensation (salaries, hourly wages, benefits,
etc.) planning and administration, motivating
employees through pay, etc.
INAPPROPRIATE TOPICS: Not given

NUMBER OF MANUSCRIPT COPIES: 2
REVIEW PERIOD: 2-4 weeks
PUBLICATION LAG TIME: 3-12 months
EARLY PUBLICATION OPTION: Yes
ACCEPTANCE RATE: 25%
AUTHORSHIP RESTRICTIONS: No

PAGE CHARGES: No
STYLE REQUIREMENTS: Chicago Manuscript
STYLE SHEET: Yes
REVISED THESES: No
STUDENT PAPERS: No
REPRINT POLICY: 100

SUBSCRIPTION ADDRESS: American Mgt. Associations
Subscription Services, Box 319
Saranac Lake, NY   12983

ANNUAL SUBSCRIPTION RATE: $20 individual, Not given - institutional
INDEXED/ABSTRACTED IN: PMA

CIRCULATION: 7500

FREQUENCY: Quarterly

JOURNAL TITLE: THE CORNELL JOURNAL OF SOCIAL RELATIONS

MANUSCRIPT ADDRESS: Editor
Department of Sociology
Uris Hall, Cornell University
Ithaca, NY 14853

TYPE OF ARTICLES: Research articles, theoretical articles, case
studies, review articles, commentaries,
unsolicited book reviews

MAJOR CONTENT AREAS: Administrative behavior, anthropology, bureaucracy, mass communication, general sociology,
human development, mass media, political sociology,
rural sociology, social change, social conflict

TOPICS PREFERRED: Not given

INAPPROPRIATE TOPICS: Not given

NUMBER OF MANUSCRIPT COPIES: 3
REVIEW PERIOD: 6-8 weeks
PUBLICATION LAG TIME: 6-8 months
EARLY PUBLICATION OPTION: No
ACCEPTANCE RATE: 35%
AUTHORSHIP RESTRICTIONS: No

PAGE CHARGES: No
STYLE REQUIREMENTS: Not given
STYLE SHEET: Yes
REVISED THESES: No
STUDENT PAPERS: No
REPRINT POLICY: 20

SUBSCRIPTION ADDRESS: Editor
Department of Sociology
Uris Hall, Cornell University
Ithaca, NY 14853

ANNUAL SUBSCRIPTION RATE: $6 individual, $6 institutional
INDEXED/ABSTRACTED IN: SA, PA

CIRCULATION: 300   FREQUENCY: Semiannually

JOURNAL TITLE: CRIME AND SOCIAL JUSTICE

MANUSCRIPT ADDRESS: PO Box 4373
Berkeley, CA 94704

TYPE OF ARTICLES: Theoretical articles, research articles, review
articles, unsolicited book reviews, case studies,
commentaries

MAJOR CONTENT AREAS: Alcoholism & drug abuse, criminology, delinquency
& crime, deviant behavior, law, poverty,
inequality, and policy, race relations, social
change, social institutions, stratification

TOPICS PREFERRED: Crime, criminal justice system

INAPPROPRIATE TOPICS: Not given

NUMBER OF MANUSCRIPT COPIES: 3
REVIEW PERIOD: 6-8 weeks
PUBLICATION LAG TIME: 3 months
EARLY PUBLICATION OPTION: No
ACCEPTANCE RATE: 5%
AUTHORSHIP RESTRICTIONS: No

PAGE CHARGES: Yes
STYLE REQUIREMENTS: Chicago Manuscript
STYLE SHEET: Yes
REVISED THESES: Yes
STUDENT PAPERS: Yes
REPRINT POLICY: 1 journal

SUBSCRIPTION ADDRESS: PO Box 4373
Berkeley, CA 94704

ANNUAL SUBSCRIPTION RATE: $6 individual, $10 institutional
INDEXED/ABSTRACTED IN: SA, API

CIRCULATION: 1000   FREQUENCY: Semiannually

JOURNAL TITLE: CRIMINAL JUSTICE AND BEHAVIOR

MANUSCRIPT ADDRESS: Stanley Brodsky
Department of Psychology
University of Alabama
University, AL 35486

TYPE OF ARTICLES: Research articles, theoretical articles, review articles

MAJOR CONTENT AREAS: Criminology, delinquency & crime, deviant behavior

TOPICS PREFERRED: Not given

INAPPROPRIATE TOPICS: Not given

NUMBER OF MANUSCRIPT COPIES: 3   PAGE CHARGES: No
REVIEW PERIOD: Not given STYLE REQUIREMENTS: Not given
PUBLICATION LAG TIME: Not given   STYLE SHEET: Yes
EARLY PUBLICATION OPTION: No   REVISED THESES: Not given
ACCEPTANCE RATE: Not given   STUDENT PAPERS: No
AUTHORSHIP RESTRICTIONS: No   REPRINT POLICY: 24

SUBSCRIPTION ADDRESS: Sage Publications
275 S Beverly Drive
Beverly Hills, CA 90212

ANNUAL SUBSCRIPTION RATE: $13.50 individual, $22.50 institutional
INDEXED/ABSTRACTED IN: PA, SA, HRA, SUSA, AC, CDL, PAIS, PRG, CC, SSCI, CJPI
CIRCULATION: Not given   FREQUENCY: Quarterly

JOURNAL TITLE: CRIMINOLOGY

MANUSCRIPT ADDRESS: Edward Sagarin, Law & Police Science Department
John Jay College of Criminal Justice
444 W 56th Street
New York, NY 10019

TYPE OF ARTICLES: Research articles, theoretical articles, review articles, case studies, commentaries

MAJOR CONTENT AREAS: Criminology, delinquency & crime, deviant behavior

TOPICS PREFERRED: Not given

INAPPROPRIATE TOPICS: Not given

NUMBER OF MANUSCRIPT COPIES: 3   PAGE CHARGES: No
REVIEW PERIOD: Not given STYLE REQUIREMENTS: Not given
PUBLICATION LAG TIME: Not given   STYLE SHEET: Yes
EARLY PUBLICATION OPTION: No   REVISED THESES: Not given
ACCEPTANCE RATE: Not given   STUDENT PAPERS: No
AUTHORSHIP RESTRICTIONS: No   REPRINT POLICY: 24

SUBSCRIPTION ADDRESS: Sage Publications
275 S Beverly Drive
Beverly Hills, CA 90212

ANNUAL SUBSCRIPTION RATE: $15 individual, $25 institutional
INDEXED/ABSTRACTED IN: HRA, SUSA, SA, PAIS, CC, SSCI, SSI, CJPI, CPL

CIRCULATION: Not given   FREQUENCY: Quarterly

JOURNAL TITLE: CURRENT ANTHROPOLOGY

MANUSCRIPT ADDRESS: University of British Columbia
Vancouver, British Columbia
Canada, V6T 1W5

TYPE OF ARTICLES: Theoretical articles, commentaries, research
articles, case studies, unsolicited book reviews,
review articles

MAJOR CONTENT AREAS: Anthropology, collective behavior, community
development, ecology, ethnic groups, groups,
rural sociology, sex roles, social change, social
issues, social mobility, social conflict

TOPICS PREFERRED: Not given

INAPPROPRIATE TOPICS: Not given

NUMBER OF MANUSCRIPT COPIES: 1	PAGE CHARGES: No	
REVIEW PERIOD: 8 weeks	STYLE REQUIREMENTS: Chicago Manuscript	
PUBLICATION LAG TIME: 9 months	STYLE SHEET: Yes	
EARLY PUBLICATION OPTION: No	REVISED THESES: No	
ACCEPTANCE RATE: 5%	STUDENT PAPERS: No	
AUTHORSHIP RESTRICTIONS: No	REPRINT POLICY: 25	

SUBSCRIPTION ADDRESS: University of Chicago Press
5801 Ellis Avenue
Chicago, IL 60637

ANNUAL SUBSCRIPTION RATE: $18 individual, $25 institutional
INDEXED/ABSTRACTED IN: Not given

CIRCULATION: 7200   FREQUENCY: Quarterly

JOURNAL TITLE: CURRENT SOCIOLOGY - LA SOCIOLOGIE CONTEMPORAINE

MANUSCRIPT ADDRESS: Department of Sociology
University of Warwick, Coventry
Warwickshire, England

TYPE OF ARTICLES: Research articles, theoretical articles, review
articles, case studies, commentaries, unsolicited
book reviews

MAJOR CONTENT AREAS: Not given

TOPICS PREFERRED: Current sociology

INAPPROPRIATE TOPICS: Not given

NUMBER OF MANUSCRIPT COPIES: Not given	PAGE CHARGES: No	
REVIEW PERIOD: 1 month	STYLE REQUIREMENTS: Not given	
PUBLICATION LAG TIME: 6 months	STYLE SHEET: Yes	
EARLY PUBLICATION OPTION: No	REVISED THESES: No	
ACCEPTANCE RATE: Not given	STUDENT PAPERS: No	
AUTHORSHIP RESTRICTIONS: No	REPRINT POLICY: 25	

SUBSCRIPTION ADDRESS: Sage Publications, Inc.
275 S Beverly Drive
Beverly Hills, CA 90212

ANNUAL SUBSCRIPTION RATE: $8 individual, $13 institutional
INDEXED/ABSTRACTED IN: Not given

CIRCULATION: 2000   FREQUENCY: Tri-yearly

JOURNAL TITLE: CYBERNETICA

MANUSCRIPT ADDRESS: Association Internationale de Cybernetique
2 rue Sergent Vrylthof, 5000
Namur, Belgium

TYPE OF ARTICLES: Research articles, theoretical articles, case studies

MAJOR CONTENT AREAS: Not given

TOPICS PREFERRED: Not given

INAPPROPRIATE TOPICS: Not given

NUMBER OF MANUSCRIPT COPIES: 2	PAGE CHARGES:	Not given
REVIEW PERIOD: 45 days	STYLE REQUIREMENTS:	Not given
PUBLICATION LAG TIME: 4 months	STYLE SHEET:	No
EARLY PUBLICATION OPTION: Not given	REVISED THESES:	Yes
ACCEPTANCE RATE: 80%	STUDENT PAPERS:	No
AUTHORSHIP RESTRICTIONS: Yes	REPRINT POLICY:	25

SUBSCRIPTION ADDRESS: Not given

ANNUAL SUBSCRIPTION RATE: $40 individual, $40 institutional
INDEXED/ABSTRACTED IN: Not given

CIRCULATION: 1000   FREQUENCY: Quarterly

JOURNAL TITLE: CYCLES

MANUSCRIPT ADDRESS: Foundation for the Study of Cycles
124 S Highland Avenue
Pittsburgh, PA 15206

TYPE OF ARTICLES: Research articles, commentaries, theoretical articles

MAJOR CONTENT AREAS: Collective behavior, human organizations, popular culture, sociology of peace

TOPICS PREFERRED: Not given

INAPPROPRIATE TOPICS: Astrology

NUMBER OF MANUSCRIPT COPIES: 1	PAGE CHARGES:	No
REVIEW PERIOD: 6 weeks	STYLE REQUIREMENTS:	Not given
PUBLICATION LAG TIME: 3 months	STYLE SHEET:	Not given
EARLY PUBLICATION OPTION: No	REVISED THESES:	Acceptable
ACCEPTANCE RATE: 50%	STUDENT PAPERS:	No
AUTHORSHIP RESTRICTIONS: No	REPRINT POLICY:	6-12

SUBSCRIPTION ADDRESS: Foundation for the Study of Cycles
124 S Highland Avenue
Pittsburgh, PA 15206

ANNUAL SUBSCRIPTION RATE: $20 individual, $15 institutional
INDEXED/ABSTRACTED IN: Not given

CIRCULATION: 2000   FREQUENCY: 9 times per year

JOURNAL TITLE: DAEDALUS

MANUSCRIPT ADDRESS: Harvard University
7 Linden Street
Cambridge, MA 02138

TYPE OF ARTICLES: Not given

MAJOR CONTENT AREAS: Not given

TOPICS PREFERRED: Not given

INAPPROPRIATE TOPICS: Not given

NUMBER OF MANUSCRIPT COPIES: 2
REVIEW PERIOD: 2 weeks
PUBLICATION LAG TIME: 3 months
EARLY PUBLICATION OPTION: No
ACCEPTANCE RATE: 5%
AUTHORSHIP RESTRICTIONS: No

PAGE CHARGES: No
STYLE REQUIREMENTS: Chicago Manuscript
STYLE SHEET: Yes
REVISED THESES: No
STUDENT PAPERS: No
REPRINT POLICY: 100

SUBSCRIPTION ADDRESS: American Academy of Arts and Sciences
165 Allandale Street
Jamaica Plain, MA 02130

ANNUAL SUBSCRIPTION RATE: $12 individual, Not given - institutional
INDEXED/ABSTRACTED IN: Not given

CIRCULATION: 52,000   FREQUENCY: Quarterly

JOURNAL TITLE: DAY CARE AND EARLY EDUCATION

MANUSCRIPT ADDRESS: Joseph M. Michalak, Editor
Behavioral Publications, Inc.
72 Fifth Avenue
New York, NY 10011
TYPE OF ARTICLES: Not given

MAJOR CONTENT AREAS: Not given

TOPICS PREFERRED: Ideas, issues, and problems of pre-school
education from birth through kindergarten

INAPPROPRIATE TOPICS: Not given

NUMBER OF MANUSCRIPT COPIES: Not given
REVIEW PERIOD: 1 month
PUBLICATION LAG TIME: 5-8 months
EARLY PUBLICATION OPTION: Not given
ACCEPTANCE RATE: 10%
AUTHORSHIP RESTRICTIONS: Not given

PAGE CHARGES: Not given
STYLE REQUIREMENTS: Not given
STYLE SHEET: Not given
REVISED THESES: Not given
STUDENT PAPERS: Not given
REPRINT POLICY: Not given

SUBSCRIPTION ADDRESS: Joseph M. Michalak, Editor
Behavioral Publications, Inc.
72 Fifth Avenue
New York, NY 10011
ANNUAL SUBSCRIPTION RATE: $9 individual, $15 institutional
INDEXED/ABSTRACTED IN: Not given

CIRCULATION: 25,000   FREQUENCY: Bimonthly

JOURNAL TITLE: DEMOGRAPHY

MANUSCRIPT ADDRESS: N. Krishnan Namboodiri, Editor
Department of Sociology
University of North Carolina
Chapel Hill, NC 27514

TYPE OF ARTICLES: Research articles, theoretical articles, review articles

MAJOR CONTENT AREAS: Demography, ecology, economy and society, family planning, marriage & divorce, migration, urban sociology, minorities, population

TOPICS PREFERRED: Not given

INAPPROPRIATE TOPICS: Not given

NUMBER OF MANUSCRIPT COPIES: 3
REVIEW PERIOD: 2-4 mos.
PUBLICATION LAG TIME: 4-8 months
EARLY PUBLICATION OPTION: No
ACCEPTANCE RATE: 16%
AUTHORSHIP RESTRICTIONS: No

PAGE CHARGES: No
STYLE REQUIREMENTS: Not given
STYLE SHEET: Yes
REVISED THESES: No
STUDENT PAPERS: No
REPRINT POLICY: None

SUBSCRIPTION ADDRESS: Population Association of America
PO Box 1418-2, B. Franklin Station
Washington, DC 20044

ANNUAL SUBSCRIPTION RATE: $25 individual, $25 institutional
INDEXED/ABSTRACTED IN: Not given

CIRCULATION: 4000   FREQUENCY: Quarterly

JOURNAL TITLE: DRUG FORUM - THE JOURNAL OF HUMAN ISSUES

MANUSCRIPT ADDRESS: Baywood Publishing Co.
43 Central Drive
Farmingdale, NY 11735

TYPE OF ARTICLES: Research articles, review articles, theoretical articles, book reviews

MAJOR CONTENT AREAS: All areas as related to drug abuse

TOPICS PREFERRED: Description and assessment of drug treatment modalities, legal issues, cultural aspects

INAPPROPRIATE TOPICS: Not given

NUMBER OF MANUSCRIPT COPIES: Not given
REVIEW PERIOD: 4-6 weeks
PUBLICATION LAG TIME: 9-12 months
EARLY PUBLICATION OPTION: No
ACCEPTANCE RATE: 50%
AUTHORSHIP RESTRICTIONS: Not given

PAGE CHARGES: Not given
STYLE REQUIREMENTS: APA
STYLE SHEET: Yes
REVISED THESES: Not given
STUDENT PAPERS: Not given
REPRINT POLICY: 20

SUBSCRIPTION ADDRESS: Baywood Publishing Company
43 Central Drive
Farmingdale, NY 11735

ANNUAL SUBSCRIPTION RATE: $35 individual, Not given institutional
INDEXED/ABSTRACTED IN: PA, EM, ACP, BA, BIS, CCSBS

CIRCULATION: 900   FREQUENCY: Not given

JOURNAL TITLE: DRUGS IN HEALTH CARE

MANUSCRIPT ADDRESS: American Society of Hospital Pharmacists
4630 Montgomery Avenue
Washington, DC 20014

TYPE OF ARTICLES: Research articles, demonstration projects, review
articles

MAJOR CONTENT AREAS: Social, economic, and administrative as related to the
drug use process

TOPICS PREFERRED: The drug use process as a unique area of
health services research and delivery

INAPPROPRIATE TOPICS: Drug abuse

NUMBER OF MANUSCRIPT COPIES: Not given	PAGE CHARGES: Not given
REVIEW PERIOD: 6 weeks	STYLE REQUIREMENTS: Index Medicus
PUBLICATION LAG TIME: 3-4 months	STYLE SHEET: Yes
EARLY PUBLICATION OPTION: No	REVISED THESES: Not given
ACCEPTANCE RATE: 50%	STUDENT PAPERS: Not given
AUTHORSHIP RESTRICTIONS: Not given	REPRINT POLICY: 20

SUBSCRIPTION ADDRESS: American Society of Hospital Pharmacists
4630 Montgomery Avenue
Washington , DC 20014

ANNUAL SUBSCRIPTION RATE: $15 individual, Not given institutional
INDEXED/ABSTRACTED IN: IPA

CIRCULATION: 800   FREQUENCY: Not given

JOURNAL TITLE: ECONOMIC AND SOCIAL REVIEW

MANUSCRIPT ADDRESS: B.A. Hutchinson, Editor
4 Burlington Road
Dublin 4, Ireland

TYPE OF ARTICLES: Not given

MAJOR CONTENT AREAS: Not given

TOPICS PREFERRED: Not given

INAPPROPRIATE TOPICS: Not given

NUMBER OF MANUSCRIPT COPIES: Not given	PAGE CHARGES: Not given
REVIEW PERIOD: 1-6 months	STYLE REQUIREMENTS: Not given
PUBLICATION LAG TIME: 2-4 months	STYLE SHEET: Not given
EARLY PUBLICATION OPTION: Not given	REVISED THESES: Not given
ACCEPTANCE RATE: 50%	STUDENT PAPERS: Not given
AUTHORSHIP RESTRICTIONS: Not given	REPRINT POLICY: 30

SUBSCRIPTION ADDRESS: B.A. Hutchinson, Editor
4 Burlington Road
Dublin 4, Ireland

ANNUAL SUBSCRIPTION RATE: $10.50 individual, $15 institutional
INDEXED/ABSTRACTED IN: Not given

CIRCULATION: 500   FREQUENCY: Quarterly

JOURNAL TITLE: ECONOMY AND SOCIETY

MANUSCRIPT ADDRESS: Routledge and Kegan Paul Ltd.
Broadway House, Newtown Road
Henley-on-Thames, England RG9 1EN

TYPE OF ARTICLES: Research articles, theoretical articles, review articles, case studies, commentaries, unsolicited book reviews

MAJOR CONTENT AREAS: Economy and society, social theory

TOPICS PREFERRED: Contemporary discussions and issues in Marxist theory and social science

INAPPROPRIATE TOPICS: Not given

NUMBER OF MANUSCRIPT COPIES: 2
REVIEW PERIOD: 6-8 wks.
PUBLICATION LAG TIME: 2-3 months
EARLY PUBLICATION OPTION: No
ACCEPTANCE RATE: Not given
AUTHORSHIP RESTRICTIONS: No

PAGE CHARGES: No
STYLE REQUIREMENTS: Chicago Manuscript
STYLE SHEET: Yes
REVISED THESES: No
STUDENT PAPERS: No
REPRINT POLICY: 25

SUBSCRIPTION ADDRESS: Routledge and Kegan Paul Ltd.
Broadway House, Newtown Road
Henley-on-Thames, England RG9 1EN

ANNUAL SUBSCRIPTION RATE: $20 individual, $20 institutional
INDEXED/ABSTRACTED IN: SA, CC

CIRCULATION: 1500   FREQUENCY: Quarterly

JOURNAL TITLE: EDUCATIONAL COMMUNICATION & TECHNOLOGY - A JOURNAL OF THEORY, RESEARCH, AND DEVELOPMENT

MANUSCRIPT ADDRESS: Dr. Robert Heinich, Editor
AVCR/ECTJ, Audio-Visual Center
Indiana University
Bloomington, IN 47401

TYPE OF ARTICLES: Research articles, theoretical articles, review articles, commentaries

MAJOR CONTENT AREAS: Educational sociology, mass communication, sociology of knowledge, mass media

TOPICS PREFERRED: Theory, development, and research related to technological processes in education.

INAPPROPRIATE TOPICS: "How I did it" type of article

NUMBER OF MANUSCRIPT COPIES: 3
REVIEW PERIOD: 2-18 mos.
PUBLICATION LAG TIME: 3-9 months
EARLY PUBLICATION OPTION: No
ACCEPTANCE RATE: 20%
AUTHORSHIP RESTRICTIONS: No

PAGE CHARGES: No
STYLE REQUIREMENTS: APA
STYLE SHEET: Yes
REVISED THESES: Acceptable
STUDENT PAPERS: Acceptable
REPRINT POLICY: 3 journals

SUBSCRIPTION ADDRESS: AVCR/ECTJ
Association for Educational Communications & Technology, 1126 16th Street NW
Washington, DC 20036

ANNUAL SUBSCRIPTION RATE: $19.50 individual, $19.50 institutional
INDEXED/ABSTRACTED IN: EI, CIJE

CIRCULATION: 7000   FREQUENCY: Quarterly

JOURNAL TITLE: EDUCATION AND URBAN SOCIETY

MANUSCRIPT ADDRESS: Jay D. Scribner
Sage Publications Inc.
275 S Beverly Drive
Beverly Hills, CA 90212

TYPE OF ARTICLES: Research articles, theoretical articles, case
studies, commentaries

MAJOR CONTENT AREAS: Educational sociology, urban sociology

TOPICS PREFERRED: Not given

INAPPROPRIATE TOPICS: Not given

NUMBER OF MANUSCRIPT COPIES: 3	PAGE CHARGES: No	
REVIEW PERIOD: Not given	STYLE REQUIREMENTS: Not given	
PUBLICATION LAG TIME: Not given	STYLE SHEET: No	
EARLY PUBLICATION OPTION: No	REVISED THESES: Not given	
ACCEPTANCE RATE: Not given	STUDENT PAPERS: No	
AUTHORSHIP RESTRICTIONS: No	REPRINT POLICY: 3	

SUBSCRIPTION ADDRESS: Sage Publications, Inc.
275 S Beverly Drive
Beverly Hills, CA 90212

ANNUAL SUBSCRIPTION RATE: $13.50 individual, $22.50 institutional
INDEXED/ABSTRACTED IN: HRA, SPAA, UAA, ERI/TE, EAA, SEA, HA, A, PAIS,
SSCI, CC, USPSD, SA
CIRCULATION: Not given   FREQUENCY: Quarterly

JOURNAL TITLE: EKISTICS

MANUSCRIPT ADDRESS: The Editor
Page Farm Road
Lincoln, MA 01773

TYPE OF ARTICLES: Research articles, theoretical articles, case
studies

MAJOR CONTENT AREAS: Anthropology, mass communication, demography,
ecology, economy and society, epidemiology,
housing and renewal, human development,
migration
TOPICS PREFERRED: Policy questions related to human settlements.

INAPPROPRIATE TOPICS: Not given

NUMBER OF MANUSCRIPT COPIES: 1	PAGE CHARGES: No	
REVIEW PERIOD: 1-52 wks.	STYLE REQUIREMENTS: Not given	
PUBLICATION LAG TIME: 3-9 months	STYLE SHEET: Not given	
EARLY PUBLICATION OPTION: Not given	REVISED THESES: Yes	
ACCEPTANCE RATE: 33%	STUDENT PAPERS: No	
AUTHORSHIP RESTRICTIONS: No	REPRINT POLICY: 10	

SUBSCRIPTION ADDRESS: Page Farm Road
Lincoln, MA 01773

ANNUAL SUBSCRIPTION RATE: $24 individual, $24 institutional
INDEXED/ABSTRACTED IN: CC,GA, CA, SUSA, EPB, RIBA/ARPA

CIRCULATION: Not given   FREQUENCY: Monthly

JOURNAL TITLE: EMERGE

MANUSCRIPT ADDRESS: Editor
PO Box 5366
Buena Park, CA 90622

TYPE OF ARTICLES: Research articles, theoretical articles, case
studies, commentaries

MAJOR CONTENT AREAS: Communes, economy and society, family formation,
human development, marriage & divorce, popular
culture, religion, sex roles, sexual behavior

TOPICS PREFERRED: Alternative lifestyles, human sexuality and sexual
behavior, social-sexual behavior, changing family
structure

INAPPROPRIATE TOPICS: Not given

NUMBER OF MANUSCRIPT COPIES: 1	PAGE CHARGES:	No
REVIEW PERIOD: 2 weeks	STYLE REQUIREMENTS:	Not given
PUBLICATION LAG TIME: 1-2 months	STYLE SHEET:	Yes
EARLY PUBLICATION OPTION: Not given	REVISED THESES:	Yes
ACCEPTANCE RATE: Not given	STUDENT PAPERS:	Yes
AUTHORSHIP RESTRICTIONS: No	REPRINT POLICY:	Not given

SUBSCRIPTION ADDRESS: PO Box 5366
Buena Park, CA 90622

ANNUAL SUBSCRIPTION RATE: $12 individual, $12 institutional
INDEXED/ABSTRACTED IN: Not given

CIRCULATION: 1500   FREQUENCY: Monthly

JOURNAL TITLE: ENVIRONMENT AND BEHAVIOR

MANUSCRIPT ADDRESS: Gary Winkel
Environmental Psychology Program
CUNY
New York, NY 10036

TYPE OF ARTICLES: Research articles, theoretical articles, review
articles, case studies, commentaries

MAJOR CONTENT AREAS: Ecology, social psychology, urban sociology

TOPICS PREFERRED: Not given

INAPPROPRIATE TOPICS: Not given

NUMBER OF MANUSCRIPT COPIES: 3	PAGE CHARGES:	No
REVIEW PERIOD: Not given	STYLE REQUIREMENTS:	Not given
PUBLICATION LAG TIME: Not given	STYLE SHEET:	Yes
EARLY PUBLICATION OPTION: No	REVISED THESES:	Not given
ACCEPTANCE RATE: Not given	STUDENT PAPERS:	No
AUTHORSHIP RESTRICTIONS: No	REPRINT POLICY:	24

SUBSCRIPTION ADDRESS: Sage Publications
275 S Beverly Drive
Beverly Hills, CA 90212

ANNUAL SUBSCRIPTION RATE: $15.60 individual, $26 institutional
INDEXED/ABSTRACTED IN: SSI, SSCI, HRA, CC, PA, PAIS, EIA, EP, SA, UAA,
SPAA

CIRCULATION: Not given   FREQUENCY: Quarterly

JOURNAL TITLE: ET.AL.

MANUSCRIPT ADDRESS: PO Box 77264
Los Angeles, CA 90007

TYPE OF ARTICLES: Not given

MAJOR CONTENT AREAS: Criminology, general sociology, human development,
social change, social theory, systems analysis,
sociobiology, social institutions, delinquency &
crime, social interaction, human organizations
TOPICS PREFERRED: Theoretical issues in the social sciences

INAPPROPRIATE TOPICS: Not given

NUMBER OF MANUSCRIPT COPIES: 2   PAGE CHARGES: No
REVIEW PERIOD: 1-2 mos.   STYLE REQUIREMENTS: ASA
PUBLICATION LAG TIME: Not given   STYLE SHEET: No
EARLY PUBLICATION OPTION: No   REVISED THESES: No
ACCEPTANCE RATE: 5-10 %   STUDENT PAPERS: Yes
AUTHORSHIP RESTRICTIONS: No   REPRINT POLICY: 4-6

SUBSCRIPTION ADDRESS: PO Box 77264
Los Angeles, CA 90007

ANNUAL SUBSCRIPTION RATE: $6 individual, $10 institutional
INDEXED/ABSTRACTED IN: SA

CIRCULATION: 500   FREQUENCY: Biannually

JOURNAL TITLE: ETHICS

MANUSCRIPT ADDRESS: University of Chicago, Cobb Hall
5811 Ellis Avenue
Chicago, IL 60637

TYPE OF ARTICLES: Theoretical articles, review articles, unsolicited
book reviews

MAJOR CONTENT AREAS: Not given

TOPICS PREFERRED: Study of the ideas and principles which form the
basis of individual and social action in ethical
theory, social science and jurisprudence.
INAPPROPRIATE TOPICS: Historical-exegetical analyses of "classic"
doctrines, highly polemics.

NUMBER OF MANUSCRIPT COPIES: 1   PAGE CHARGES: No
REVIEW PERIOD: 2-5 mos. STYLE REQUIREMENTS: Chicago Manuscript
PUBLICATION LAG TIME: 4-18 months   STYLE SHEET: Yes
EARLY PUBLICATION OPTION: No   REVISED THESES: No
ACCEPTANCE RATE: 6 1/2 %   STUDENT PAPERS: No
AUTHORSHIP RESTRICTIONS: No   REPRINT POLICY: None

SUBSCRIPTION ADDRESS: University of Chicago Press
Subscriptions Department
5801 Ellis Avenue
Chicago, IL 60637
ANNUAL SUBSCRIPTION RATE: $10.50 individual, $14 institutional
INDEXED/ABSTRACTED IN: SSI, PI, CC, BSMS, ABC:PSG

CIRCULATION: 3200   FREQUENCY: Quarterly

JOURNAL TITLE: ETHNICITY

MANUSCRIPT ADDRESS: William C. McCready
NORC, 6030 S Ellis Avenue
Chicago, IL 60637

TYPE OF ARTICLES: Research articles, theoretical articles, case
studies, commentaries

MAJOR CONTENT AREAS: Ethnic groups, social diversity, (religious,
ethnic, regional and linguistic.)

TOPICS PREFERRED: Interdisciplinary research articles on ethnic and
social diversityin the United States with secondary
interest in other geographic areas.
INAPPROPRIATE TOPICS: Not given

NUMBER OF MANUSCRIPT COPIES:	3	PAGE CHARGES:	Not given
REVIEW PERIOD:	Variable	STYLE REQUIREMENTS:	ASA
PUBLICATION LAG TIME:	1 year	STYLE SHEET:	Yes
EARLY PUBLICATION OPTION:	No	REVISED THESES:	No
ACCEPTANCE RATE:	55%	STUDENT PAPERS:	No
AUTHORSHIP RESTRICTIONS:	No	REPRINT POLICY:	50

SUBSCRIPTION ADDRESS: Academic Press, Inc.
111 Fifth Avenue
New York, NY 10003

ANNUAL SUBSCRIPTION RATE: Not given- individual, $32 institutional
INDEXED/ABSTRACTED IN: Not given

CIRCULATION: Not given   FREQUENCY: Quarterly

JOURNAL TITLE: ETHNOLOGY

MANUSCRIPT ADDRESS: Department of Anthropology
University of Pittsburgh
Pittsburgh, PA 15260

TYPE OF ARTICLES: Research articles, case studies

MAJOR CONTENT AREAS: Anthropology, social structure, stratification,
urban sociology

TOPICS PREFERRED: Social and cultural anthropological articles

INAPPROPRIATE TOPICS: Not given

NUMBER OF MANUSCRIPT COPIES:	1	PAGE CHARGES:	No
REVIEW PERIOD:	1-2 mos.	STYLE REQUIREMENTS:	Not given
PUBLICATION LAG TIME:	3 months	STYLE SHEET:	No
EARLY PUBLICATION OPTION:	No	REVISED THESES:	Yes
ACCEPTANCE RATE:	25%	STUDENT PAPERS:	No
AUTHORSHIP RESTRICTIONS:	No	REPRINT POLICY:	None

SUBSCRIPTION ADDRESS: Department of Anthropology
University of Pittsburgh
Pittsburgh, PA 15260

ANNUAL SUBSCRIPTION RATE: $10 individual, $15 institutional
INDEXED/ABSTRACTED IN: Not given

CIRCULATION: 3500   FREQUENCY: Quarterly

JOURNAL TITLE: EUROPEAN JOURNAL OF SOCIAL PSYCHOLOGY

MANUSCRIPT ADDRESS: Professor Arnold Upmeyer
Technische Universitat Berlin
Institute fur Psychologie
Dovestr., 1-5, 1000 Berlin (West) 10, Germany

TYPE OF ARTICLES: Research articles, theoretical articles, book
reviews, short research notes

MAJOR CONTENT AREAS: Social psychology

TOPICS PREFERRED: Social psychology predominantly of European
origin

INAPPROPRIATE TOPICS: Experimental studies without theoretical
background.

NUMBER OF MANUSCRIPT COPIES:	4	PAGE CHARGES:	No
REVIEW PERIOD:	1 1/2 yrs	STYLE REQUIREMENTS:	APA
PUBLICATION LAG TIME:	2 years	STYLE SHEET:	No
EARLY PUBLICATION OPTION:	No	REVISED THESES:	No
ACCEPTANCE RATE:	20%	STUDENT PAPERS:	No
AUTHORSHIP RESTRICTIONS:	No	REPRINT POLICY:	50

SUBSCRIPTION ADDRESS: Not given

ANNUAL SUBSCRIPTION RATE: Not given
INDEXED/ABSTRACTED IN: PA

CIRCULATION: Not given   FREQUENCY: Quarterly

JOURNAL TITLE: EUROPEAN JOURNAL OF SOCIOLOGY

MANUSCRIPT ADDRESS: Nusee de l'Homme
75 116 Paris, France

TYPE OF ARTICLES: Not given

MAJOR CONTENT AREAS: Not given

TOPICS PREFERRED: Not given

INAPPROPRIATE TOPICS: Not given

NUMBER OF MANUSCRIPT COPIES:	Not given	PAGE CHARGES:	Not given
REVIEW PERIOD:	Not given	STYLE REQUIREMENTS:	Not given
PUBLICATION LAG TIME:	Not given	STYLE SHEET:	Not given
EARLY PUBLICATION OPTION:	Not given	REVISED THESES:	Not given
ACCEPTANCE RATE:	50%	STUDENT PAPERS:	Not given
AUTHORSHIP RESTRICTIONS:	Not given	REPRINT POLICY:	50

SUBSCRIPTION ADDRESS: Nusee de l'Homme
75 116 Paris, France

ANNUAL SUBSCRIPTION RATE: $8 individual, Not given institutional
INDEXED/ABSTRACTED IN: Not given

CIRCULATION: 1500   FREQUENCY: Semiannually

JOURNAL TITLE: EVALUATION: A FORUM FOR HUMAN SERVICE
DECISION-MAKERS
MANUSCRIPT ADDRESS: 501 Park Avenue, South
Minneapolis, MN 55415

TYPE OF ARTICLES: Research articles, case studies, theoretical
articles, commentaries

MAJOR CONTENT AREAS: Aging and aged, counseling, epidemiology, social
planning, mental health & illness, social change,
social interaction, social issues, social policy,
social theory, systems analysis

TOPICS PREFERRED: Evaluation, planned change, policy analysis

INAPPROPRIATE TOPICS: Not given

NUMBER OF MANUSCRIPT COPIES: 2   PAGE CHARGES: No
REVIEW PERIOD: 3-6 months STYLE REQUIREMENTS: APA
PUBLICATION LAG TIME: 6-12 months   STYLE SHEET: Yes
EARLY PUBLICATION OPTION: No   REVISED THESES: No
ACCEPTANCE RATE: 25%   STUDENT PAPERS: No
AUTHORSHIP RESTRICTIONS: No   REPRINT POLICY: 5 journals

SUBSCRIPTION ADDRESS: 501 Park Avenue, South
Minneapolis, MN 55415

ANNUAL SUBSCRIPTION RATE: Not given
INDEXED/ABSTRACTED IN: BSD, GRAD, AEP, WFSD, GB, GPE

CIRCULATION: 30,000   FREQUENCY: Semiannually

JOURNAL TITLE: EXCEPTIONAL CHILDREN

MANUSCRIPT ADDRESS: 1920 Association Drive
Reston, VA 22091

TYPE OF ARTICLES: Research articles, theoretical articles, commentaries, model programs, review articles, case
studies, unsolicited book reviews

MAJOR CONTENT AREAS: Administrative behavior, adolescence, sex roles,
social change, social issues, social psychology,
values, law, minorities, ethnic groups

TOPICS PREFERRED: Exceptional child education, professional issues
and trends

INAPPROPRIATE TOPICS: Personal experience accounts

NUMBER OF MANUSCRIPT COPIES: 5   PAGE CHARGES: No
REVIEW PERIOD: 3 months STYLE REQUIREMENTS: APA
PUBLICATION LAG TIME: 6-9 months   STYLE SHEET: Yes
EARLY PUBLICATION OPTION: Yes   REVISED THESES: No
ACCEPTANCE RATE: 15%   STUDENT PAPERS: Yes
AUTHORSHIP RESTRICTIONS: No   REPRINT POLICY: 2 journals

SUBSCRIPTION ADDRESS: 1920 Association Drive
Reston, VA 22091

ANNUAL SUBSCRIPTION RATE: $20 individual, $20 institutional
INDEXED/ABSTRACTED IN: PA, ECEA, ASW, LLBA, CIJE

CIRCULATION: 68,000   FREQUENCY: 8 times per year

JOURNAL TITLE: FAMILY COORDINATOR

MANUSCRIPT ADDRESS: Dr. James Walters
Department of Child & Family Development
Dawson Hall, University of Georgia
Athens, GA 30602

TYPE OF ARTICLES: Commentaries, review articles, theoretical
articles, research articles, unsolicited
book reviews, case studies

MAJOR CONTENT AREAS: Adolescence, aging and aged, communes,
counseling, death & dying, delinquency &
crime, deviant behavior, ethnic groups, law,
marriage & divorce, race relations, values

TOPICS PREFERRED: Marriage & family

INAPPROPRIATE TOPICS: Research studies involving small, nonrepresen-
tative samples

NUMBER OF MANUSCRIPT COPIES: Not given   PAGE CHARGES: No
REVIEW PERIOD: 4 months   STYLE REQUIREMENTS: APA
PUBLICATION LAG TIME: 12-18 months   STYLE SHEET: Yes
EARLY PUBLICATION OPTION: No   REVISED THESES: No
ACCEPTANCE RATE: 25%   STUDENT PAPERS: Yes
AUTHORSHIP RESTRICTIONS: No   REPRINT POLICY: 5

SUBSCRIPTION ADDRESS: National Council on Family Relations
1219 University Avenue Southeast
Minneapolis, MN 55414

ANNUAL SUBSCRIPTION RATE: $15 individual, $15 institutional
INDEXED/ABSTRACTED IN: IBS, CIJE, SSCI, PA, CDA, SA

CIRCULATION: 7000   FREQUENCY: Quarterly

JOURNAL TITLE: FAMILY PLANNING PERSPECTIVES

MANUSCRIPT ADDRESS: 515 Madison Avenue
New York, NY 10022

TYPE OF ARTICLES: Research articles, review articles, case
studies, commentaries

MAJOR CONTENT AREAS: Adolescence, demography, family formation,
family planning, marriage and divorce, medical
sociology, social planning, population, public
health, sex roles, social change, social issues

TOPICS PREFERRED: Fertility - and population-related subjects

INAPPROPRIATE TOPICS: Not given

NUMBER OF MANUSCRIPT COPIES: 2   PAGE CHARGES: No
REVIEW PERIOD: 6-8 weeks STYLE REQUIREMENTS: Chicago Manuscript
PUBLICATION LAG TIME: 4 months   STYLE SHEET: Yes
EARLY PUBLICATION OPTION: Yes   REVISED THESES: Acceptable
ACCEPTANCE RATE: Not given   STUDENT PAPERS: Not given
AUTHORSHIP RESTRICTIONS: No   REPRINT POLICY: 25

SUBSCRIPTION ADDRESS: 515 Madison Avenue
New York, NY 10022

ANNUAL SUBSCRIPTION RATE: $25 individual, $25 institutional
INDEXED/ABSTRACTED IN: AEP, CINL, IM, N, PI, CICNRD, SPD, M, EA,
IGCC/RCSC
CIRCULATION: 30,000   FREQUENCY: Bimonthly

JOURNAL TITLE: FAMILY PROCESS

MANUSCRIPT ADDRESS: 149 East 78th Street
New York, NY 10021

TYPE OF ARTICLES: Research articles, theoretical articles, review
articles, case studies, commentaries, unsolicited
book reviews

MAJOR CONTENT AREAS: Anthropology, marriage & divorce, mental health
& illness, social institutions, social
interaction, social theory

TOPICS PREFERRED: Family research and treatment

INAPPROPRIATE TOPICS: Not given

NUMBER OF MANUSCRIPT COPIES: 2   PAGE CHARGES: No
REVIEW PERIOD: 8-10 wks. STYLE REQUIREMENTS: Not given
PUBLICATION LAG TIME: 3-6 months   STYLE SHEET: Yes
EARLY PUBLICATION OPTION: No   REVISED THESES: No
ACCEPTANCE RATE: 15%   STUDENT PAPERS: No
AUTHORSHIP RESTRICTIONS: No   REPRINT POLICY: None

SUBSCRIPTION ADDRESS: 149 East 78th Street
New York, NY 10021

ANNUAL SUBSCRIPTION RATE: $12 individual, $20 institutional
INDEXED/ABSTRACTED IN: ISI, PA, ASW, SA

CIRCULATION: 6000   FREQUENCY: Quarterly

JOURNAL TITLE: FAMILY THERAPY

MANUSCRIPT ADDRESS: Libra Publishers, Inc.
PO Box 165, 391 Willets Road
Roslyn Heights, L.I., NY 11577

TYPE OF ARTICLES: Case studies, theoretical articles, research
articles, commentaries

MAJOR CONTENT AREAS: Adolescence, aging and aged, counseling,
criminology, deviant behavior, family planning,
health and illness, human organizations,marriage
and divorce, social planning, social psychology

TOPICS PREFERRED: Case studies of family therapy

INAPPROPRIATE TOPICS: Not given

NUMBER OF MANUSCRIPT COPIES: 2   PAGE CHARGES: No
REVIEW PERIOD: 2-3 weeks STYLE REQUIREMENTS: Chicago Manuscript
PUBLICATION LAG TIME: 6 months   STYLE SHEET: Yes
EARLY PUBLICATION OPTION: No   REVISED THESES: No
ACCEPTANCE RATE: 30%   STUDENT PAPERS: No
AUTHORSHIP RESTRICTIONS: No   REPRINT POLICY: None

SUBSCRIPTION ADDRESS: Libra Publishers, Inc.
PO Box 165, 391 Willets Road
Roslyn Heights, L.I., NY 11577

ANNUAL SUBSCRIPTION RATE: $16 individual, $20 institutional
INDEXED/ABSTRACTED IN: Not given

CIRCULATION: 1000   FREQUENCY: Tri-yearly

JOURNAL TITLE: FEDERAL PROBATION

MANUSCRIPT ADDRESS: Donal L. Chamlee, Editor
Probation Div.
U.S. Supreme Court
Washington, DC   20544
TYPE OF ARTICLES: Not given

MAJOR CONTENT AREAS: Not given

TOPICS PREFERRED: Correctional philosophy and practice with a
special interest in criminal justice policy
issues
INAPPROPRIATE TOPICS: Academic research

NUMBER OF MANUSCRIPT COPIES: Not given   PAGE CHARGES: Not given
REVIEW PERIOD: 1-2 months STYLE REQUIREMENTS: Not given
PUBLICATION LAG TIME: 3-9 months   STYLE SHEET: Not given
EARLY PUBLICATION OPTION: Not given   REVISED THESES: Not given
ACCEPTANCE RATE: 25%   STUDENT PAPERS: Not given
AUTHORSHIP RESTRICTIONS: Not given   REPRINT POLICY: Not given

SUBSCRIPTION ADDRESS: Donal L. Chamlee, Editor
Probation Div.
U.S. Supreme Court
Washington, DC   20544
ANNUAL SUBSCRIPTION RATE: Free
INDEXED/ABSTRACTED IN: Not given

CIRCULATION: 35,000   FREQUENCY: Quarterly

JOURNAL TITLE: FOUNDATION NEWS

MANUSCRIPT ADDRESS: 888 Seventh Avenue
New York, NY   10019

TYPE OF ARTICLES: Case studies, theoretical articles, commentaries

MAJOR CONTENT AREAS: Administrative behavior, adolescence, aging and
aged, ethnic groups, leadership, marriage and
divorce, social conflict, sex roles, sexual
behavior, social theory, urban sociology, values
TOPICS PREFERRED: Improvement of the "human condition", especially
insofar as they have been supported by foundations

INAPPROPRIATE TOPICS: Not given

NUMBER OF MANUSCRIPT COPIES: 1   PAGE CHARGES: No
REVIEW PERIOD: 3 weeks   STYLE REQUIREMENTS: Not given
PUBLICATION LAG TIME: 3-9 months   STYLE SHEET: Yes
EARLY PUBLICATION OPTION: No   REVISED THESES: No
ACCEPTANCE RATE: 40%   STUDENT PAPERS: Acceptable
AUTHORSHIP RESTRICTIONS: No   REPRINT POLICY: 3 journals

SUBSCRIPTION ADDRESS: Box 783 Old Chelsea Station
New York, NY   10011

ANNUAL SUBSCRIPTION RATE: $20 individual, $20 institutional
INDEXED/ABSTRACTED IN: UIS, RRBC

CIRCULATION: 11,000   FREQUENCY: Bimonthly

JOURNAL TITLE: THE FUTURIST

MANUSCRIPT ADDRESS: World Future Society
PO Box 30369, Bethesda Branch
Washington, DC 20014

TYPE OF ARTICLES: Research articles, theoretical articles, review
articles, case studies, commentaries, unsolicited
book reviews

MAJOR CONTENT AREAS: Not given

TOPICS PREFERRED: Topics dealing only with the future.

INAPPROPRIATE TOPICS: "Crystal ball" type manuscripts

NUMBER OF MANUSCRIPT COPIES:	2	PAGE CHARGES: Not given
REVIEW PERIOD:	6 months	STYLE REQUIREMENTS: Chicago Manuscript
PUBLICATION LAG TIME:	6 months	STYLE SHEET: Yes
EARLY PUBLICATION OPTION:	No	REVISED THESES: Yes
ACCEPTANCE RATE:	4%	STUDENT PAPERS: No
AUTHORSHIP RESTRICTIONS:	No	REPRINT POLICY: 10

SUBSCRIPTION ADDRESS: World Future Society
PO Box 30369, Bethesda Branch
Washington, DC 20014

ANNUAL SUBSCRIPTION RATE: $15 individual, $90-$150 institutional
INDEXED/ABSTRACTED IN: Not given

CIRCULATION: 23,000   FREQUENCY: Bimonthly

JOURNAL TITLE: GENETIC PSYCHOLOGY MONOGRAPHS

MANUSCRIPT ADDRESS: Managing Editor, The Journal Press
Box 543, 2 Commercial Street
Provincetown, MA 02657

TYPE OF ARTICLES: Research articles, theoretical articles, review
articles

MAJOR CONTENT AREAS: Adolescence, aging and aged, human development

TOPICS PREFERRED: Not given

INAPPROPRIATE TOPICS: Clinical case histories

NUMBER OF MANUSCRIPT COPIES:	2	PAGE CHARGES: No
REVIEW PERIOD:	1 month	STYLE REQUIREMENTS: Not given
PUBLICATION LAG TIME:	1 year	STYLE SHEET: Yes
EARLY PUBLICATION OPTION:	Yes	REVISED THESES: Yes
ACCEPTANCE RATE:	40%	STUDENT PAPERS: Yes
AUTHORSHIP RESTRICTIONS:	Yes	REPRINT POLICY: 200

SUBSCRIPTION ADDRESS: Managing Editor, The Journal Press
Box 543, 2 Commercial Street
Provincetown, MA 02657

ANNUAL SUBSCRIPTION RATE: $30 individual, $30 institutional
INDEXED/ABSTRACTED IN: IM, PA, ASW, BA, BAMS, ECEA, EM

CIRCULATION: 1200   FREQUENCY: Quarterly

JOURNAL TITLE: GEORGIA SOCIAL SCIENCE JOURNAL

MANUSCRIPT ADDRESS: Ronald K. Templeton, Editor
204 Pine Valley Drive
Athens, GA 30601

TYPE OF ARTICLES: Not given

MAJOR CONTENT AREAS: Not given

TOPICS PREFERRED: Not given

INAPPROPRIATE TOPICS: Not given

NUMBER OF MANUSCRIPT COPIES: Not given
REVIEW PERIOD: 6 weeks
PUBLICATION LAG TIME: 1 year
EARLY PUBLICATION OPTION: Not given
ACCEPTANCE RATE: 75%
AUTHORSHIP RESTRICTIONS: Not given

PAGE CHARGES: Not given
STYLE REQUIREMENTS: Not given
STYLE SHEET: Not given
REVISED THESES: Not given
STUDENT PAPERS: Not given
REPRINT POLICY: 3

SUBSCRIPTION ADDRESS: Ronald K. Templeton, Editor
204 Pine Valley Drive
Athens, GA 30601

ANNUAL SUBSCRIPTION RATE: $5 individual, $5 institutional
INDEXED/ABSTRACTED IN: Not given

CIRCULATION: 600   FREQUENCY: Tri-yearly

JOURNAL TITLE: GERIATRICS

MANUSCRIPT ADDRESS: 4015 W 65th Street
Minneapolis, MN 55435

TYPE OF ARTICLES: Review articles, case studies

MAJOR CONTENT AREAS: Aging and aged

TOPICS PREFERRED: Medical papers concerning aging that are of practical clinical value.

INAPPROPRIATE TOPICS: Not given

NUMBER OF MANUSCRIPT COPIES: 1
REVIEW PERIOD: 1 month
PUBLICATION LAG TIME: 3 months
EARLY PUBLICATION OPTION: No
ACCEPTANCE RATE: Not given
AUTHORSHIP RESTRICTIONS: No

PAGE CHARGES: No
STYLE REQUIREMENTS: Not given
STYLE SHEET: Yes
REVISED THESES: No
STUDENT PAPERS: No
REPRINT POLICY: None

SUBSCRIPTION ADDRESS: Harcourt Brace Janonovich Publications
1 East First Street
Duluth, MN 55802

ANNUAL SUBSCRIPTION RATE: $15 individual, $15 institutional
INDEXED/ABSTRACTED IN: IM

CIRCULATION: 40,000   FREQUENCY: Monthly

JOURNAL TITLE: THE GERONTOLOGIST

MANUSCRIPT ADDRESS: Elias S. Cohen
136 Farwood Road
Philadelphia, PA 19151

TYPE OF ARTICLES: Applied research articles, commentaries,
theoretical articles

MAJOR CONTENT AREAS: Aging and aged, demography, health and illness,
housing and renewal

TOPICS PREFERRED: Aging

INAPPROPRIATE TOPICS: Not given

NUMBER OF MANUSCRIPT COPIES: 3	PAGE CHARGES:	No
REVIEW PERIOD: 60 days	STYLE REQUIREMENTS:	APA
PUBLICATION LAG TIME: 4-6 months	STYLE SHEET:	Yes
EARLY PUBLICATION OPTION: No	REVISED THESES:	Acceptable
ACCEPTANCE RATE: Not given	STUDENT PAPERS:	Acceptable
AUTHORSHIP RESTRICTIONS: No	REPRINT POLICY:	None

SUBSCRIPTION ADDRESS: Gerontological Society
One Dupont Circle #520
Washington, DC 20036

ANNUAL SUBSCRIPTION RATE: $20 individual, $20 institutional
INDEXED/ABSTRACTED IN: Not given

CIRCULATION: 7000   FREQUENCY: Bimonthly

JOURNAL TITLE: GROUP PSYCHOTHERAPY, PSCYCHODRAMA AND
SOCIOMETRY
MANUSCRIPT ADDRESS: PO Box 311
Beacon, NY 12508

TYPE OF ARTICLES: Research articles, case studies

MAJOR CONTENT AREAS: Administrative behavior, adolescence, aging and
aged, deviant behavior, health and illness, human
development, marriage and divorce, medical
sociology, social conflict, sex roles, suicide
TOPICS PREFERRED: Not given

INAPPROPRIATE TOPICS: Not given

NUMBER OF MANUSCRIPT COPIES: 2	PAGE CHARGES:	Yes
REVIEW PERIOD: Not given	STYLE REQUIREMENTS:	APA
PUBLICATION LAG TIME: 6 months	STYLE SHEET:	Yes
EARLY PUBLICATION OPTION: No	REVISED THESES:	Yes
ACCEPTANCE RATE: Not given	STUDENT PAPERS:	Yes
AUTHORSHIP RESTRICTIONS: No	REPRINT POLICY:	None

SUBSCRIPTION ADDRESS: PO Box 311
Beacon, NY 12508

ANNUAL SUBSCRIPTION RATE: $14 individual, $14 institutional
INDEXED/ABSTRACTED IN: Not given

CIRCULATION: 1500   FREQUENCY: Annually

JOURNAL TITLE: GROWTH AND CHANGE: A JOURNAL OF REGIONAL
DEVELOPMENT

MANUSCRIPT ADDRESS: Executive Editor
644 Maxwelton Court
Lexington , KY 40506

TYPE OF ARTICLES: Research articles, case studies, theoretical
articles, review articles

MAJOR CONTENT AREAS: Community development, demography, ecology,
housing and renewal, migration, social planning,
political sociology, population, public health,
rural sociology, social change

TOPICS PREFERRED: Planning and regional development - policy
oriented articles based on sound theory

INAPPROPRIATE TOPICS: Historical pieces, articles on foreign subjects
with no connection to regional development

NUMBER OF MANUSCRIPT COPIES: 3	PAGE CHARGES:	Not given
REVIEW PERIOD: 6 months	STYLE REQUIREMENTS:	Chicago Manuscript
PUBLICATION LAG TIME: Not given	STYLE SHEET:	Yes
EARLY PUBLICATION OPTION: No	REVISED THESES:	Acceptable
ACCEPTANCE RATE: 25%	STUDENT PAPERS:	No
AUTHORSHIP RESTRICTIONS: No	REPRINT POLICY:	None

SUBSCRIPTION ADDRESS: 644 Maxwelton Court
Lexington, KY 40506

ANNUAL SUBSCRIPTION RATE: Not given
INDEXED/ABSTRACTED IN: JEL, CC, UAA, ABC PS, LH, GPE, B-D

CIRCULATION: 1250   FREQUENCY: Quarterly

JOURNAL TITLE: HANDBOOK OF INTERNATIONAL SOCIOMETRY

MANUSCRIPT ADDRESS: Beacon House, Inc.
PO Box 311
Beacon , NY 12508

TYPE OF ARTICLES: Research articles, review articles, theoretical
articles

MAJOR CONTENT AREAS: Psychotherapy as applied to groups

TOPICS PREFERRED: Sociometry, psychodrama, group psychotherapy,
group dynamics

INAPPROPRIATE TOPICS: Not given

NUMBER OF MANUSCRIPT COPIES: Not given	PAGE CHARGES:	Not given
REVIEW PERIOD: 6-8 weeks	STYLE REQUIREMENTS:	APA
PUBLICATION LAG TIME: 1 year	STYLE SHEET:	Yes
EARLY PUBLICATION OPTION: No	REVISED THESES:	Not given
ACCEPTANCE RATE: Not given	STUDENT PAPERS:	Not given
AUTHORSHIP RESTRICTIONS: Not given	REPRINT POLICY:	Not given

SUBSCRIPTION ADDRESS: Beacon House, Inc.
P O Box 311
Beacon, NY 12508

ANNUAL SUBSCRIPTION RATE: $14 individual, Not given institutional
INDEXED/ABSTRACTED IN: PA, SA, BS

CIRCULATION: 500   FREQUENCY: Not given

JOURNAL TITLE: HARVARD BUSINESS REVIEW

MANUSCRIPT ADDRESS: Mr. E.H. Knox, Editor
Soldiers Field
Boston, MA 02163

TYPE OF ARTICLES: Not given

MAJOR CONTENT AREAS: Not given

TOPICS PREFERRED: Not given

INAPPROPRIATE TOPICS: Not given

NUMBER OF MANUSCRIPT COPIES:	Not given	PAGE CHARGES:	Not given
REVIEW PERIOD:	1-2 mos.	STYLE REQUIREMENTS:	Not given
PUBLICATION LAG TIME:	1-6 months	STYLE SHEET:	Not given
EARLY PUBLICATION OPTION:	Not given	REVISED THESES:	Not given
ACCEPTANCE RATE:	5%	STUDENT PAPERS:	Not given
AUTHORSHIP RESTRICTIONS:	Not given	REPRINT POLICY:	100

SUBSCRIPTION ADDRESS: Mr. E.H. Knox, Editor
Soldiers Field
Boston, MA 02163

ANNUAL SUBSCRIPTION RATE: $15 individual, $15 institutional
INDEXED/ABSTRACTED IN: Not given

CIRCULATION: 150,000   FREQUENCY: Bimonthly

JOURNAL TITLE: HARVARD EDUCATIONAL REVIEW

MANUSCRIPT ADDRESS: 13 Appian Way
Longfellow Hall
Cambridge, MA 02138

TYPE OF ARTICLES: Theoretical articles, research articles, case
studies, review articles, commentaries,
unsolicited book reviews
MAJOR CONTENT AREAS: Adolescence, educational sociology, ethnic groups,
poverty, inequality, and policy, sex roles,
social change, social issues, socialization,
social psychology, stratification
TOPICS PREFERRED: Not given

INAPPROPRIATE TOPICS: Not given

NUMBER OF MANUSCRIPT COPIES:	3	PAGE CHARGES:	No
REVIEW PERIOD:	2 months	STYLE REQUIREMENTS:	APA, MLA
PUBLICATION LAG TIME:	6 months	STYLE SHEET:	Yes
EARLY PUBLICATION OPTION:	No	REVISED THESES:	No
ACCEPTANCE RATE:	6%	STUDENT PAPERS:	No
AUTHORSHIP RESTRICTIONS:	No	REPRINT POLICY:	20

SUBSCRIPTION ADDRESS: 13 Appian Way
Longfellow Hall
Cambridge, MA 02138

ANNUAL SUBSCRIPTION RATE: $15 individual, $20 institutional
INDEXED/ABSTRACTED IN: EI, BRI, CIJE, PA, SA, HA, SEA, USPSD

CIRCULATION: 14,000   FREQUENCY: Quarterly

JOURNAL TITLE: HEALTH AND SOCIAL WORK

MANUSCRIPT ADDRESS: Editorial Office
National Association of Social Workers
2 Park Avenue
New York, NY 10016

TYPE OF ARTICLES: Theoretical articles, case studies, research
articles, commentaries

MAJOR CONTENT AREAS: Aging and aged, counseling, family planning,
medical sociology, public health, sexual
behavior, social issues, suicide

TOPICS PREFERRED: The role of the social workers in new areas of
medical treatment

INAPPROPRIATE TOPICS: Not given

NUMBER OF MANUSCRIPT COPIES: 3	PAGE CHARGES:	No
REVIEW PERIOD: 2-4 mos.	STYLE REQUIREMENTS:	Not given
PUBLICATION LAG TIME: 3-8 months	STYLE SHEET:	Yes
EARLY PUBLICATION OPTION: No	REVISED THESES:	No
ACCEPTANCE RATE: 25-30%	STUDENT PAPERS:	No
AUTHORSHIP RESTRICTIONS: No	REPRINT POLICY:	5

SUBSCRIPTION ADDRESS: Publications Sales
National Association of Social Workers
49 Sheridan Avenue
Albany, NY 12210

ANNUAL SUBSCRIPTION RATE: $30 individual, Not given- institutional
INDEXED/ABSTRACTED IN: ASW, IM, EM, DSHA, AHMS, MCR

CIRCULATION: 4500   FREQUENCY: Quarterly

JOURNAL TITLE: HEALTH SERVICES RESEARCH

MANUSCRIPT ADDRESS: J. David Amundson, Editor
840 N Lake Shore Drive
Chicago, IL 60611

TYPE OF ARTICLES: Research articles, commentaries, review articles,
theoretical articles, case studies, unsolicited
book reviews

MAJOR CONTENT AREAS: Administrative behavior, bureaucracy, collective
behavior, economy and society, health and illness,
human organizations, medical sociology, public
health, systems analysis, social planning

TOPICS PREFERRED: Health service problem areas

INAPPROPRIATE TOPICS: Sociological, anthropological studies without
application

NUMBER OF MANUSCRIPT COPIES: 3	PAGE CHARGES:	No
REVIEW PERIOD: 3 months	STYLE REQUIREMENTS:	Chicago Manuscript
PUBLICATION LAG TIME: 3 months	STYLE SHEET:	Yes
EARLY PUBLICATION OPTION: No	REVISED THESES:	No
ACCEPTANCE RATE: 20%	STUDENT PAPERS:	No
AUTHORSHIP RESTRICTIONS: No	REPRINT POLICY:	50

SUBSCRIPTION ADDRESS: William S. Childs
Circulation Manager
840 N Lake Shore Drive
Chicago, IL 60611

ANNUAL SUBSCRIPTION RATE: $20 individual, $20 institutional
INDEXED/ABSTRACTED IN: IM, HLI, MEDSOC, EM,HA, INI, AHMS, CC

CIRCULATION: 2200   FREQUENCY: Quarterly

JOURNAL TITLE: HEURISTICS

MANUSCRIPT ADDRESS: Editor, Heuristics
Dept. of Sociology
Northern Illinois University
DeKalb, IL 60115
TYPE OF ARTICLES: Theoretical articles, research articles, case
studies

MAJOR CONTENT AREAS: Criminology, collective behavior, groups, human
organizations, rural sociology, sex roles, race
relations, religion, values, social theory,
social issues
TOPICS PREFERRED: Not given

INAPPROPRIATE TOPICS: Literature review papers

NUMBER OF MANUSCRIPT COPIES: 3   PAGE CHARGES: No
REVIEW PERIOD: 2 months STYLE REQUIREMENTS: ASA
PUBLICATION LAG TIME: 6 months   STYLE SHEET: Yes
EARLY PUBLICATION OPTION: No   REVISED THESES: Yes
ACCEPTANCE RATE: 40-50%   STUDENT PAPERS: Yes
AUTHORSHIP RESTRICTIONS: No   REPRINT POLICY: 1

SUBSCRIPTION ADDRESS: Editor, Heuristics
Dept. of Sociology
Northern Illinois University

ANNUAL SUBSCRIPTION RATE: $3 individual, $5 institutional
INDEXED/ABSTRACTED IN: Not given

CIRCULATION: 80   FREQUENCY: Biannually

JOURNAL TITLE: HIGHER EDUCATION

MANUSCRIPT ADDRESS: Professor Alec Ross
Department of Educational Research
University of Lancaster
Bailrigg, Lancaster, England
TYPE OF ARTICLES: Research articles, review articles, unsolicited
book reviews

MAJOR CONTENT AREAS: Education

TOPICS PREFERRED: Comparative education, educational planning,
new developments in higher education in all
countries
INAPPROPRIATE TOPICS: Not given

NUMBER OF MANUSCRIPT COPIES: 3   PAGE CHARGES: No
REVIEW PERIOD: Not given STYLE REQUIREMENTS: Chicago Manuscript
PUBLICATION LAG TIME: 4 months   STYLE SHEET: Yes
EARLY PUBLICATION OPTION: Not given   REVISED THESES: No
ACCEPTANCE RATE: Not given   STUDENT PAPERS: No
AUTHORSHIP RESTRICTIONS: No   REPRINT POLICY: 50

SUBSCRIPTION ADDRESS: Elsevier Scientific Publishing Company
Journal Division
PO Box 211
Amsterdam, The Netherlands
ANNUAL SUBSCRIPTION RATE: $21 individual, $45.60 institutional
INDEXED/ABSTRACTED IN: BEI, BIAU, CSPA, CC/SBS, CIJE, SEA

CIRCULATION: 1000   FREQUENCY: Quarterly

JOURNAL TITLE: HOMOSEXUAL COUNSELING JOURNAL

MANUSCRIPT ADDRESS: 30 East 60th Street
Room 708
New York, NY 10022

TYPE OF ARTICLES: Research articles, review articles,
theoretical articles; the emphasis
is on practicality and clinical experience

MAJOR CONTENT AREAS: Counseling (with homosexuals)

TOPICS PREFERRED: Counseling with homosexuals and their
families

INAPPROPRIATE TOPICS: Those unrelated to counseling with homosexuals

NUMBER OF MANUSCRIPT COPIES:	Not given	PAGE CHARGES:	Not given
REVIEW PERIOD:	2 months	STYLE REQUIREMENTS:	APA
PUBLICATION LAG TIME:	2 months	STYLE SHEET:	Yes
EARLY PUBLICATION OPTION:	Yes	REVISED THESES:	Not given
ACCEPTANCE RATE:	20%	STUDENT PAPERS:	Not given
AUTHORSHIP RESTRICTIONS:	Not given	REPRINT POLICY:	Not given

SUBSCRIPTION ADDRESS: 30 East 60th Street
Room 708
New York, NY 10022

ANNUAL SUBSCRIPTION RATE: $10 individual, $15 institutional
INDEXED/ABSTRACTED IN: PA

CIRCULATION: 700 FREQUENCY: Not given

JOURNAL TITLE: HISTORY AND THEORY

MANUSCRIPT ADDRESS: Wesleyan Station
Middletown, CT 06457

TYPE OF ARTICLES: Research articles, theoretical articles

MAJOR CONTENT AREAS: Demography, sociology of knowledge, social
theory

TOPICS PREFERRED: Philosophy of history, historiography

INAPPROPRIATE TOPICS: Not given

NUMBER OF MANUSCRIPT COPIES:	1	PAGE CHARGES:	No
REVIEW PERIOD:	2 months	STYLE REQUIREMENTS:	Not given
PUBLICATION LAG TIME:	Not given	STYLE SHEET:	Yes
EARLY PUBLICATION OPTION:	No	REVISED THESES:	Not given
ACCEPTANCE RATE:	14%	STUDENT PAPERS:	No
AUTHORSHIP RESTRICTIONS:	No	REPRINT POLICY:	25

SUBSCRIPTION ADDRESS: Wesleyan Station
Middletown, CT 06457

ANNUAL SUBSCRIPTION RATE: $10 individual, $16 institutional
INDEXED/ABSTRACTED IN: HA, PI, SSHI, SA, CRIS, USPSD

CIRCULATION: 2600 FREQUENCY: Quarterly

JOURNAL TITLE: HOSPITAL & HEALTH SERVICES ADMINISTRATION

MANUSCRIPT ADDRESS: 840 N Lake Shore Drive
Chicago, IL 60611

TYPE OF ARTICLES: Research articles, theoretical articles,
organization, evaluation, communication,
public relations
MAJOR CONTENT AREAS: Administrative behavior, leadership

TOPICS PREFERRED: Any facets of administration

INAPPROPRIATE TOPICS: Not given

NUMBER OF MANUSCRIPT COPIES:	4	PAGE CHARGES:	No
REVIEW PERIOD:	3 months	STYLE REQUIREMENTS:	Chicago Manuscript
PUBLICATION LAG TIME:	6 months	STYLE SHEET:	Yes
EARLY PUBLICATION OPTION:	No	REVISED THESES:	Acceptable
ACCEPTANCE RATE:	30%	STUDENT PAPERS:	No
AUTHORSHIP RESTRICTIONS:	No	REPRINT POLICY:	6

SUBSCRIPTION ADDRESS: 840 N Lake Shore Drive
Chicago, IL 60611

ANNUAL SUBSCRIPTION RATE: $5 individual, $5 institutional
INDEXED/ABSTRACTED IN: Not given

CIRCULATION: 12,500   FREQUENCY: Quarterly

JOURNAL TITLE: HUMAN BEHAVIOR MAGAZINE

MANUSCRIPT ADDRESS: Manson Western Corp.
12031 Wilshire Boulevard
Los Angeles, CA 90025

TYPE OF ARTICLES: Review articles, case studies, commentaries

MAJOR CONTENT AREAS: Adolescence, aging and aged, alcoholism & drug
abuse, anthropology, collective behavior,
consumerism, criminology, death & dying

TOPICS PREFERRED: Not given

INAPPROPRIATE TOPICS: How-to articles, self-help

NUMBER OF MANUSCRIPT COPIES:	1	PAGE CHARGES:	No
REVIEW PERIOD:	1 1/2 mos	STYLE REQUIREMENTS:	Not given
PUBLICATION LAG TIME:	2-5 months	STYLE SHEET:	Yes
EARLY PUBLICATION OPTION:	No	REVISED THESES:	Yes
ACCEPTANCE RATE:	Not given	STUDENT PAPERS:	No
AUTHORSHIP RESTRICTIONS:	No	REPRINT POLICY:	3 journals

SUBSCRIPTION ADDRESS: 12031 Wilshire Boulevard
Los Angeles, CA 90025

ANNUAL SUBSCRIPTION RATE: $14 individual, Not given-institutional
INDEXED/ABSTRACTED IN: Not given

CIRCULATION: 100,000   FREQUENCY: Monthly

JOURNAL TITLE: HUMAN BIOLOGY

MANUSCRIPT ADDRESS: Dr. Gabriel W. Lasker
Department of Anatomy, Wayne State Univ.
School of Medicine, 540 East Canfield St.
Detroit, MI 48201

TYPE OF ARTICLES: Research articles, review articles, theoretical
articles

MAJOR CONTENT AREAS: Aging and aged, demography,health and illness,
human development, population, public health,
anthropology, ecology, evolution

TOPICS PREFERRED: Human biological adaptation

INAPPROPRIATE TOPICS: Not given

NUMBER OF MANUSCRIPT COPIES:	3	PAGE CHARGES:	Yes
REVIEW PERIOD:	4 weeks	STYLE REQUIREMENTS:	Not given
PUBLICATION LAG TIME:	1 year	STYLE SHEET:	Yes
EARLY PUBLICATION OPTION:	No	REVISED THESES:	No
ACCEPTANCE RATE:	50%	STUDENT PAPERS:	No
AUTHORSHIP RESTRICTIONS:	No	REPRINT POLICY:	25

SUBSCRIPTION ADDRESS: Wayne State University Press
5959 Woodward Avenue
Detroit, MI 48202

ANNUAL SUBSCRIPTION RATE: $15 individual, $20 institutional
INDEXED/ABSTRACTED IN: Not given

CIRCULATION: 1723   FREQUENCY: Quarterly

JOURNAL TITLE: HUMAN DEVELOPMENT

MANUSCRIPT ADDRESS: Klaus F. Riegel, Dept. of Psychology
University of Michigan
Ann Arbor, MI 48104

TYPE OF ARTICLES: Theoretical articles, review articles

MAJOR CONTENT AREAS: Developmental, general, history & systems,
social issues

TOPICS PREFERRED: Theoretical contributions and integrative
reviews

INAPPROPRIATE TOPICS: Research reports

NUMBER OF MANUSCRIPT COPIES:	Not given	PAGE CHARGES:	Not given
REVIEW PERIOD:	6 weeks	STYLE REQUIREMENTS:	APA
PUBLICATION LAG TIME:	4 months	STYLE SHEET:	Yes
EARLY PUBLICATION OPTION:	No	REVISED THESES:	Not given
ACCEPTANCE RATE:	25%	STUDENT PAPERS:	Not given
AUTHORSHIP RESTRICTIONS:	Not given	REPRINT POLICY:	Not given

SUBSCRIPTION ADDRESS: Albert J. Phiebig
PO Box 352
White Plains, NY 10602

ANNUAL SUBSCRIPTION RATE: $36 individual, $60 institutional
INDEXED/ABSTRACTED IN: PA, AA, BEI, BS, CCSBS, CIJE, EI, LLBA, WSA

CIRCULATION: 1500   FREQUENCY: Not given

JOURNAL TITLE: HUMAN ECOLOGY

MANUSCRIPT ADDRESS: Professors Susan H. Lees, Daniel G. Bates
Box 792, Hunter College
695 Park Avenue
New York, NY 10011

TYPE OF ARTICLES: Research articles, theoretical articles, case studies

MAJOR CONTENT AREAS: Anthropology, demography, ecology, evolution, systems analysis

TOPICS PREFERRED: Not given

INAPPROPRIATE TOPICS: Not given

NUMBER OF MANUSCRIPT COPIES:	3	PAGE CHARGES:	No
REVIEW PERIOD:	Not given	STYLE REQUIREMENTS:	Not given
PUBLICATION LAG TIME:	Not given	STYLE SHEET:	Yes
EARLY PUBLICATION OPTION:	No	REVISED THESES:	No
ACCEPTANCE RATE:	Not given	STUDENT PAPERS:	No
AUTHORSHIP RESTRICTIONS:	No	REPRINT POLICY:	None

SUBSCRIPTION ADDRESS: Plenum Publishing Corporation
227 West 17th Street
New York, NY 10011

ANNUAL SUBSCRIPTION RATE: $14 individual, $35 institutional
INDEXED/ABSTRACTED IN: AI, BA, EI, EM, CC, SSA, URS

CIRCULATION: 2000   FREQUENCY: Quarterly

JOURNAL TITLE: HUMANITAS

MANUSCRIPT ADDRESS: Center for the Study of Spirituality
Institute of Man
Duquesne University
Pittsburgh, PA 15219

TYPE OF ARTICLES: Not given

MAJOR CONTENT AREAS: Adolescence, aging and aged, anthropology, counseling, death and dying, general sociology, human development, sociology of peace, social planning, values, religion, social change

TOPICS PREFERRED: Topics relevant to human development

INAPPROPRIATE TOPICS: Obscure philosophical topics

NUMBER OF MANUSCRIPT COPIES:	1	PAGE CHARGES:	No
REVIEW PERIOD:	4 months	STYLE REQUIREMENTS:	Not given
PUBLICATION LAG TIME:	2 weeks	STYLE SHEET:	Yes
EARLY PUBLICATION OPTION:	Not given	REVISED THESES:	Acceptable
ACCEPTANCE RATE:	50%	STUDENT PAPERS:	Acceptable
AUTHORSHIP RESTRICTIONS:	No	REPRINT POLICY:	25

SUBSCRIPTION ADDRESS: Publication Manager
Institute of Man
Pittsburgh, PA 15219

ANNUAL SUBSCRIPTION RATE: $10 individual, $10 institutional
INDEXED/ABSTRACTED IN: ISSN

CIRCULATION: 1200   FREQUENCY: Tri-yearly

JOURNAL TITLE: HUMAN MOSAIC

MANUSCRIPT ADDRESS: Department of Anthropology
Tulane University
New Orleans, LA 70118

TYPE OF ARTICLES: Research articles, case studies, theoretical
articles, review articles, commentaries,
unsolicited book reviews

MAJOR CONTENT AREAS: Anthropology, collective behavior, ecology,
ethnic groups, evolution, family formation,
general sociology, groups, human organizations, marriage & divorce, migration, population

TOPICS PREFERRED: Not given

INAPPROPRIATE TOPICS: Not given

NUMBER OF MANUSCRIPT COPIES:	1	PAGE CHARGES:	No
REVIEW PERIOD:	3 months	STYLE REQUIREMENTS:	AAA
PUBLICATION LAG TIME:	1 month	STYLE SHEET:	Yes
EARLY PUBLICATION OPTION:	No	REVISED THESES:	No
ACCEPTANCE RATE:	50%	STUDENT PAPERS:	Yes
AUTHORSHIP RESTRICTIONS:	Yes	REPRINT POLICY:	2 journals

SUBSCRIPTION ADDRESS: Department of Anthropology
Tulane University
New Orleans, LA 70118

ANNUAL SUBSCRIPTION RATE: $3.50 individual, $3.50 institutional
INDEXED/ABSTRACTED IN: SA

CIRCULATION: 85   FREQUENCY: Semiannually

JOURNAL TITLE: HUMAN ORGANIZATION

MANUSCRIPT ADDRESS: 1703 New Hampshire Avenue NW
Washington, DC 20009

TYPE OF ARTICLES: Research articles, theoretical articles, case
studies, commentaries

MAJOR CONTENT AREAS: Administrative behavior, aging and aged, race
relations, criminology, demography, human
organization, sex roles, social change, social
conflict, social mobility, social movements

TOPICS PREFERRED: Applied social science

INAPPROPRIATE TOPICS: Personal professional histories and programmatic
statements

NUMBER OF MANUSCRIPT COPIES:	4	PAGE CHARGES:	No
REVIEW PERIOD:	2 months	STYLE REQUIREMENTS:	AAA
PUBLICATION LAG TIME:	1 year	STYLE SHEET:	Yes
EARLY PUBLICATION OPTION:	Yes	REVISED THESES:	Yes
ACCEPTANCE RATE:	15%	STUDENT PAPERS:	No
AUTHORSHIP RESTRICTIONS:	No	REPRINT POLICY:	Not given

SUBSCRIPTION ADDRESS: 1703 New Hampshire Avenue NW
Washington, DC 20009

ANNUAL SUBSCRIPTION RATE: $17 individual, $25 institutional
INDEXED/ABSTRACTED IN: Not given

CIRCULATION: 4000   FREQUENCY: Quarterly

JOURNAL TITLE: HUMAN RELATIONS

MANUSCRIPT ADDRESS: Coordinator Editor, Human Relations
University of Pennsylvania, Wharton School
Management and Behavioral Science Center
Philadelphia, PA 19174

TYPE OF ARTICLES: Theoretical developments, new methods, review articles,
reports of empirical research including qualitative and/or
quantitative data

MAJOR CONTENT AREAS: Innovative contributions in emerging fields of work
relating to understanding the complexities of human
problems

TOPICS PREFERRED: Articles dealing with a broad spectrum of human
problems and approaches toward the integration of
the social sciences

INAPPROPRIATE TOPICS: Not given

NUMBER OF MANUSCRIPT COPIES: 2	PAGE CHARGES:	No
REVIEW PERIOD: Not given	STYLE REQUIREMENTS:	Not given
PUBLICATION LAG TIME: Not given	STYLE SHEET:	Yes
EARLY PUBLICATION OPTION: Not given	REVISED THESES:	Not given
ACCEPTANCE RATE: Not given	STUDENT PAPERS:	Not given
AUTHORSHIP RESTRICTIONS: Not given	REPRINT POLICY:	50

SUBSCRIPTION ADDRESS: Plenum Publishing Corporation
227 West 17 Street
New York, New York 10011

ANNUAL SUBSCRIPTION RATE: $22 APA member, $32.50 individual, $65 institutional
INDEXED/ABSTRACTED IN: Not given

CIRCULATION: Not given   FREQUENCY: Monthly

JOURNAL TITLE: HUMAN RESOURCE MANAGEMENT

MANUSCRIPT ADDRESS: Graduate School of Business Administration
University of Michigan
Ann Arbor, MI 48109

TYPE OF ARTICLES: Research articles, theoretical articles, case
studies

MAJOR CONTENT AREAS: Administrative behavior, bureaucracy, human
organizations, labor force/labor relations,
minorities, occupations & careers, organizations, society & institutions

TOPICS PREFERRED: Not given

INAPPROPRIATE TOPICS: Not given

NUMBER OF MANUSCRIPT COPIES: 3	PAGE CHARGES:	No
REVIEW PERIOD: 6 weeks	STYLE REQUIREMENTS:	Not given
PUBLICATION LAG TIME: 8 months	STYLE SHEET:	No
EARLY PUBLICATION OPTION: No	REVISED THESES:	Yes
ACCEPTANCE RATE: 15%	STUDENT PAPERS:	No
AUTHORSHIP RESTRICTIONS: No	REPRINT POLICY:	Not given

SUBSCRIPTION ADDRESS: Graduate School of Business Administration
University of Michigan
Ann Arbor, MI 48109

ANNUAL SUBSCRIPTION RATE: $8 individual, $8 institutional
INDEXED/ABSTRACTED IN: PMA, MC, TMA, MR, PTA

CIRCULATION: 8500   FREQUENCY: Quarterly

JOURNAL TITLE: IMPROVING COLLEGE AND UNIVERSITY TEACHING

MANUSCRIPT ADDRESS: D.M. Goode, Editor
Oregon State University Press
PO Box 689, Oregon State University
Corvallis, OR 97331

TYPE OF ARTICLES: Research articles, commentaries, theoretical articles, case studies

MAJOR CONTENT AREAS: Articles on college and university teaching

TOPICS PREFERRED: Same as above

INAPPROPRIATE TOPICS: Not given

NUMBER OF MANUSCRIPT COPIES: 1	PAGE CHARGES: No
REVIEW PERIOD: 1 month	STYLE REQUIREMENTS: U.S. Gov't.
PUBLICATION LAG TIME: Not given	STYLE SHEET: Not given
EARLY PUBLICATION OPTION: Not given	REVISED THESES: Acceptable
ACCEPTANCE RATE: Not given	STUDENT PAPERS: Not given
AUTHORSHIP RESTRICTIONS: No	REPRINT POLICY: None

SUBSCRIPTION ADDRESS: D.M. Goode, Editor
Oregon State University Press
PO Box 689, Oregon State University
Corvallis, OR 97331

ANNUAL SUBSCRIPTION RATE: $9 individual, Not given - institutional

INDEXED/ABSTRACTED IN: EI

CIRCULATION: 2500   FREQUENCY: Not given

JOURNAL TITLE: THE INDIAN HISTORIAN

MANUSCRIPT ADDRESS: Jeannette Henry, Editor
1451 Masonic Avenue
San Francisco, CA 94117

TYPE OF ARTICLES: Not given

MAJOR CONTENT AREAS: Not given

TOPICS PREFERRED: History, culture, current affairs, arts and literature of the American Indian

INAPPROPRIATE TOPICS: Not given

NUMBER OF MANUSCRIPT COPIES: Not given	PAGE CHARGES: Not given
REVIEW PERIOD: 1-5 mos.	STYLE REQUIREMENTS: Not given
PUBLICATION LAG TIME: 1-8 mos.	STYLE SHEET: Not given
EARLY PUBLICATION OPTION: Not given	REVISED THESES: Not given
ACCEPTANCE RATE: 50%	STUDENT PAPERS: Not given
AUTHORSHIP RESTRICTIONS: Not given	REPRINT POLICY: Not given

SUBSCRIPTION ADDRESS: Jeannette Henry, Editor
1451 Masonic Avenue
San Francisco, CA 94117

ANNUAL SUBSCRIPTION RATE: $6 individual, $6 institutional

INDEXED/ABSTRACTED IN: Not given

CIRCULATION: 5600   FREQUENCY: Quarterly

JOURNAL TITLE: INDUSTRIAL AND LABOR RELATIONS REVIEW

MANUSCRIPT ADDRESS: Editor
Cornell University
Box 1000
Ithaca, NY 14853

TYPE OF ARTICLES: Research articles, commentaries, theoretical
articles, review articles, case studies,
unsolicited book reviews

MAJOR CONTENT AREAS: Administrative behavior, bureaucracy, collective
behavior, economy and society, human organizations,
industrial sociology, labor law, leadership,
minorities, occupations & careers

TOPICS PREFERRED: Labor economics, collective bargaining, manpower
programs, social security & pensions,
organizational management

INAPPROPRIATE TOPICS: Not given

NUMBER OF MANUSCRIPT COPIES: 3
REVIEW PERIOD: 12 weeks
PUBLICATION LAG TIME: 9 months
EARLY PUBLICATION OPTION: No
ACCEPTANCE RATE: 15%
AUTHORSHIP RESTRICTIONS: No

PAGE CHARGES: No
STYLE REQUIREMENTS: Chicago Manuscript
STYLE SHEET: Yes
REVISED THESES: Acceptable
STUDENT PAPERS: No
REPRINT POLICY: None

SUBSCRIPTION ADDRESS: Circulation Manager
Cornell University
Box 1000
Ithaca, NY 14853

ANNUAL SUBSCRIPTION RATE: $12 individual, $14 institutional
INDEXED/ABSTRACTED IN: BRI, BPAIS, BPI, EAA, IPRL, JEL, PMA, PHRA, WSA,
WRA, PA, SA

CIRCULATION: 4500   FREQUENCY: Quarterly

JOURNAL TITLE: INDUSTRIAL RELATIONS: A JOURNAL
OF ECONOMY AND SOCIETY

MANUSCRIPT ADDRESS: Institute of Industrial Relations
University of California
Berkeley, CA 94720

TYPE OF ARTICLES: Research articles, case studies

MAJOR CONTENT AREAS: Administrative behavior, systems analysis,
economy and society, human organizations,
sociology of knowledge, labor force/labor
relations, organizations, social mobility

TOPICS PREFERRED: Aspects of the employment relationship --
developments in the fields of labor economics,
sociology, psychology, political science, law

INAPPROPRIATE TOPICS: Not given

NUMBER OF MANUSCRIPT COPIES: 2
REVIEW PERIOD: 4-6 weeks
PUBLICATION LAG TIME: 3-6 months
EARLY PUBLICATION OPTION: No
ACCEPTANCE RATE: 5%
AUTHORSHIP RESTRICTIONS: No

PAGE CHARGES: No
STYLE REQUIREMENTS: Not given
STYLE SHEET: Yes
REVISED THESES: Acceptable
STUDENT PAPERS: No
REPRINT POLICY: 1 journal

SUBSCRIPTION ADDRESS: Institute of Industrial Relations
University of California
Berkeley, CA 94720

ANNUAL SUBSCRIPTION RATE: $10 individual, $12 institutional
INDEXED/ABSTRACTED IN: JEL

CIRCULATION: 2500   FREQUENCY: Tri-yearly

JOURNAL TITLE: INSTITUT DE SOCIOLOGIE REVUE

MANUSCRIPT ADDRESS: Avenue Jeanne 44
1050 Brussels, Belgium

TYPE OF ARTICLES: Research articles, theoretical articles, case
studies, unsolicited book reviews

MAJOR CONTENT AREAS: Not given

TOPICS PREFERRED: Not given

INAPPROPRIATE TOPICS: Commentaries on widely-publicized author's books

NUMBER OF MANUSCRIPT COPIES: 2   PAGE CHARGES: Yes
REVIEW PERIOD: 6 months   STYLE REQUIREMENTS: French Sociological
PUBLICATION LAG TIME: 1 year   STYLE SHEET: Yes
EARLY PUBLICATION OPTION: No   REVISED THESES: Yes
ACCEPTANCE RATE: 50%   STUDENT PAPERS: Yes
AUTHORSHIP RESTRICTIONS: No   REPRINT POLICY: 25

SUBSCRIPTION ADDRESS: Editions de l'Universite de Bruxelles
Parc Leopold, B-1040 Brussels, Belgium

ANNUAL SUBSCRIPTION RATE: Not given - individual, Not given - institutional
INDEXED/ABSTRACTED IN: CC

CIRCULATION: 800   FREQUENCY: Quarterly

JOURNAL TITLE: INTELLECT

MANUSCRIPT ADDRESS: 1860 Broadway
New York, NY 10023

TYPE OF ARTICLES: Commentaries, case studies, research articles,
theoretical articles

MAJOR CONTENT AREAS: Adolescence, aging and aged, alcoholism & drug
abuse, anthropology, bureaucracy, collective
behavior, deviant behavior, human development,
law, marriage & divorce, religion, sex roles
TOPICS PREFERRED: Not given

INAPPROPRIATE TOPICS: Not given

NUMBER OF MANUSCRIPT COPIES: 1   PAGE CHARGES: No
REVIEW PERIOD: 2-3 weeks STYLE REQUIREMENTS: Not given
PUBLICATION LAG TIME: 2-8 months   STYLE SHEET: Yes
EARLY PUBLICATION OPTION: No   REVISED THESES: No
ACCEPTANCE RATE: 10-15%   STUDENT PAPERS: No
AUTHORSHIP RESTRICTIONS: No   REPRINT POLICY: 5 journals

SUBSCRIPTION ADDRESS: 1860 Broadway
New York, NY 10023

ANNUAL SUBSCRIPTION RATE: $12.50 individual, $17.50 institutional
INDEXED/ABSTRACTED IN: Not given

CIRCULATION: 40,000   FREQUENCY: Monthly

JOURNAL TITLE: INTERNATIONAL DEVELOPMENT REVIEW

MANUSCRIPT ADDRESS: 1346 Connecticut Avenue NW
Washington, DC 20036

TYPE OF ARTICLES: Case studies, commentaries, review articles,
research articles

MAJOR CONTENT AREAS: Administrative behavior, anthropology, economy
and society, human organizations, modernization,
population, social change, social issues, social
policy

TOPICS PREFERRED: We deal with problems of modernization in the Third
World countries and related international issues.

INAPPROPRIATE TOPICS: Not given

NUMBER OF MANUSCRIPT COPIES: Not given	PAGE CHARGES:	No
REVIEW PERIOD: 2 1/2 mos	STYLE REQUIREMENTS:	Not given
PUBLICATION LAG TIME: 3-6 months	STYLE SHEET:	Yes
EARLY PUBLICATION OPTION: Not given	REVISED THESES:	No
ACCEPTANCE RATE: 10-20%	STUDENT PAPERS:	No
AUTHORSHIP RESTRICTIONS: No	REPRINT POLICY:	15 journals

SUBSCRIPTION ADDRESS: 1346 Connecticut Avenue NW
Washington, DC 20036

ANNUAL SUBSCRIPTION RATE: $12 individual, $12 institutional
INDEXED/ABSTRACTED IN: ABC PS, CC, IIMMI, PAIS, SSI, SPAA, SA

CIRCULATION: 8200   FREQUENCY: Quarterly

JOURNAL TITLE: INTERNATIONAL FAMILY PLANNING DIGEST

MANUSCRIPT ADDRESS: Alan Guttmacher Institute
515 Madison Avenue
New York, NY 10022

TYPE OF ARTICLES: Research articles, case studies, summaries of
papers presented at scientific meetings, research
findings

MAJOR CONTENT AREAS: Adolescence, demography, epidemiology, family
formation, family planning, marriage & divorce,
social planning, population, public health, sex
roles, sexual behavior, social issues

TOPICS PREFERRED: Fertility and population

INAPPROPRIATE TOPICS: Not given

NUMBER OF MANUSCRIPT COPIES: 2	PAGE CHARGES:	No
REVIEW PERIOD: Not given	STYLE REQUIREMENTS:	Chicago Manuscript
PUBLICATION LAG TIME: Not given	STYLE SHEET:	Not given
EARLY PUBLICATION OPTION: Not given	REVISED THESES:	Acceptable
ACCEPTANCE RATE: Not given	STUDENT PAPERS:	No
AUTHORSHIP RESTRICTIONS: No	REPRINT POLICY:	None

SUBSCRIPTION ADDRESS: Alan Guttmacher Institute
515 Madison Avenue
New York, NY 10022

ANNUAL SUBSCRIPTION RATE: Available only to overseas readers
INDEXED/ABSTRACTED IN: Not given

CIRCULATION: 24,000   FREQUENCY: Quarterly

JOURNAL TITLE: INTERNATIONAL INTERACTIONS

MANUSCRIPT ADDRESS: Department of Political Science
University of North Carolina
Chapel Hill, NC 27514

TYPE OF ARTICLES: Research articles, theoretical articles, case
studies, commentaries, review articles

MAJOR CONTENT AREAS: Forecasting theory and methodology, models of
world order, population and international tension,
trend analysis, historical analysis of interaction
patterns, events analysis, civil-military relations
TOPICS PREFERRED: Not given

INAPPROPRIATE TOPICS: Not given

NUMBER OF MANUSCRIPT COPIES: 3	PAGE CHARGES:	No
REVIEW PERIOD: 2-4 mos.	STYLE REQUIREMENTS:	Harvard
PUBLICATION LAG TIME: 6 months	STYLE SHEET:	Yes
EARLY PUBLICATION OPTION: No	REVISED THESES:	No
ACCEPTANCE RATE: 10-20 %	STUDENT PAPERS:	No
AUTHORSHIP RESTRICTIONS: No	REPRINT POLICY:	None

SUBSCRIPTION ADDRESS: Gordon and Breach, Science Publishers, Inc.
One Park Avenue
New York, NY 10016

ANNUAL SUBSCRIPTION RATE: $21 individual, $39 institutional
INDEXED/ABSTRACTED IN: Not given

CIRCULATION: Not given   FREQUENCY: 8 times per year

JOURNAL TITLE: INTERNATIONAL JOURNAL OF THE ADDICTIONS

MANUSCRIPT ADDRESS: Ms. Angela Cartier, Ed. Asst.
333 Jackson Avenue
West Hempstead, NY 11552

TYPE OF ARTICLES: Research articles, theoretical articles,
review articles, research notes, clinical notes

MAJOR CONTENT AREAS: Not given

TOPICS PREFERRED: Not given

INAPPROPRIATE TOPICS: Not given

NUMBER OF MANUSCRIPT COPIES: 3	PAGE CHARGES:	No
REVIEW PERIOD: 3 months	STYLE REQUIREMENTS:	APA
PUBLICATION LAG TIME: 1 1/2 years	STYLE SHEET:	Yes
EARLY PUBLICATION OPTION: No	REVISED THESES:	Yes
ACCEPTANCE RATE: Not given	STUDENT PAPERS:	No
AUTHORSHIP RESTRICTIONS: No	REPRINT POLICY:	20

SUBSCRIPTION ADDRESS: Marcel Dekke, Journals
PO Box 11305
Church Street Station
New York, NY 10249
ANNUAL SUBSCRIPTION RATE: Not given
INDEXED/ABSTRACTED IN: Not given

CIRCULATION: 1500   FREQUENCY: 8 times per year

JOURNAL TITLE: INTERNATIONAL JOURNAL OF COMPARATIVE SOCIOLOGY

MANUSCRIPT ADDRESS: Professor K. Ishwaran
Department of Sociology
York University, 4700 Keele Street
Dounsview, Ontario, Canada

TYPE OF ARTICLES: Research articles, theoretical articles, review articles, case studies

MAJOR CONTENT AREAS: Social sciences

TOPICS PREFERRED: Comparative sociology

INAPPROPRIATE TOPICS: Non-comparative sociology

NUMBER OF MANUSCRIPT COPIES: 2
REVIEW PERIOD: 3-6 mos.
PUBLICATION LAG TIME: 1 year
EARLY PUBLICATION OPTION: Yes
ACCEPTANCE RATE: 2%
AUTHORSHIP RESTRICTIONS: No

PAGE CHARGES: No
STYLE REQUIREMENTS: ASA
STYLE SHEET: No
REVISED THESES: No
STUDENT PAPERS: No
REPRINT POLICY: 25

SUBSCRIPTION ADDRESS: E.J. Brill
Leiden, Holland

ANNUAL SUBSCRIPTION RATE: Not given
INDEXED/ABSTRACTED IN: Not given

CIRCULATION: Not given   FREQUENCY: Quarterly

JOURNAL TITLE: INTERNATIONAL JOURNAL OF CONTEMPORARY SOCIOLOGY

MANUSCRIPT ADDRESS: Dr. Raj P. Mohan, Book Review Editor
Department of Sociology-Anthropology
Auburn University
Auburn, AL 36830

TYPE OF ARTICLES: Theoretical articles, research articles, commentaries, case studies, review articles, unsolicited book reviews, cross-cultural studies

MAJOR CONTENT AREAS: Aging and aged, anthropology, collective behavior, communes, community development, criminology, death & dying, evolution, medical sociology, public health, values

TOPICS PREFERRED: Not given

INAPPROPRIATE TOPICS: Not given

NUMBER OF MANUSCRIPT COPIES: 2
REVIEW PERIOD: 6-8 weeks
PUBLICATION LAG TIME: 1 year
EARLY PUBLICATION OPTION: Yes
ACCEPTANCE RATE: 50%
AUTHORSHIP RESTRICTIONS: No

PAGE CHARGES: Yes
STYLE REQUIREMENTS: Not given
STYLE SHEET: Yes
REVISED THESES: Yes
STUDENT PAPERS: Yes
REPRINT POLICY: None

SUBSCRIPTION ADDRESS: International Journal of Contemporary Sociology
PO Box 114, Rakes Marg, Pili Kothi, G.T. Road
Ghaziabad (U.P.) India

ANNUAL SUBSCRIPTION RATE: $12 individual, $20 institutional
INDEXED/ABSTRACTED IN: SA, EA, CC, HA, UB

CIRCULATION: 1500   FREQUENCY: Quarterly

JOURNAL TITLE: INTERNATIONAL JOURNAL OF COOPERATIVE DEVELOPMENT

MANUSCRIPT ADDRESS: Mrs. Mary Jean McGrath, Editor
University of Wisconsin
610 Langdon St.
Madison, WI 53706
TYPE OF ARTICLES: Research articles, book reviews

MAJOR CONTENT AREAS: Not given

TOPICS PREFERRED: Economic or social development work
associated with cooperatives

INAPPROPRIATE TOPICS: Not given

NUMBER OF MANUSCRIPT COPIES:	Not given	PAGE CHARGES:	Not given
REVIEW PERIOD:	1-4 mos.	STYLE REQUIREMENTS:	Not given
PUBLICATION LAG TIME:	4-12 months	STYLE SHEET:	Not given
EARLY PUBLICATION OPTION:	Not given	REVISED THESES:	Not given
ACCEPTANCE RATE:	75%	STUDENT PAPERS:	Not given
AUTHORSHIP RESTRICTIONS:	Not given	REPRINT POLICY:	10

SUBSCRIPTION ADDRESS: Mrs. Mary Jean McGrath, Editor
University of Wisconsin
610 Langdon St.
Madison, WI 53706
ANNUAL SUBSCRIPTION RATE: Not given
INDEXED/ABSTRACTED IN: Not given

CIRCULATION: 5000   FREQUENCY: Quarterly

JOURNAL TITLE: INTERNATIONAL JOURNAL OF ETHNIC STUDIES

MANUSCRIPT ADDRESS: Anthony L. LaRuffa, Editor
Herbert H. Lehman College
Dept. of Anthropology
Bedford Park Blvd. West, Bronx, NY 10468
TYPE OF ARTICLES: Not given

MAJOR CONTENT AREAS: Not given

TOPICS PREFERRED: Dynamics of inter-ethnic relations; ethnic
identity; interplay between ethnicity & the
political structure
INAPPROPRIATE TOPICS: Not given

NUMBER OF MANUSCRIPT COPIES:	Not given	PAGE CHARGES:	Not given
REVIEW PERIOD:	1-3 months	STYLE REQUIREMENTS:	Not given
PUBLICATION LAG TIME:	6 months	STYLE SHEET:	Not given
EARLY PUBLICATION OPTION:	Not given	REVISED THESES:	Not given
ACCEPTANCE RATE:	45%	STUDENT PAPERS:	Not given
AUTHORSHIP RESTRICTIONS:	Not given	REPRINT POLICY:	Not given

SUBSCRIPTION ADDRESS: Anthony L. LaRuffa, Editor
Herbert H. Lehman College
Dept. of Anthropology
Bedford Park Blvd. West, Bronx, NY 10468
ANNUAL SUBSCRIPTION RATE: $11 individual, $41 institutional
INDEXED/ABSTRACTED IN: Not given

CIRCULATION: Not given   FREQUENCY: Quarterly

JOURNAL TITLE: INTERNATIONAL JOURNAL OF GROUP PSYCHOTHERAPY

MANUSCRIPT ADDRESS: Dr. Saul Schlidbuigh
372 Bleecher Street
New York, NY 10014

TYPE OF ARTICLES: Research articles, theoretical articles, review
articles, case studies

MAJOR CONTENT AREAS: Adolescence, aging and aged, death & dying, deviant
behavior, groups, human development, mental health
& illness, sexual behavior, social psychology,
suicide, social interaction

TOPICS PREFERRED: Group psychotherapy

INAPPROPRIATE TOPICS: Not given

NUMBER OF MANUSCRIPT COPIES: 3	PAGE CHARGES:	Yes
REVIEW PERIOD: 6 months	STYLE REQUIREMENTS:	Chicago Manuscript
PUBLICATION LAG TIME: 1 year	STYLE SHEET:	Yes
EARLY PUBLICATION OPTION: No	REVISED THESES:	No
ACCEPTANCE RATE: 30%	STUDENT PAPERS:	No
AUTHORSHIP RESTRICTIONS: No	REPRINT POLICY:	None

SUBSCRIPTION ADDRESS: 315 Fifth Avenue
New York, NY 10016

ANNUAL SUBSCRIPTION RATE: $22 individual, $34 institutional
INDEXED/ABSTRACTED IN: PA

CIRCULATION: 5000   FREQUENCY: Quarterly

JOURNAL TITLE: INTERNATIONAL JOURNAL OF OFFENDER THERAPY
AND COMPARATIVE CRIMINOLOGY

MANUSCRIPT ADDRESS: 199 Gloucester Place
London NW1 6BU, England

TYPE OF ARTICLES: Clinical articles preferred; research articles,
review articles, theoretical articles

MAJOR CONTENT AREAS: Offender therapy

TOPICS PREFERRED: Treatment techniques

INAPPROPRIATE TOPICS: Not given

NUMBER OF MANUSCRIPT COPIES: Not given	PAGE CHARGES:	Not given
REVIEW PERIOD: 1-2 mos.	STYLE REQUIREMENTS:	Not given
PUBLICATION LAG TIME: 1-2 years	STYLE SHEET:	Yes
EARLY PUBLICATION OPTION: No	REVISED THESES:	Not given
ACCEPTANCE RATE: 25%	STUDENT PAPERS:	Not given
AUTHORSHIP RESTRICTIONS: Not given	REPRINT POLICY:	10

SUBSCRIPTION ADDRESS: 199 Gloucester Place
London NW1 6BU, England

ANNUAL SUBSCRIPTION RATE: $20 individual, Not given institutional
INDEXED/ABSTRACTED IN: PA,ASW, SA, ACP, CCSBS, ICS, LLBA

CIRCULATION: 3000   FREQUENCY: Not given

JOURNAL TITLE: INTERNATIONAL JOURNAL OF SOCIAL PSYCHIATRY

MANUSCRIPT ADDRESS: Prof. Marvin K. Opler, Dept. of Anthropology & Psychiatry, State Univ. of New York, 4242 Ridge Lea Road Buffalo, NY 14226

TYPE OF ARTICLES: Research articles, review articles, theoretical articles, book reviews, clinical articles

MAJOR CONTENT AREAS: Behavior therapy, clinical, community, psychotherapy, social

TOPICS PREFERRED: Psycho-social psychotherapy, community psychotherapy

INAPPROPRIATE TOPICS: Not given

NUMBER OF MANUSCRIPT COPIES: Not given	PAGE CHARGES:	Not given
REVIEW PERIOD: 5 weeks	STYLE REQUIREMENTS:	APA
PUBLICATION LAG TIME: 5 months	STYLE SHEET:	No
EARLY PUBLICATION OPTION: No	REVISED THESES:	Not given
ACCEPTANCE RATE: 50%	STUDENT PAPERS:	Not given
AUTHORSHIP RESTRICTIONS: Not given	REPRINT POLICY:	1

SUBSCRIPTION ADDRESS: 18 Park Avenue London NW11 7SJ, England

ANNUAL SUBSCRIPTION RATE: $15 individual, $20 institutional

INDEXED/ABSTRACTED IN: PA, ASW, BI, BS, CCSBS, IBSS, PRAJ, WSA

CIRCULATION: 2500   FREQUENCY: Not given

JOURNAL TITLE: INTERNATIONAL JOURNAL OF SOCIOLOGY

MANUSCRIPT ADDRESS: c/o M.E. Sharpe, Inc. 901 North Broadway White Plains, NY 10603

TYPE OF ARTICLES: Research articles, theoretical articles, case studies, commentaries, review articles

MAJOR CONTENT AREAS: Administrative behavior, adolescence, anthropology, collective behavior, mass communication, economy and society, human development, human organization, minorities, modernization, race relations

TOPICS PREFERRED: World sociology - new developments, national or area trends, fields or national achievements not generally known in English, Marxist sociology

INAPPROPRIATE TOPICS: Not given

NUMBER OF MANUSCRIPT COPIES: 1	PAGE CHARGES:	No
REVIEW PERIOD: 1 month	STYLE REQUIREMENTS:	Chicago Manuscript
PUBLICATION LAG TIME: 3-6 months	STYLE SHEET:	Yes
EARLY PUBLICATION OPTION: No	REVISED THESES:	Yes
ACCEPTANCE RATE: 100%	STUDENT PAPERS:	No
AUTHORSHIP RESTRICTIONS: No	REPRINT POLICY:	3 journals

SUBSCRIPTION ADDRESS: M.E. Sharpe, Inc. 901 North Broadway White Plains, NY 10603

ANNUAL SUBSCRIPTION RATE: $20 individual, $70 institutional

INDEXED/ABSTRACTED IN: Not given

CIRCULATION: 300   FREQUENCY: Quarterly

JOURNAL TITLE: INTERNATIONAL JOURNAL OF SOCIOLOGY OF THE FAMILY

MANUSCRIPT ADDRESS: Man Singh Das, Ph.D. , Editor
Department of Sociology
Northern Illinois University
DeKalb, IL 60115

TYPE OF ARTICLES: Research articles, case studies, theoretical
articles, review articles, unsolicited book
reviews

MAJOR CONTENT AREAS: Family formation, family planning, marriage &
divorce, sex roles, sexual behavior

TOPICS PREFERRED: Cross-national, cross-cultural, and interdisciplinary research

INAPPROPRIATE TOPICS: Not given

NUMBER OF MANUSCRIPT COPIES: 3   PAGE CHARGES: No
REVIEW PERIOD: 6-8 weeks STYLE REQUIREMENTS: ASA
PUBLICATION LAG TIME: 12-18 months   STYLE SHEET: Yes
EARLY PUBLICATION OPTION: Yes   REVISED THESES: Yes
ACCEPTANCE RATE: 40%   STUDENT PAPERS: No
AUTHORSHIP RESTRICTIONS: No   REPRINT POLICY: None

SUBSCRIPTION ADDRESS: Vikas Publishing House
5 Ansari Road
New Delhi-110002
India

ANNUAL SUBSCRIPTION RATE: $7.50 individual, $14 institutional
INDEXED/ABSTRACTED IN: SA, CC:BSES

CIRCULATION: 1000   FREQUENCY: Semiannually

JOURNAL TITLE: INTERNATIONAL JOURNAL OF SYMBOLOGY

MANUSCRIPT ADDRESS: Ray A. Craddick, Co-Editor
Department of Psychology
Georgia State University
Atlanta, GA 30303

TYPE OF ARTICLES: Not given

MAJOR CONTENT AREAS: Aging and aged, alcoholism & drug abuse, counseling, criminology, death & dying, deviant behavior,
ecology, groups, health and illness, housing and
renewal, human development, human organizations

TOPICS PREFERRED: Not given

INAPPROPRIATE TOPICS: Not given

NUMBER OF MANUSCRIPT COPIES: 3   PAGE CHARGES: No
REVIEW PERIOD: 3 months STYLE REQUIREMENTS: Not given
PUBLICATION LAG TIME: 6-15 months   STYLE SHEET: No
EARLY PUBLICATION OPTION: No   REVISED THESES: No
ACCEPTANCE RATE: 50%   STUDENT PAPERS: Not given
AUTHORSHIP RESTRICTIONS: No   REPRINT POLICY: 50

SUBSCRIPTION ADDRESS: Ray A. Craddick, Co-Editor
Department of Psychology
Georgia State University
Atlanta, GA 30303

ANNUAL SUBSCRIPTION RATE: $11 individual, $20 institutional
INDEXED/ABSTRACTED IN: Not given

CIRCULATION: 280   FREQUENCY: Tri-yearly

JOURNAL TITLE: INTERNATIONAL MIGRATION REVIEW

MANUSCRIPT ADDRESS: Editor
209 Flagg Place
Staten Island, NY 10304

TYPE OF ARTICLES: Research articles, theoretical articles, case
studies, immigration policies and legislative
developments

MAJOR CONTENT AREAS: Demography, economy and society, ethnic groups,
migration, population

TOPICS PREFERRED: Theory of migration, immigration policies; migrant
workers, migration and ethnicity

INAPPROPRIATE TOPICS: Not given

NUMBER OF MANUSCRIPT COPIES: 2	PAGE CHARGES:	No
REVIEW PERIOD: 3-5 mos.	STYLE REQUIREMENTS:	Chicago Manuscript
PUBLICATION LAG TIME: 3-6 months	STYLE SHEET:	Yes
EARLY PUBLICATION OPTION: Yes	REVISED THESES:	Yes
ACCEPTANCE RATE: 20%	STUDENT PAPERS:	Yes
AUTHORSHIP RESTRICTIONS: No	REPRINT POLICY:	2 journals

SUBSCRIPTION ADDRESS: IMR Subscription Department
Center for Migration Studies
209 Flagg Place
Staten Island, NY 10304

ANNUAL SUBSCRIPTION RATE: Not given

INDEXED/ABSTRACTED IN: SA, HA, A:HL, CC/BSMS, BSSH, CNRS

CIRCULATION: 2500   FREQUENCY: Quarterly

JOURNAL TITLE: INTERNATIONAL REVIEW OF ADMINISTRATIVE SCIENCES

MANUSCRIPT ADDRESS: The Assistant Editor, IRAS,
Rue de la Charité 25-
B 1040 Brussels, Belgium

TYPE OF ARTICLES: Research article, commentaries, theoretical articles

MAJOR CONTENT AREAS: Administrative behavior, bureaucracy, community
development , economy and society, human organi-
zations, law, modernization, political sociology,
public health, social change, social policy

TOPICS PREFERRED: National public administration, administrative
law

INAPPROPRIATE TOPICS: Business administration

NUMBER OF MANUSCRIPT COPIES: 2	PAGE CHARGES:	No
REVIEW PERIOD: 15-30days	STYLE REQUIREMENTS:	Not given
PUBLICATION LAG TIME: 6-9 months	STYLE SHEET:	No
EARLY PUBLICATION OPTION: No	REVISED THESES:	No
ACCEPTANCE RATE: 15-25%	STUDENT PAPERS:	No
AUTHORSHIP RESTRICTIONS: No	REPRINT POLICY:	25

SUBSCRIPTION ADDRESS: Publications Service
Rue de la Charité 25 -
B 1040 Brussels, Belgium

ANNUAL SUBSCRIPTION RATE: $40 individual, $40 institutional

INDEXED/ABSTRACTED IN: Not given

CIRCULATION: Not given   FREQUENCY: Quarterly

JOURNAL TITLE: INTERNATIONAL REVIEW OF MODERN SOCIOLOGY

MANUSCRIPT ADDRESS: Man Singh Das, Ph.D., Editor
Department of Sociology
Northern Illinois University
DeKalb, IL 60115

TYPE OF ARTICLES: Research articles, case studies, theoretical
articles, review articles, unsolicited book
reviews

MAJOR CONTENT AREAS: Aging and aged, collective behavior, deviant
behavior, economy and society, educational
sociology, general sociology, medical sociology,
social planning, political sociology

TOPICS PREFERRED: Cross - national, cross - cultural, and
inter-disciplinary research

INAPPROPRIATE TOPICS: Not given

NUMBER OF MANUSCRIPT COPIES: 3	PAGE CHARGES:	No
REVIEW PERIOD: 6-8 weeks	STYLE REQUIREMENTS:	ASA
PUBLICATION LAG TIME: 12-18 months	STYLE SHEET:	Yes
EARLY PUBLICATION OPTION: Yes	REVISED THESES:	Yes
ACCEPTANCE RATE: 40%	STUDENT PAPERS:	No
AUTHORSHIP RESTRICTIONS: No	REPRINT POLICY:	None

SUBSCRIPTION ADDRESS: Vikas Publishing House
5 Ansari Road
New Delhi - 110002
India

ANNUAL SUBSCRIPTION RATE: $7.50 individual, $14.00 institutional

INDEXED/ABSTRACTED IN: SA, CC:BSES

CIRCULATION: 1000   FREQUENCY: Semiannually

JOURNAL TITLE: INTERNATIONAL REVIEW OF SOCIAL HISTORY

MANUSCRIPT ADDRESS: Herengracht 262-266
Amsterdam, The Netherlands

TYPE OF ARTICLES: Articles on the history of the working class
movement, research articles

MAJOR CONTENT AREAS: Labor force/labor relations, social conflict,
social movements, stratification

TOPICS PREFERRED: History of the working-class movement

INAPPROPRIATE TOPICS: Not given

NUMBER OF MANUSCRIPT COPIES: 1	PAGE CHARGES:	No
REVIEW PERIOD: 6 months	STYLE REQUIREMENTS:	Not given
PUBLICATION LAG TIME: 12 months	STYLE SHEET:	Yes
EARLY PUBLICATION OPTION: No	REVISED THESES:	No
ACCEPTANCE RATE: 20%	STUDENT PAPERS:	No
AUTHORSHIP RESTRICTIONS: No	REPRINT POLICY:	20

SUBSCRIPTION ADDRESS: Van Gorcum Publications
PO Box 43
Assen - The Netherlands

ANNUAL SUBSCRIPTION RATE: $26 individual, $26 institutional

INDEXED/ABSTRACTED IN: Not given

CIRCULATION: 1200   FREQUENCY: Tri-yearly

JOURNAL TITLE: INTERNATIONAL SOCIAL SCIENCE JOURNAL

MANUSCRIPT ADDRESS: UNESCO
7 Place de Fontenoy, 75700
Paris, France

TYPE OF ARTICLES: Theoretical articles, research articles, review articles

MAJOR CONTENT AREAS: Social sciences

TOPICS PREFERRED: International or cross-national character

INAPPROPRIATE TOPICS: Highly technical material, polemical texts, small local studies

NUMBER OF MANUSCRIPT COPIES:	1	PAGE CHARGES:	No
REVIEW PERIOD:	1 month	STYLE REQUIREMENTS:	Not given
PUBLICATION LAG TIME:	9-12 months	STYLE SHEET:	Yes
EARLY PUBLICATION OPTION:	Yes	REVISED THESES:	No
ACCEPTANCE RATE:	Not given	STUDENT PAPERS:	No
AUTHORSHIP RESTRICTIONS:	No	REPRINT POLICY:	25

SUBSCRIPTION ADDRESS: Unipub
Box 433
Murray Hill Station, NY 10016

ANNUAL SUBSCRIPTION RATE: $12 individual, Not given - institutional
INDEXED/ABSTRACTED IN: Not given

CIRCULATION: 7000   FREQUENCY: Quarterly

JOURNAL TITLE: INTERNATIONAL STUDIES QUARTERLY

MANUSCRIPT ADDRESS: Jonathan Wilkenfeld
Department of Government
University of Maryland
College Park, MD 20742

TYPE OF ARTICLES: Research articles, theoretical articles, review articles, case studies, commentaries

MAJOR CONTENT AREAS: Sociology of peace, political sociology

TOPICS PREFERRED: Not given

INAPPROPRIATE TOPICS: Not given

NUMBER OF MANUSCRIPT COPIES:	3	PAGE CHARGES:	No
REVIEW PERIOD:	Not given	STYLE REQUIREMENTS:	Not given
PUBLICATION LAG TIME:	Not given	STYLE SHEET:	Yes
EARLY PUBLICATION OPTION:	No	REVISED THESES:	Not given
ACCEPTANCE RATE:	Not given	STUDENT PAPERS:	No
AUTHORSHIP RESTRICTIONS:	No	REPRINT POLICY:	24

SUBSCRIPTION ADDRESS: Sage Publications
275 S Beverly Drive
Beverly Hills, CA 90212

ANNUAL SUBSCRIPTION RATE: Not given - individual, $26 institutional
INDEXED/ABSTRACTED IN: PRR, IPSA, HRA, SUSA, ABC PS, US PSD, PAIS, SSCI, SSI, CC
CIRCULATION: Not given   FREQUENCY: Quarterly

JOURNAL TITLE: ISSUES IN CRIMINOLOGY

MANUSCRIPT ADDRESS: June Kress, Editor
101 Haviland Hall
University of California
Berkeley, CA 94720
TYPE OF ARTICLES: Critical theoretical articles

MAJOR CONTENT AREAS: Not given

TOPICS PREFERRED: Crime, criminology and the criminal justice
system

INAPPROPRIATE TOPICS: Not given

NUMBER OF MANUSCRIPT COPIES: Not given
REVIEW PERIOD: 3 months
PUBLICATION LAG TIME: 2 months
EARLY PUBLICATION OPTION: Not given
ACCEPTANCE RATE: 10%
AUTHORSHIP RESTRICTIONS: Not given

PAGE CHARGES: Not given
STYLE REQUIREMENTS: Not given
STYLE SHEET: Not given
REVISED THESES: Not given
STUDENT PAPERS: Not given
REPRINT POLICY: 25

SUBSCRIPTION ADDRESS: June Kress, Editor
101 Haviland Hall
University of California
Berkeley, CA 94720
ANNUAL SUBSCRIPTION RATE: $5 individual, $6 institutional
INDEXED/ABSTRACTED IN: Not given

CIRCULATION: 1000   FREQUENCY: Semiannually

JOURNAL TITLE: JEWISH JOURNAL OF SOCIOLOGY

MANUSCRIPT ADDRESS: Maurice Freedman
55 New Cavendish Street
London W1M 8BT, England

TYPE OF ARTICLES: Research articles, case studies, theoretical
articles, commentaries, review articles

MAJOR CONTENT AREAS: Anthropology, demography, ethnic groups, general
sociology, marriage & divorce, migration,
minorities, political sociology, population, race
relations, religion, social conflict
TOPICS PREFERRED: The sociology of the Jews

INAPPROPRIATE TOPICS: Not given

NUMBER OF MANUSCRIPT COPIES: 2
REVIEW PERIOD: 2 months
PUBLICATION LAG TIME: 6 months
EARLY PUBLICATION OPTION: Not given
ACCEPTANCE RATE: Not given
AUTHORSHIP RESTRICTIONS: No

PAGE CHARGES: No
STYLE REQUIREMENTS: Not given
STYLE SHEET: Yes
REVISED THESES: Yes
STUDENT PAPERS: No
REPRINT POLICY: 30

SUBSCRIPTION ADDRESS: Maurice Freedman
55 New Cavendish Street
London W1M 8BT, England

ANNUAL SUBSCRIPTION RATE: $7.50 individual, $7.50 institutional
INDEXED/ABSTRACTED IN: Not given

CIRCULATION: Not given   FREQUENCY: Semiannually

JOURNAL TITLE: JEWISH SOCIAL STUDIES

MANUSCRIPT ADDRESS: 250 West 57th Street
Room 904
New York, NY 10019

TYPE OF ARTICLES: Research articles, any type of well-documented
original social study referring to the Jewish
population.

MAJOR CONTENT AREAS: Aging and aged, anthropology, collective behavior,
death & dying, economy and society, ethnic groups,
population, race relations, rural sociology, sex
roles, social ideology, stratification

TOPICS PREFERRED: Not given

INAPPROPRIATE TOPICS: Not given

NUMBER OF MANUSCRIPT COPIES: 3	PAGE CHARGES:	No
REVIEW PERIOD: 12 months	STYLE REQUIREMENTS:	Chicago Manuscript
PUBLICATION LAG TIME: 12 months	STYLE SHEET:	Yes
EARLY PUBLICATION OPTION: Yes	REVISED THESES:	Yes
ACCEPTANCE RATE: 40%	STUDENT PAPERS:	No
AUTHORSHIP RESTRICTIONS: No	REPRINT POLICY:	50

SUBSCRIPTION ADDRESS: 250 West 57th Street
Room 904
New York, NY 10019

ANNUAL SUBSCRIPTION RATE: $20 individual, $20 institutional
INDEXED/ABSTRACTED IN: SSI, BRI

CIRCULATION: 1500   FREQUENCY: Quarterly

JOURNAL TITLE: JOURNAL FOR THE SCIENTIFIC STUDY OF RELIGION

MANUSCRIPT ADDRESS: Dr. Richard Gorsuch
Graduate School of Social Work
University of Texas at Arlington
Arlington, TX 76019

TYPE OF ARTICLES: Research articles, theoretical articles, review
articles, commentaries, case studies

MAJOR CONTENT AREAS: Religion

TOPICS PREFERRED: Religion: its nature, development and impact

INAPPROPRIATE TOPICS: Non-scientific papers

NUMBER OF MANUSCRIPT COPIES: 3	PAGE CHARGES:	No
REVIEW PERIOD: 2-3 months	STYLE REQUIREMENTS:	APA
PUBLICATION LAG TIME: 3-6 months	STYLE SHEET:	Yes
EARLY PUBLICATION OPTION: No	REVISED THESES:	Acceptable
ACCEPTANCE RATE: 15-20%	STUDENT PAPERS:	No
AUTHORSHIP RESTRICTIONS: No	REPRINT POLICY:	None

SUBSCRIPTION ADDRESS: S.S.S.R.
St. John's University
Jamaica, NY 11439

ANNUAL SUBSCRIPTION RATE: $15 individual, $15 institutional
INDEXED/ABSTRACTED IN: Not given

CIRCULATION: 2500   FREQUENCY: Quarterly

JOURNAL TITLE: JOURNAL OF ABNORMAL PSYCHOLOGY

MANUSCRIPT ADDRESS: Dr. Leonard D. Eron
University of Illinois at Chicago Circle
PO Box 4348, Department of Psychology
Chicago, IL   60680

TYPE OF ARTICLES: Not given

MAJOR CONTENT AREAS: Psychopathology, normal processes in abnormal
individuals, pathological or atypical features
of the behavior of normal persons, experimental
studies with human or animal subjects

TOPICS PREFERRED: Not given

INAPPROPRIATE TOPICS: Not given

NUMBER OF MANUSCRIPT COPIES:	3	PAGE CHARGES:	No
REVIEW PERIOD:	2 months	STYLE REQUIREMENTS:	APA
PUBLICATION LAG TIME:	10 months	STYLE SHEET:	Yes
EARLY PUBLICATION OPTION:	No	REVISED THESES:	No
ACCEPTANCE RATE:	28%	STUDENT PAPERS:	No
AUTHORSHIP RESTRICTIONS:	No	REPRINT POLICY:	20

SUBSCRIPTION ADDRESS: APA
Subscription Section
1200 17th Street
Washington, DC   20036

ANNUAL SUBSCRIPTION RATE: $12 member, $28 nonmember
INDEXED/ABSTRACTED IN: PA

CIRCULATION: 6320   FREQUENCY: Bimonthly

JOURNAL TITLE: JOURNAL OF THE AMERICAN ACADEMY OF CHILD
PSYCHIATRY

MANUSCRIPT ADDRESS: 333 Cedar Street
New Haven, CT   06510

TYPE OF ARTICLES: Research articles, review articles, theoretical
articles

MAJOR CONTENT AREAS: Behavior therapy, community, developmental,
mental retardation, psychoanalysis, psychotherapy

TOPICS PREFERRED: Clinical and basic research related to child
psychiatry

INAPPROPRIATE TOPICS: Anecdotal case studies

NUMBER OF MANUSCRIPT COPIES:	Not given	PAGE CHARGES:	Not given
REVIEW PERIOD:	3 months	STYLE REQUIREMENTS:	Not given
PUBLICATION LAG TIME:	9 months	STYLE SHEET:	Yes
EARLY PUBLICATION OPTION:	Yes	REVISED THESES:	Not given
ACCEPTANCE RATE:	18%	STUDENT PAPERS:	Not given
AUTHORSHIP RESTRICTIONS:	Not given	REPRINT POLICY:	Not given

SUBSCRIPTION ADDRESS: Journals Dept., Yale University Press
92-A Yale Station
New Haven, CT   06520

ANNUAL SUBSCRIPTION RATE: $17.50 individual, Not given institutional
INDEXED/ABSTRACTED IN: PA, CCSBS, IPAPL, LLBA

CIRCULATION: 3300   FREQUENCY: Not given

JOURNAL TITLE: JOURNAL OF AMERICAN FOLKLORE

MANUSCRIPT ADDRESS: Dr. Jan Harold Brunvand
Department of English
University of Utah
Salt Lake City, UT   84112

TYPE OF ARTICLES: Research articles, theoretical articles, commentaries, notes and queries

MAJOR CONTENT AREAS: Anthropology, folklore

TOPICS PREFERRED: Professional folklore research articles

INAPPROPRIATE TOPICS: Heavily statistical or abstract

NUMBER OF MANUSCRIPT COPIES:	1	PAGE CHARGES:	No
REVIEW PERIOD:	3 months	STYLE REQUIREMENTS:	Chicago Manuscript
PUBLICATION LAG TIME:	6 months	STYLE SHEET:	Yes
EARLY PUBLICATION OPTION:	No	REVISED THESES:	Yes
ACCEPTANCE RATE:	10%	STUDENT PAPERS:	No
AUTHORSHIP RESTRICTIONS:	No	REPRINT POLICY:	25

SUBSCRIPTION ADDRESS: 1703 New Hampshire Avenue NW
Washington, DC   20009

ANNUAL SUBSCRIPTION RATE: $18 individual, $18 institutional
INDEXED/ABSTRACTED IN: Not given

CIRCULATION: 3000   FREQUENCY: Quarterly

JOURNAL TITLE: JOURNAL OF AMERICAN FORENSIC ASSOCIATION

MANUSCRIPT ADDRESS: David Zorefsky
School of Speech
Northwestern University
Evanston, IL   60200

TYPE OF ARTICLES: Theoretical articles, research articles, commentaries, unsolicited book reviews, review articles,
case studies

MAJOR CONTENT AREAS: Mass communication, law

TOPICS PREFERRED: Argumentation, debate, persuasion

INAPPROPRIATE TOPICS: Not given

NUMBER OF MANUSCRIPT COPIES:	2	PAGE CHARGES:	No
REVIEW PERIOD:	8-12 wks.	STYLE REQUIREMENTS:	MLA
PUBLICATION LAG TIME:	6-10 months	STYLE SHEET:	Yes
EARLY PUBLICATION OPTION:	No	REVISED THESES:	Yes
ACCEPTANCE RATE:	25%	STUDENT PAPERS:	No
AUTHORSHIP RESTRICTIONS:	No	REPRINT POLICY:	10

SUBSCRIPTION ADDRESS: Larry K. Hannah
Eastern Montana College
Billings, MT   59101

ANNUAL SUBSCRIPTION RATE: $13 individual, $15 institutional
INDEXED/ABSTRACTED IN: ERIC

CIRCULATION: 1300   FREQUENCY: Quarterly

JOURNAL TITLE: JOURNAL OF THE AMERICAN GERIATRICS SOCIETY

MANUSCRIPT ADDRESS: 10 Columbus Circle
Suite 1470
New York, NY 10019

TYPE OF ARTICLES: Research articles, case studies

MAJOR CONTENT AREAS: Aging and aged

TOPICS PREFERRED: Clinical papers in field of aging and aged

INAPPROPRIATE TOPICS: Not given

NUMBER OF MANUSCRIPT COPIES: 2	PAGE CHARGES:	No
REVIEW PERIOD: 1 month	STYLE REQUIREMENTS:	Index Medicus
PUBLICATION LAG TIME: 6 months	STYLE SHEET:	Yes
EARLY PUBLICATION OPTION: No	REVISED THESES:	No
ACCEPTANCE RATE: Not given	STUDENT PAPERS:	No
AUTHORSHIP RESTRICTIONS: No	REPRINT POLICY:	None

SUBSCRIPTION ADDRESS: 10 Columbus Circle
Suite 1470
New York, NY 10019

ANNUAL SUBSCRIPTION RATE: $30 individual, $30 institutional
INDEXED/ABSTRACTED IN: BSISBA, LLBA

CIRCULATION: 8000   FREQUENCY: Monthly

JOURNAL TITLE: JOURNAL OF THE AMERICAN MEDICAL ASSOCIATION

MANUSCRIPT ADDRESS: W.R. Barclay, M.D., Editor, JAMA
535 North Dearborn Street
Chicago, Illinois   60610

TYPE OF ARTICLES: Original articles, research articles, case studies,
commentaries, theoretical articles, review articles

MAJOR CONTENT AREAS: Not given

TOPICS PREFERRED: Not given

INAPPROPRIATE TOPICS: Not given

NUMBER OF MANUSCRIPT COPIES: Not given	PAGE CHARGES:	No
REVIEW PERIOD: 10 days	STYLE REQUIREMENTS:	AMA
PUBLICATION LAG TIME: 3-6 months	STYLE SHEET:	Yes
EARLY PUBLICATION OPTION: Yes	REVISED THESES:	No
ACCEPTANCE RATE: 20%	STUDENT PAPERS:	Yes
AUTHORSHIP RESTRICTIONS: No	REPRINT POLICY:	None

SUBSCRIPTION ADDRESS: Fulfillment Department--JAMA
535 N. Dearborn Street
Chicago, Illinois   60610

ANNUAL SUBSCRIPTION RATE: $30 individual, $30 institutional
INDEXED/ABSTRACTED IN: IM; EM; CC; others

CIRCULATION: 250,000   FREQUENCY: Weekly

JOURNAL TITLE: JOURNAL OF THE AMERICAN PSYCHOANALYTIC ASSOCIATION

MANUSCRIPT ADDRESS: Dr. Harold Blum, Editor
23 The Hemlock
Roslyn Estate, NY 11576

TYPE OF ARTICLES: Research articles, theoretical articles, case
studies, review articles

MAJOR CONTENT AREAS: Adolescence, aging and aged, alcoholism & drug
abuse, death & dying, deviant behavior, human
development, mental health & illness, social
psychology, suicide, sexual behavior

TOPICS PREFERRED: Psychoanalysis

INAPPROPRIATE TOPICS: Not given

NUMBER OF MANUSCRIPT COPIES: 3	PAGE CHARGES:	Yes
REVIEW PERIOD: 6 months	STYLE REQUIREMENTS:	Chicago Manuscript
PUBLICATION LAG TIME: 1 year	STYLE SHEET:	Yes
EARLY PUBLICATION OPTION: No	REVISED THESES:	No
ACCEPTANCE RATE: 30%	STUDENT PAPERS:	No
AUTHORSHIP RESTRICTIONS: Not given	REPRINT POLICY:	None

SUBSCRIPTION ADDRESS: 315 Fifth Avenue
New York, NY 10016

ANNUAL SUBSCRIPTION RATE: $27.50 individual, $40 institutional
INDEXED/ABSTRACTED IN: PA

CIRCULATION: 5500   FREQUENCY: Quarterly

JOURNAL TITLE: JOURNAL OF THE AMERICAN STATISTICAL ASSOCIATION

MANUSCRIPT ADDRESS: Dr. S. Fienberg, Department of Applied Statistics
University of Minnesota
1994 Buford Avenue
St. Paul, MN 55108

TYPE OF ARTICLES: Research articles, review articles

MAJOR CONTENT AREAS: Consumerism, criminology, demography, epidemiology,
labor force/labor relations, law, migration, social
mobility, sociometry

TOPICS PREFERRED: Not given

INAPPROPRIATE TOPICS: Not given

NUMBER OF MANUSCRIPT COPIES: 4	PAGE CHARGES:	Yes
REVIEW PERIOD: 2-15 mos.	STYLE REQUIREMENTS:	JASA
PUBLICATION LAG TIME: 5-9 months	STYLE SHEET:	Yes
EARLY PUBLICATION OPTION: No	REVISED THESES:	Not given
ACCEPTANCE RATE: 15%	STUDENT PAPERS:	No
AUTHORSHIP RESTRICTIONS: No	REPRINT POLICY:	None

SUBSCRIPTION ADDRESS: Department of Applied Statistics
University of Minnesota
1994 Buford Avenue
St. Paul, MN 55108

ANNUAL SUBSCRIPTION RATE: $30 individual, $30 institutional
INDEXED/ABSTRACTED IN: CIS, JEL, MC, MRSTMA

CIRCULATION: 16,000   FREQUENCY: Quarterly

JOURNAL TITLE: JOURNAL OF ANTHROPOLOGICAL RESEARCH

MANUSCRIPT ADDRESS: The University of New Mexico
Albuquerque, NM 87131

TYPE OF ARTICLES: Theoretical articles, research articles,
solicited book reviews

MAJOR CONTENT AREAS: Anthropology

TOPICS PREFERRED: General anthropology (including archaeology,
biological, cultural-social and linguistics)
of the world
INAPPROPRIATE TOPICS: Not given

NUMBER OF MANUSCRIPT COPIES: 1
REVIEW PERIOD: 3 months
PUBLICATION LAG TIME: 9 months
EARLY PUBLICATION OPTION: No
ACCEPTANCE RATE: 20%
AUTHORSHIP RESTRICTIONS: No

PAGE CHARGES: No
STYLE REQUIREMENTS: Chicago Manuscript
STYLE SHEET: Yes
REVISED THESES: Acceptable
STUDENT PAPERS: No
REPRINT POLICY: 50

SUBSCRIPTION ADDRESS: The University of New Mexico
Albuquerque, NM 87131

ANNUAL SUBSCRIPTION RATE: $7 individual, $12 institutional
INDEXED/ABSTRACTED IN: SSI,SA, AA

CIRCULATION: 2300   FREQUENCY: Quarterly

JOURNAL TITLE: JOURNAL OF APPLIED BEHAVIORAL SCIENCE

MANUSCRIPT ADDRESS: Manuscript Editor
PO Box 9155
Rosslyn Station
Arlington, VA 22209
TYPE OF ARTICLES: Research articles, theoretical articles, case
studies

MAJOR CONTENT AREAS: Planned change theories, strategies, values,
small group theory, applied behavioral science

TOPICS PREFERRED: Interplay among theory, practice and values in
the domain of planned change, strategies of social
intervention, small group theory
INAPPROPRIATE TOPICS: Not given

NUMBER OF MANUSCRIPT COPIES: 4
REVIEW PERIOD: 10 weeks
PUBLICATION LAG TIME: 18 months
EARLY PUBLICATION OPTION: No
ACCEPTANCE RATE: 10%
AUTHORSHIP RESTRICTIONS: No

PAGE CHARGES: No
STYLE REQUIREMENTS: APA
STYLE SHEET: Yes
REVISED THESES: Not given
STUDENT PAPERS: Not given
REPRINT POLICY: 3 journals

SUBSCRIPTION ADDRESS: Subscription Administrator
PO Box 9155
Rosslyn Station
Arlington, VA 22209
ANNUAL SUBSCRIPTION RATE: $19 individual, $19 institutional
INDEXED/ABSTRACTED IN: ASW, WRA, EAA, SA, ABC PS

CIRCULATION: 6000   FREQUENCY: Quarterly

JOURNAL TITLE: JOURNAL OF APPLIED PSYCHOLOGY

MANUSCRIPT ADDRESS: John Campbell, Department of Psychology
Elliott Hall
University of Minnesota
Minneapolis, MN 55455

TYPE OF ARTICLES: Not given

MAJOR CONTENT AREAS: Journal is devoted primarily to original
investigations that contribute new
knowledge and understanding to any field
of applied psychology except clinical psychology

TOPICS PREFERRED: Not given

INAPPROPRIATE TOPICS: Not given

NUMBER OF MANUSCRIPT COPIES:	3	PAGE CHARGES:	No
REVIEW PERIOD:	6 weeks	STYLE REQUIREMENTS:	APA
PUBLICATION LAG TIME:	12 months	STYLE SHEET:	Yes
EARLY PUBLICATION OPTION:	No	REVISED THESES:	No
ACCEPTANCE RATE:	15%	STUDENT PAPERS:	No
AUTHORSHIP RESTRICTIONS:	No	REPRINT POLICY:	20

SUBSCRIPTION ADDRESS: APA
Subscription Section
1200 17th Street NW
Washington, DC 20036

ANNUAL SUBSCRIPTION RATE: $12 member, $30 nonmember
INDEXED/ABSTRACTED IN: PA

CIRCULATION: 6075   FREQUENCY: Bimonthly

JOURNAL TITLE: JOURNAL OF APPLIED SOCIAL PSYCHOLOGY

MANUSCRIPT ADDRESS: Dr. Peter Suedfeld, Editor, Dept. of Psychology
Univ. of British Columbia, 2075 Westbrook Pl.
Vancouver, B.C. V6T 1W5, Canada

TYPE OF ARTICLES: Research articles, theoretical articles, review
articles, applications based on research

MAJOR CONTENT AREAS: Social

TOPICS PREFERRED: Any research in social psychology of actual
or potential applicable value

INAPPROPRIATE TOPICS: Research in education

NUMBER OF MANUSCRIPT COPIES:	Not given	PAGE CHARGES:	Not given
REVIEW PERIOD:	3 months	STYLE REQUIREMENTS:	APA
PUBLICATION LAG TIME:	1 year	STYLE SHEET:	No
EARLY PUBLICATION OPTION:	No	REVISED THESES:	Not given
ACCEPTANCE RATE:	15-20%	STUDENT PAPERS:	Not given
AUTHORSHIP RESTRICTIONS:	Not given	REPRINT POLICY:	Not given

SUBSCRIPTION ADDRESS: Scripta Publishing Co.
1511 K Street, NW
Washington, DC 20005

ANNUAL SUBSCRIPTION RATE: $18 individual, $36 institutional
INDEXED/ABSTRACTED IN: PA, EM, CSPA, CCSBS, CIJE, WSA

CIRCULATION: Not given   FREQUENCY: Not given

JOURNAL TITLE: JOURNAL OF THE ASSOCIATION FOR THE STUDY OF PERCEPTION

MANUSCRIPT ADDRESS: Editor
Box 744
DeKalb, IL 60115

TYPE OF ARTICLES: Research articles, theoretical articles, review articles, case studies, commentaries

MAJOR CONTENT AREAS: Adolescence, aging and aged, counseling, deviant behavior, groups, human development, human organizations, mental health & illness, sex roles, social change, social institutions

TOPICS PREFERRED: All topics dealing with perception

INAPPROPRIATE TOPICS: Not given

NUMBER OF MANUSCRIPT COPIES: 1
REVIEW PERIOD: 3-6 mos.
PUBLICATION LAG TIME: 3-6 months
EARLY PUBLICATION OPTION: No
ACCEPTANCE RATE: 50%
AUTHORSHIP RESTRICTIONS: No

PAGE CHARGES: No
STYLE REQUIREMENTS: APA
STYLE SHEET: Yes
REVISED THESES: No
STUDENT PAPERS: Yes
REPRINT POLICY: 10

SUBSCRIPTION ADDRESS: Box 744
DeKalb, IL 60115

ANNUAL SUBSCRIPTION RATE: $5 individual, $5 institutional
INDEXED/ABSTRACTED IN: UM,EI

CIRCULATION: 250

FREQUENCY: Semiannually

JOURNAL TITLE: JOURNAL OF BEHAVIOR THERAPY AND EXPERIMENTAL PSYCHIATRY

MANUSCRIPT ADDRESS: Dr. Joseph Wolpe, Editor
Temple U. Medical School, Eastern Pa.
Psychiatric Institute, Henry Avenue
Philadelphia, PA 19129

TYPE OF ARTICLES: Research articles, case reports; should have follow-up data of at least six months' duration

MAJOR CONTENT AREAS: Behavior therapy/applied behavior analysis, experimental psychiatry

TOPICS PREFERRED: New methods, target behaviors, or populations; observations of considerable interest

INAPPROPRIATE TOPICS: Smoking, eating and addictive behaviors with less than one year follow-up

NUMBER OF MANUSCRIPT COPIES: Not given
REVIEW PERIOD: 3-5 months
PUBLICATION LAG TIME: 3 months
EARLY PUBLICATION OPTION: No
ACCEPTANCE RATE: 25-35%
AUTHORSHIP RESTRICTIONS: Not given

PAGE CHARGES: Not given
STYLE REQUIREMENTS: APA
STYLE SHEET: Yes
REVISED THESES: Not given
STUDENT PAPERS: Not given
REPRINT POLICY: Not given

SUBSCRIPTION ADDRESS: Pergamon Press, Inc.
Maxwell House, Fairview Park
Elmsford, NY 10523

ANNUAL SUBSCRIPTION RATE: $25 individual, $55 institutional
INDEXED/ABSTRACTED IN: PA, IM, CCSBS, LLBA, PRG

CIRCULATION: 4200

FREQUENCY: Not given

JOURNAL TITLE: JOURNAL OF BIOLOGICAL PSYCHOLOGY/WORM RUNNER'S DIGEST

MANUSCRIPT ADDRESS: PO Box 644
Ann Arbor, MI 48107

TYPE OF ARTICLES: Research articles, theoretical articles, review articles, commentaries, unsolicited book reviews, case studies

MAJOR CONTENT AREAS: Educational sociology, general sociology, human development, sociology of knowledge, medical sociology, mental health & illness, sociology of science, social change, social issues

TOPICS PREFERRED: Experimental, biological psychology, behavior modification, theoretical articles in psychology, sociology, social sciences

INAPPROPRIATE TOPICS: Not given

NUMBER OF MANUSCRIPT COPIES: 2	PAGE CHARGES:	No
REVIEW PERIOD: 3-6 mos.	STYLE REQUIREMENTS:	APA
PUBLICATION LAG TIME: 6-12 months	STYLE SHEET:	Yes
EARLY PUBLICATION OPTION: No	REVISED THESES:	Acceptable
ACCEPTANCE RATE: 90%	STUDENT PAPERS:	Yes
AUTHORSHIP RESTRICTIONS: No	REPRINT POLICY:	100

SUBSCRIPTION ADDRESS: PO Box 644
Ann Arbor, MI 48107

ANNUAL SUBSCRIPTION RATE: $5 individual, $5 institutional
INDEXED/ABSTRACTED IN: CC:BSMS, SA, UM

CIRCULATION: 1000   FREQUENCY: Semiannually

JOURNAL TITLE: JOURNAL OF BLACK STUDIES

MANUSCRIPT ADDRESS: Molefi Asante, Department of Black Studies
State University of New York
Buffalo, NY 14226

TYPE OF ARTICLES: Research articles, theoretical articles, review articles, case studies, commentaries

MAJOR CONTENT AREAS: Anthropology, economy and society, ethnic groups, general sociology, minorities, political sociology, race relations, social issues, society & institutions, urban sociology

TOPICS PREFERRED: Not given

INAPPROPRIATE TOPICS: Not given

NUMBER OF MANUSCRIPT COPIES: 3	PAGE CHARGES:	No
REVIEW PERIOD: Not given	STYLE REQUIREMENTS:	Not given
PUBLICATION LAG TIME: Not given	STYLE SHEET:	Yes
EARLY PUBLICATION OPTION: No	REVISED THESES:	Not given
ACCEPTANCE RATE: Not given	STUDENT PAPERS:	No
AUTHORSHIP RESTRICTIONS: No	REPRINT POLICY:	24

SUBSCRIPTION ADDRESS: Sage Publications
275 S Beverly Drive
Beverly Hills, CA 90212

ANNUAL SUBSCRIPTION RATE: $12 individual, $20 institutional
INDEXED/ABSTRACTED IN: SA, HRA, SUSA, HA, ASW, UAA, IPSA, A

CIRCULATION: Not given   FREQUENCY: Quarterly

JOURNAL TITLE: JOURNAL OF BROADCASTING

MANUSCRIPT ADDRESS: School of Journalism
University of Georgia
Athens, GA 30602

TYPE OF ARTICLES: Research articles, theoretical articles, case
studies, review articles, commentaries, unsolicited
book reviews

MAJOR CONTENT AREAS: Mass communication, mass media, popular culture,
public opinion, socialization

TOPICS PREFERRED: Not given

INAPPROPRIATE TOPICS: Bibliographies

NUMBER OF MANUSCRIPT COPIES: 2	PAGE CHARGES:	No
REVIEW PERIOD: 2 months	STYLE REQUIREMENTS:	Not given
PUBLICATION LAG TIME: 12 months	STYLE SHEET:	Yes
EARLY PUBLICATION OPTION: No	REVISED THESES:	Yes
ACCEPTANCE RATE: 20%	STUDENT PAPERS:	No
AUTHORSHIP RESTRICTIONS: No	REPRINT POLICY:	4

SUBSCRIPTION ADDRESS: 1771 N Street, NW
Washington, DC 20036

ANNUAL SUBSCRIPTION RATE: $17.50 individual, $17.50 institutional
INDEXED/ABSTRACTED IN: SA, JT

CIRCULATION: 1800   FREQUENCY: Quarterly

JOURNAL TITLE: JOURNAL OF COMMUNICATION

MANUSCRIPT ADDRESS: Editor
3620 Walnut Street
Philadelphia, PA 19104

TYPE OF ARTICLES: Research articles, review articles

MAJOR CONTENT AREAS: Adolescence, aging and aged, mass communication,
consumerism, ethnic groups, health and illness,
law, mass media, popular culture, public opinion,
race relations, sex roles, social ideology

TOPICS PREFERRED: Not given

INAPPROPRIATE TOPICS: Not given

NUMBER OF MANUSCRIPT COPIES: 2	PAGE CHARGES:	No
REVIEW PERIOD: 6 months	STYLE REQUIREMENTS:	Not given
PUBLICATION LAG TIME: 6-8 months	STYLE SHEET:	No
EARLY PUBLICATION OPTION: No	REVISED THESES:	Yes
ACCEPTANCE RATE: 5%	STUDENT PAPERS:	No
AUTHORSHIP RESTRICTIONS: No	REPRINT POLICY:	1 journal

SUBSCRIPTION ADDRESS: PO Box 13358
Philadelphia, PA 19101

ANNUAL SUBSCRIPTION RATE: $15 individual, $15 institutional
INDEXED/ABSTRACTED IN: XUM, HA, USPD, ERIC, EI

CIRCULATION: 6500   FREQUENCY: Quarterly

JOURNAL TITLE: JOURNAL OF THE COMMUNITY DEVELOPMENT SOCIETY

MANUSCRIPT ADDRESS: Jerry Robinson, Jr. Editor
305 Mumford Hall
University of Illinois
Urbana, IL 61801

TYPE OF ARTICLES: Case studies, research articles, theoretical articles, commentaries, review articles

MAJOR CONTENT AREAS: Community development, housing and renewal, human organizations, industrial sociology, leadership, organizations, social planning, public health, rural sociology, social conflict, social policy

TOPICS PREFERRED: Community development

INAPPROPRIATE TOPICS: Not given

NUMBER OF MANUSCRIPT COPIES:	4	PAGE CHARGES:	No
REVIEW PERIOD:	2-3 months	STYLE REQUIREMENTS:	ASA
PUBLICATION LAG TIME:	3-9 months	STYLE SHEET:	Yes
EARLY PUBLICATION OPTION:	No	REVISED THESES:	No
ACCEPTANCE RATE:	10-20%	STUDENT PAPERS:	Yes
AUTHORSHIP RESTRICTIONS:	No	REPRINT POLICY:	2 journals

SUBSCRIPTION ADDRESS: Jerry Robinson, Jr. Editor
305 Mumford Hall
University of Illinois
Urbana, IL 61801

ANNUAL SUBSCRIPTION RATE: $15 individual, $15 institutional
INDEXED/ABSTRACTED IN: ASW

CIRCULATION: 1000   FREQUENCY: Semiannually

JOURNAL TITLE: JOURNAL OF COMMUNITY HEALTH

MANUSCRIPT ADDRESS: Robert L. Kane, M.D. , Editor
Department of Family and Community Medicine
50 North Medical Drive
Salt Lake City, UT 84132

TYPE OF ARTICLES: Research articles, commentaries, review articles, theoretical articles, case studies

MAJOR CONTENT AREAS: Health and illness, medical sociology, poverty, inequality, and policy, public health, social policy

TOPICS PREFERRED: Well done evaluations, policy-relevant material

INAPPROPRIATE TOPICS: Simple reports of projects

NUMBER OF MANUSCRIPT COPIES:	3	PAGE CHARGES:	No
REVIEW PERIOD:	1 month	STYLE REQUIREMENTS:	Index Medicus
PUBLICATION LAG TIME:	6 months	STYLE SHEET:	Yes
EARLY PUBLICATION OPTION:	No	REVISED THESES:	Yes
ACCEPTANCE RATE:	25%	STUDENT PAPERS:	Yes
AUTHORSHIP RESTRICTIONS:	No	REPRINT POLICY:	None

SUBSCRIPTION ADDRESS: Vittorio Maestro, Managing Editor
Human Sciences Press
72 Fifth Avenue
New York, NY 10011

ANNUAL SUBSCRIPTION RATE: $15 individual, $35 institutional
INDEXED/ABSTRACTED IN: IM, CIJE, CMHR, HRA, AHMS, SA, CLS:SWHC

CIRCULATION: 1500   FREQUENCY: Quarterly

JOURNAL TITLE: JOURNAL OF COMPARATIVE FAMILY STUDIES

MANUSCRIPT ADDRESS: Dr. George Kirian, Editor
University of Calgary
2920 24th Avenue NW
Calgary, Alberta, Canada T2N 1N4

TYPE OF ARTICLES: Research articles,theoretical articles, case
studies, commentaries, review articles,
unsolicited book reviews

MAJOR CONTENT AREAS: Adolescence, aging and aged, anthropology, communes,
death & dying, demography, family formation,family
planning, marriage & divorce, sex roles, sexual
behavior

TOPICS PREFERRED: Cross-cultural studies on family - national as
well as international

INAPPROPRIATE TOPICS: Not given

NUMBER OF MANUSCRIPT COPIES:	2	PAGE CHARGES: No
REVIEW PERIOD:	6 months	STYLE REQUIREMENTS: ASA
PUBLICATION LAG TIME:	3 months	STYLE SHEET: Yes
EARLY PUBLICATION OPTION:	Not given	REVISED THESES: Yes
ACCEPTANCE RATE:	75%	STUDENT PAPERS: No
AUTHORSHIP RESTRICTIONS:	No	REPRINT POLICY: None

SUBSCRIPTION ADDRESS: Dr. George Kirian, Editor
University of Calgary
2920 24th Avenue NW
Calgary, Alberta, Canada T2N 1N4

ANNUAL SUBSCRIPTION RATE: $16 individual, $21 institutional
INDEXED/ABSTRACTED IN: Not given

CIRCULATION: 600   FREQUENCY: Tri-yearly

JOURNAL TITLE: JOURNAL OF CONFLICT RESOLUTION

MANUSCRIPT ADDRESS: Bruce Russett
Box 3532
New Haven, CT 06520

TYPE OF ARTICLES: Research articles, theoretical articles, review
articles, case studies, commentaries

MAJOR CONTENT AREAS: Sociology of peace

TOPICS PREFERRED: Not given

INAPPROPRIATE TOPICS: Not given

NUMBER OF MANUSCRIPT COPIES:	3	PAGE CHARGES: No
REVIEW PERIOD:	Not given	STYLE REQUIREMENTS: Not given
PUBLICATION LAG TIME:	Not given	STYLE SHEET: Yes
EARLY PUBLICATION OPTION:	No	REVISED THESES: Not given
ACCEPTANCE RATE:	Not given	STUDENT PAPERS: No
AUTHORSHIP RESTRICTIONS:	No	REPRINT POLICY: 24

SUBSCRIPTION ADDRESS: Sage Publications, Inc.
275 S Beverly Drive
Beverly Hills, CA 90212

ANNUAL SUBSCRIPTION RATE: $16.80 individual, $28 institutional
INDEXED/ABSTRACTED IN: IPSA, PA, ABC PS, SA, SEA, ASW, HRA, SPA, PAIS,
CC, SSCI, SSI, SUSA
CIRCULATION: Not given   FREQUENCY: Quarterly

JOURNAL TITLE: JOURNAL OF CONSULTING AND CLINICAL PSYCHOLOGY

MANUSCRIPT ADDRESS: Brendan Maher
1120 William James Hall
Harvard University, 33 Kirkland Street
Cambridge, MA 02138

TYPE OF ARTICLES: Not given

MAJOR CONTENT AREAS: The development, validity, and use of techniques of diagnosis and treatment in disordered behavior, studies of populations of clinical interest, such as hospital, prison, rehabilitation, geriatric

TOPICS PREFERRED: Not given

INAPPROPRIATE TOPICS: Not given

NUMBER OF MANUSCRIPT COPIES:	3	PAGE CHARGES:	No
REVIEW PERIOD:	4 months	STYLE REQUIREMENTS:	APA
PUBLICATION LAG TIME:	10 months	STYLE SHEET:	Yes
EARLY PUBLICATION OPTION:	No	REVISED THESES:	No
ACCEPTANCE RATE:	18%	STUDENT PAPERS:	No
AUTHORSHIP RESTRICTIONS:	No	REPRINT POLICY:	20

SUBSCRIPTION ADDRESS: APA, Subscription Section
1200 17th Street NW
Washington, DC 20036

ANNUAL SUBSCRIPTION RATE: $14 member, $32 nonmember
INDEXED/ABSTRACTED IN: PA

CIRCULATION: 8900   FREQUENCY: Bimonthly

JOURNAL TITLE: JOURNAL OF CONSUMER AFFAIRS

MANUSCRIPT ADDRESS: Weaver Building
Penn State University
University Park, PA 16802

TYPE OF ARTICLES: Research articles, review articles, theoretical articles, commentaries, case studies, unsolicited book reviews

MAJOR CONTENT AREAS: Collective behavior, consumerism, economy and society, poverty, inequality, and policy, social institutions, social policy, economics, consumer decisions

TOPICS PREFERRED: Consumer affairs, economics of consumption

INAPPROPRIATE TOPICS: Not given

NUMBER OF MANUSCRIPT COPIES:	3	PAGE CHARGES:	No
REVIEW PERIOD:	2-3 mos.	STYLE REQUIREMENTS:	Chicago Manuscript
PUBLICATION LAG TIME:	3-4 months	STYLE SHEET:	Yes
EARLY PUBLICATION OPTION:	Yes	REVISED THESES:	Yes
ACCEPTANCE RATE:	15%	STUDENT PAPERS:	No
AUTHORSHIP RESTRICTIONS:	No	REPRINT POLICY:	5

SUBSCRIPTION ADDRESS: ACCI
Stanley Hall
University of Missouri
Columbia, MO 65201

ANNUAL SUBSCRIPTION RATE: $15 individual, $20 institutional
INDEXED/ABSTRACTED IN: BEI, PAIS, SSCI, MI

CIRCULATION: 3500   FREQUENCY: Semiannually

JOURNAL TITLE: JOURNAL OF CRIMINAL LAW & CRIMINOLOGY

MANUSCRIPT ADDRESS: 357 East Chicago Avenue
Chicago, IL 60611

TYPE OF ARTICLES: Articles in the fields of criminal law and
criminology, research articles

MAJOR CONTENT AREAS: Alcoholism & drug abuse, criminology, deviant
behavior, educational sociology, general
sociology, law, mental health & illness, race
relations, rehabilitation, sex roles

TOPICS PREFERRED: Criminal law, criminology

INAPPROPRIATE TOPICS: Taxation, real estate

NUMBER OF MANUSCRIPT COPIES: 2	PAGE CHARGES:	No
REVIEW PERIOD: 3-5 weeks	STYLE REQUIREMENTS:	Not given
PUBLICATION LAG TIME: 3-4 months	STYLE SHEET:	Yes
EARLY PUBLICATION OPTION: Yes	REVISED THESES:	Acceptable
ACCEPTANCE RATE: 45%	STUDENT PAPERS:	Acceptable
AUTHORSHIP RESTRICTIONS: No	REPRINT POLICY:	50

SUBSCRIPTION ADDRESS: The Williams & Wilkins Co.
428 East Preston Street
Baltimore, MD 21202

ANNUAL SUBSCRIPTION RATE: $20 individual, $25 institutional
INDEXED/ABSTRACTED IN: ILP, CCLP, SA

CIRCULATION: 3500   FREQUENCY: Quarterly

JOURNAL TITLE: JOURNAL OF CROSS-CULTURAL PSYCHOLOGY

MANUSCRIPT ADDRESS: Walter J. Lonner
Department of Psychology
Western Washington State College
Bellingham, WA 98225

TYPE OF ARTICLES: Research articles, theoretical articles, review
articles, case studies, commentaries

MAJOR CONTENT AREAS: Social psychology

TOPICS PREFERRED: Not given

INAPPROPRIATE TOPICS: Not given

NUMBER OF MANUSCRIPT COPIES: 3	PAGE CHARGES:	No
REVIEW PERIOD: Not given	STYLE REQUIREMENTS:	Not given
PUBLICATION LAG TIME: Not given	STYLE SHEET:	Yes
EARLY PUBLICATION OPTION: No	REVISED THESES:	Not given
ACCEPTANCE RATE: Not given	STUDENT PAPERS:	No
AUTHORSHIP RESTRICTIONS: No	REPRINT POLICY:	24

SUBSCRIPTION ADDRESS: Sage Publications
275 S Beverly Drive
Beverly Hills, CA 90212

ANNUAL SUBSCRIPTION RATE: $13.50 individual, $22.50 institutional
INDEXED/ABSTRACTED IN: SUSA, HRA, PA, AA, SSCI, CC, PRG

CIRCULATION: Not given   FREQUENCY: Quarterly

JOURNAL TITLE: JOURNAL OF DEVELOPING AREAS

MANUSCRIPT ADDRESS: Western Illinois University
Macomb, IL 61455

TYPE OF ARTICLES: Research articles, theoretical articles, case
studies, analytical survey articles, review
articles, commentaries, unsolicited book reviews
MAJOR CONTENT AREAS: Not given

TOPICS PREFERRED: Articles which deal with the humanistic aspects
of the development process

INAPPROPRIATE TOPICS: Economics

NUMBER OF MANUSCRIPT COPIES: 2	PAGE CHARGES:	No
REVIEW PERIOD: 2-4 months	STYLE REQUIREMENTS:	Chicago Manuscript
PUBLICATION LAG TIME: 12-18 months	STYLE SHEET:	Yes
EARLY PUBLICATION OPTION: No	REVISED THESES:	No
ACCEPTANCE RATE: 9-11%	STUDENT PAPERS:	No
AUTHORSHIP RESTRICTIONS: No	REPRINT POLICY:	50

SUBSCRIPTION ADDRESS: Western Illinois University
Macomb, IL 61455

ANNUAL SUBSCRIPTION RATE: $12 individual, $16 institutional
INDEXED/ABSTRACTED IN: Not given

CIRCULATION: 1440   FREQUENCY: Quarterly

JOURNAL TITLE: THE JOURNAL OF DEVELOPMENT STUDIES

MANUSCRIPT ADDRESS: The Secretary
Frank Cass & Co. Ltd.
11 Gainsborough Road
London E11 1RS, England
TYPE OF ARTICLES: Research articles, theoretical articles, case
studies, review articles, commentaries,
unsolicited book reviews
MAJOR CONTENT AREAS: Administrative behavior, anthropology, economy
and society, human development, industrial
sociology, leadership, migration, population

TOPICS PREFERRED: Wage determination, politics of planning,
relevance of theories of bureaucracy and
democracy to development
INAPPROPRIATE TOPICS: Trivial extensions of neo-classical economic
theory, mechanical econometrics

NUMBER OF MANUSCRIPT COPIES: 2	PAGE CHARGES:	No
REVIEW PERIOD: 3-12 wks.	STYLE REQUIREMENTS:	Not given
PUBLICATION LAG TIME: 1 year	STYLE SHEET:	Yes
EARLY PUBLICATION OPTION: No	REVISED THESES:	Acceptable
ACCEPTANCE RATE: 10%	STUDENT PAPERS:	Acceptable
AUTHORSHIP RESTRICTIONS: No	REPRINT POLICY:	25

SUBSCRIPTION ADDRESS: Subscription Department
Frank Cass & Co., Ltd.
11 Gainsborough Road
London E11 1RS, England
ANNUAL SUBSCRIPTION RATE: $37.50 individual, $49.50 institutional
INDEXED/ABSTRACTED IN: Not given

CIRCULATION: 1500   FREQUENCY: Quarterly

JOURNAL TITLE: JOURNAL OF DIVORCE

MANUSCRIPT ADDRESS: Esther Oshiver Fisher, J.D., Ed.D.
1050 Park Avenue
New York, N.Y. 10028

TYPE OF ARTICLES: Research, theoretical, case studies

MAJOR CONTENT AREAS: Clinical issues, psychotherapy, human sexuality,
sociological & legal aspects of divorce

TOPICS PREFERRED: Any concerned with the divorce process

INAPPROPRIATE TOPICS: Those unrelated to divorce

NUMBER OF MANUSCRIPT COPIES:	3	PAGE CHARGES:	None
REVIEW PERIOD:	2 months	STYLE REQUIREMENTS:	APA
PUBLICATION LAG TIME:	6 months	STYLE SHEET:	Yes
EARLY PUBLICATION OPTION:	No	REVISED THESES:	Yes
ACCEPTANCE RATE:	Not yet known	STUDENT PAPERS:	Not given
AUTHORSHIP RESTRICTIONS:	None	REPRINT POLICY:	10 reprints

SUBSCRIPTION ADDRESS: The Haworth Press
149 Fifth Avenue
New York, N.Y. 10010

ANNUAL SUBSCRIPTION RATE: $18 individuals; $35 institutions
INDEXED/ABSTRACTED IN: Not yet known (new journal)

CIRCULATION: 1,000   FREQUENCY: Quarterly

JOURNAL TITLE: JOURNAL OF EDUCATIONAL PSYCHOLOGY

MANUSCRIPT ADDRESS: Joanna Williams
Teachers College, Box 238
Columbia University
New York, NY 10027
TYPE OF ARTICLES: Not given

MAJOR CONTENT AREAS: Publishes original investigations and theoretical
papers dealing with learning and cognition,
especially as they relate to problems of instruc-
tion, and with psychological development
TOPICS PREFERRED: Not given

INAPPROPRIATE TOPICS: Not given

NUMBER OF MANUSCRIPT COPIES:	3	PAGE CHARGES:	No
REVIEW PERIOD:	2 months	STYLE REQUIREMENTS:	APA
PUBLICATION LAG TIME:	9 months	STYLE SHEET:	Yes
EARLY PUBLICATION OPTION:	No	REVISED THESES:	No
ACCEPTANCE RATE:	15%	STUDENT PAPERS:	No
AUTHORSHIP RESTRICTIONS:	No	REPRINT POLICY:	20

SUBSCRIPTION ADDRESS: APA, Subscription Section
1200 17th Street NW
Washington, DC 20036

ANNUAL SUBSCRIPTION RATE: $12 members , $30 nonmembers
INDEXED/ABSTRACTED IN: PA

CIRCULATION: 6225   FREQUENCY: Bimonthly

JOURNAL TITLE: JOURNAL OF EDUCATIONAL THOUGHT

MANUSCRIPT ADDRESS: Room 514, Education Tower
The University of Calgary
2920-24th Avenue NW
Calgary, Alberta, T2N, 1N4, Canada

TYPE OF ARTICLES: Theoretical articles, promoting speculative, critical thought about theory and practice of education in a variety of disciplines

MAJOR CONTENT AREAS: Not given

TOPICS PREFERRED: Educational

INAPPROPRIATE TOPICS: Not given

NUMBER OF MANUSCRIPT COPIES:	3	PAGE CHARGES:	No
REVIEW PERIOD:	3 months	STYLE REQUIREMENTS:	MLA
PUBLICATION LAG TIME:	3-6 months	STYLE SHEET:	Yes
EARLY PUBLICATION OPTION:	Not given	REVISED THESES:	Acceptable
ACCEPTANCE RATE:	Not given	STUDENT PAPERS:	No
AUTHORSHIP RESTRICTIONS:	No	REPRINT POLICY:	5 journals

SUBSCRIPTION ADDRESS: Room 514, Education Tower
The University of Calgary
2920-24th Avenue NW
Calgary, Alberta, T2N 1N4, Canada

ANNUAL SUBSCRIPTION RATE: $6.50 individual, $6.50 institutional

INDEXED/ABSTRACTED IN: Not given

CIRCULATION: Not given   FREQUENCY: Tri-yearly

JOURNAL TITLE: THE JOURNAL OF EMOTIONAL EDUCATION

MANUSCRIPT ADDRESS: Bea Langerman, Editor
112 E 19th Street
New York, NY 10003

TYPE OF ARTICLES: Not given

MAJOR CONTENT AREAS: Not given

TOPICS PREFERRED: Milieu therapy

INAPPROPRIATE TOPICS: Not given

NUMBER OF MANUSCRIPT COPIES:	Not given	PAGE CHARGES:	Not given
REVIEW PERIOD:	1 month	STYLE REQUIREMENTS:	Not given
PUBLICATION LAG TIME:	6 months	STYLE SHEET:	Not given
EARLY PUBLICATION OPTION:	Not given	REVISED THESES:	Not given
ACCEPTANCE RATE:	66%	STUDENT PAPERS:	Not given
AUTHORSHIP RESTRICTIONS:	Not given	REPRINT POLICY:	0

SUBSCRIPTION ADDRESS: Bea Langerman, Editor
112 E 19th Street
New York, NY 10003

ANNUAL SUBSCRIPTION RATE: $5 individual, Not given institutional

INDEXED/ABSTRACTED IN: Not given

CIRCULATION: Not given   FREQUENCY: Quarterly

JOURNAL TITLE: THE JOURNAL OF ETHNIC STUDIES

MANUSCRIPT ADDRESS: The Editor
Western Washington State College
Bellingham, WA 98225

TYPE OF ARTICLES: Commentaries, theoretical articles, research
articles, review articles

MAJOR CONTENT AREAS: Economy and society, ethnic groups, human
development, migration, minorities, poverty,
inequality, and policy, race relations, social
change, social conflict, social ideology
TOPICS PREFERRED: Ethnic studies

INAPPROPRIATE TOPICS: Case studies which are limited and have no focus,
no ideology, no personal position

NUMBER OF MANUSCRIPT COPIES: 2
REVIEW PERIOD: 1-6 months
PUBLICATION LAG TIME: 3-6 months
EARLY PUBLICATION OPTION: No
ACCEPTANCE RATE: 20%
AUTHORSHIP RESTRICTIONS: No

PAGE CHARGES: No
STYLE REQUIREMENTS: Chicago Manuscript
STYLE SHEET: Yes
REVISED THESES: No
STUDENT PAPERS: No
REPRINT POLICY: 5

SUBSCRIPTION ADDRESS: Western Washington State College
Bellingham, WA 98225

ANNUAL SUBSCRIPTION RATE: $8 individual, $10 institutional
INDEXED/ABSTRACTED IN: JPC, UCIS, MLA, SA, HS

CIRCULATION: 700   FREQUENCY: Quarterly

JOURNAL TITLE: JOURNAL OF EXPERIMENTAL PSYCHOLOGY: GENERAL

MANUSCRIPT ADDRESS: Gregory A. Kimble
Department of Psychology
Duke University
Durham, NC 27706
TYPE OF ARTICLES: Not given

MAJOR CONTENT AREAS: Articles of experimental psychology involving a
longer, more integrative report that is judged
to be of interest to the entire community of
experimental psychologists.
TOPICS PREFERRED: Not given

INAPPROPRIATE TOPICS: Not given

NUMBER OF MANUSCRIPT COPIES: 3
REVIEW PERIOD: 2 months
PUBLICATION LAG TIME: 12 months
EARLY PUBLICATION OPTION: No
ACCEPTANCE RATE: 36%
AUTHORSHIP RESTRICTIONS: No

PAGE CHARGES: No
STYLE REQUIREMENTS: APA
STYLE SHEET: Yes
REVISED THESES: No
STUDENT PAPERS: No
REPRINT POLICY: 20

SUBSCRIPTION ADDRESS: APA, Subscription Section
1200 17th Street NW
Washington, DC 20036

ANNUAL SUBSCRIPTION RATE: $7 member, $14 nonmember
INDEXED/ABSTRACTED IN: PA

CIRCULATION: 4080   FREQUENCY: Quarterly

JOURNAL TITLE: JOURNAL OF EXPERIMENTAL PSYCHOLOGY: HUMAN LEARNING AND MEMORY

MANUSCRIPT ADDRESS: Lyle E. Bourne, Jr.
Department of Psychology
University of Colorado
Boulder, CO 80309

TYPE OF ARTICLES: Experimental studies on fundamental acquisition, retention, and transfer processes in human behavior

MAJOR CONTENT AREAS: Not given

TOPICS PREFERRED: Not given

INAPPROPRIATE TOPICS: Not given

NUMBER OF MANUSCRIPT COPIES: 3	PAGE CHARGES: No
REVIEW PERIOD: 5 weeks	STYLE REQUIREMENTS: APA
PUBLICATION LAG TIME: 10 months	STYLE SHEET: Yes
EARLY PUBLICATION OPTION: No	REVISED THESES: No
ACCEPTANCE RATE: 24%	STUDENT PAPERS: No
AUTHORSHIP RESTRICTIONS: No	REPRINT POLICY: 20

SUBSCRIPTION ADDRESS: APA
Subscription Section
1200 17th Street NW
Washington, DC 20036

ANNUAL SUBSCRIPTION RATE: $12 member, $24 nonmember

INDEXED/ABSTRACTED IN: PA

CIRCULATION: 4190   FREQUENCY: Bimonthly

JOURNAL TITLE: JOURNAL OF EXPERIMENTAL PSYCHOLOGY: HUMAN PERCEPTION AND PERFORMANCE

MANUSCRIPT ADDRESS: Michael I. Posner
Department of Psychology
University of Oregon
Eugene, OR 97403

TYPE OF ARTICLES: Experimental studies designed to foster under-standing of information-processing operations and their relation to experience and performance

MAJOR CONTENT AREAS: Not given

TOPICS PREFERRED: Not given

INAPPROPRIATE TOPICS: Not given

NUMBER OF MANUSCRIPT COPIES: 3	PAGE CHARGES: No
REVIEW PERIOD: 5 weeks	STYLE REQUIREMENTS: APA
PUBLICATION LAG TIME: 10 months	STYLE SHEET: Yes
EARLY PUBLICATION OPTION: No	REVISED THESES: No
ACCEPTANCE RATE: 23%	STUDENT PAPERS: No
AUTHORSHIP RESTRICTIONS: No	REPRINT POLICY: 20

SUBSCRIPTION ADDRESS: APA, Subscription Section
1200 17th Street NW
Washington, DC 20036

ANNUAL SUBSCRIPTION RATE: $10 member, $20 nonmember

INDEXED/ABSTRACTED IN: PA

CIRCULATION: Not given   FREQUENCY: Quarterly

JOURNAL TITLE: JOURNAL OF EXPERIMENTAL SOCIAL PSYCHOLOGY

MANUSCRIPT ADDRESS: A. Doob, Editor
Dept. of Psychology, University of Toronto
Toronto, Ontario, Canada

TYPE OF ARTICLES: Research articles, review articles, theoretical
articles, methodological notes

MAJOR CONTENT AREAS: Social

TOPICS PREFERRED: Not given

INAPPROPRIATE TOPICS: Not given

NUMBER OF MANUSCRIPT COPIES: Not given	PAGE CHARGES: Not given
REVIEW PERIOD: 6 weeks	STYLE REQUIREMENTS: APA
PUBLICATION LAG TIME: 8 months	STYLE SHEET: No
EARLY PUBLICATION OPTION: No	REVISED THESES: Not given
ACCEPTANCE RATE: 15%	STUDENT PAPERS: Not given
AUTHORSHIP RESTRICTIONS: Not given	REPRINT POLICY: Not given

SUBSCRIPTION ADDRESS: Academic Press
111 Fifth Avenue
New York, NY 10003

ANNUAL SUBSCRIPTION RATE: $40 individual, Not given institutional
INDEXED/ABSTRACTED IN: PA, CSPA, CCSBS, CIJE, WSA

CIRCULATION: Not given   FREQUENCY: Not given

JOURNAL TITLE: JOURNAL OF FAMILY HISTORY

MANUSCRIPT ADDRESS: The Editor
Clark University
Worcester, MA 01610

TYPE OF ARTICLES: Research articles, review articles, theoretical
articles, research reports, description of sources

MAJOR CONTENT AREAS: Anthropology, demography, economy and society,
family formation, family planning, marriage &
divorce, modernization, population, sex roles,
sexual behavior, social structure, socialization
TOPICS PREFERRED: The history of the family, kinship, demography,
and sex roles

INAPPROPRIATE TOPICS: Contemporary sociology without historical information or interpretation

NUMBER OF MANUSCRIPT COPIES: 2	PAGE CHARGES: No
REVIEW PERIOD: 1-6 mos.	STYLE REQUIREMENTS: ASA
PUBLICATION LAG TIME: 6-9 months	STYLE SHEET: Yes
EARLY PUBLICATION OPTION: No	REVISED THESES: Acceptable
ACCEPTANCE RATE: 20%	STUDENT PAPERS: No
AUTHORSHIP RESTRICTIONS: No	REPRINT POLICY: Not given

SUBSCRIPTION ADDRESS: National Council on Family Relations
1219 University Avenue SE
Minneapolis, MN 55414

ANNUAL SUBSCRIPTION RATE: $15 individual, $18 institutional
INDEXED/ABSTRACTED IN: Not given

CIRCULATION: 800   FREQUENCY: Quarterly

JOURNAL TITLE: JOURNAL OF FAMILY LAW

MANUSCRIPT ADDRESS: Journal of Family Law
University of Louisville School of Law
Louisville, Kentucky   40208

TYPE OF ARTICLES: Research, theoretical, commentaries

MAJOR CONTENT AREAS: Family law

TOPICS PREFERRED: Family law

INAPPROPRIATE TOPICS: Articles on foreign law

NUMBER OF MANUSCRIPT COPIES: 1
REVIEW PERIOD: 2 weeks
PUBLICATION LAG TIME: 4 months
EARLY PUBLICATION OPTION: No
ACCEPTANCE RATE: 50%
AUTHORSHIP RESTRICTIONS: None

PAGE CHARGES: No
STYLE REQUIREMENTS: Uniform Syst of Citation
STYLE SHEET: Yes
REVISED THESES: No
STUDENT PAPERS: Yes
REPRINT POLICY: 45

SUBSCRIPTION ADDRESS: same as editorial address

ANNUAL SUBSCRIPTION RATE: $15
INDEXED/ABSTRACTED IN: Index to Legal Periodicals

CIRCULATION: 1,000   FREQUENCY: Quarterly

JOURNAL TITLE: THE JOURNAL OF GENERAL PSYCHOLOGY

MANUSCRIPT ADDRESS: Managing Editor
The Journal Press
Box 543, 2 Commercial Street
Provincetown, MA 02657

TYPE OF ARTICLES: Research articles, theoretical articles

MAJOR CONTENT AREAS: Experimental, physiological, and comparative
psychology, human and animal laboratory studies,
and mathematical and other theoretical investigations are appropriate

TOPICS PREFERRED: Not given

INAPPROPRIATE TOPICS: Not given

NUMBER OF MANUSCRIPT COPIES: 2
REVIEW PERIOD: 1 month
PUBLICATION LAG TIME: 1 year
EARLY PUBLICATION OPTION: No
ACCEPTANCE RATE: 50%
AUTHORSHIP RESTRICTIONS: No

PAGE CHARGES: No
STYLE REQUIREMENTS: Not given
STYLE SHEET: Yes
REVISED THESES: Acceptable
STUDENT PAPERS: Not given
REPRINT POLICY: 100

SUBSCRIPTION ADDRESS: Managing Editor
The Journal Press
Box 543, 2 Commercial Street
Provincetown, MA 02657

ANNUAL SUBSCRIPTION RATE: $30 individual, $30 institutional
INDEXED/ABSTRACTED IN: ASW, BA,BAMS, DSHA, ECEA, IM, EM, PA

CIRCULATION: 1700   FREQUENCY: Quarterly

JOURNAL TITLE: JOURNAL OF GENETIC PSYCHOLOGY

MANUSCRIPT ADDRESS: Managing Editor
The Journal Press
Box 543, 2 Commercial Street
Provincetown, MA 02657

TYPE OF ARTICLES: Research articles, theoretical articles, review articles

MAJOR CONTENT AREAS: Aging and aged, human development, clinical psychology

TOPICS PREFERRED: Not given

INAPPROPRIATE TOPICS: Not given

NUMBER OF MANUSCRIPT COPIES:	2	PAGE CHARGES: Yes
REVIEW PERIOD:	6 weeks	STYLE REQUIREMENTS: Not given
PUBLICATION LAG TIME:	1 year	STYLE SHEET: Yes
EARLY PUBLICATION OPTION:	No	REVISED THESES: Not given
ACCEPTANCE RATE:	50%	STUDENT PAPERS: Not given
AUTHORSHIP RESTRICTIONS:	No	REPRINT POLICY: 100

SUBSCRIPTION ADDRESS: Managing Editor
The Journal Press
Box 543, 2 Commercial Street
Provincetown, MA 02657

ANNUAL SUBSCRIPTION RATE: $30 individual, $30 institutional
INDEXED/ABSTRACTED IN: ASW, BA, BAMS, ECEA, IM, EM, PA, DSHA

CIRCULATION: 1600   FREQUENCY: Quarterly

JOURNAL TITLE: JOURNAL OF GERIATRIC PSYCHIATRY

MANUSCRIPT ADDRESS: Dr. David Blau
90 Forest Avenue
Newton Center, MA 02748

TYPE OF ARTICLES: Research articles, theoretical articles, case studies, review articles

MAJOR CONTENT AREAS: Aging and aged, alcoholism & drug abuse, anthropology, death & dying, delinquency & crime, deviant behavior, health & illness, human development, mental health & illness

TOPICS PREFERRED: Aging and aged

INAPPROPRIATE TOPICS: Not given

NUMBER OF MANUSCRIPT COPIES:	3	PAGE CHARGES: Yes
REVIEW PERIOD:	6 months	STYLE REQUIREMENTS: Chicago Manuscript
PUBLICATION LAG TIME:	1 year	STYLE SHEET: Yes
EARLY PUBLICATION OPTION:	No	REVISED THESES: No
ACCEPTANCE RATE:	30%	STUDENT PAPERS: No
AUTHORSHIP RESTRICTIONS:	No	REPRINT POLICY: None

SUBSCRIPTION ADDRESS: 315 Fifth Avenue
New York, NY 10016

ANNUAL SUBSCRIPTION RATE: $16.50 individual, $25 institutional
INDEXED/ABSTRACTED IN: PA

CIRCULATION: 1200   FREQUENCY: Semiannually

JOURNAL TITLE: JOURNAL OF HEALTH AND SOCIAL BEHAVIOR

MANUSCRIPT ADDRESS: Mary E.W. Goss, Editor
Cornell University Medical College, A-623
1300 York Avenue
New York, NY 10021

TYPE OF ARTICLES: Research articles, theoretical articles, review articles, case studies

MAJOR CONTENT AREAS: Health and illness, medical sociology, mental & illness, organizational studies, health care delivery systems

TOPICS PREFERRED: Empirical studies, theoretical analyses, synthesizing reviews

INAPPROPRIATE TOPICS: Not given

NUMBER OF MANUSCRIPT COPIES: Not given	PAGE CHARGES: No
REVIEW PERIOD: 10 weeks	STYLE REQUIREMENTS: ASA
PUBLICATION LAG TIME: 9 months	STYLE SHEET: Yes
EARLY PUBLICATION OPTION: No	REVISED THESES: Yes
ACCEPTANCE RATE: 18%	STUDENT PAPERS: No
AUTHORSHIP RESTRICTIONS: No	REPRINT POLICY: None

SUBSCRIPTION ADDRESS: American Sociological Association
1722 N Street NW
Washington, DC 20036

ANNUAL SUBSCRIPTION RATE: $8 individual, $12 institutional
INDEXED/ABSTRACTED IN: SSCI, BA, IM, PA, SSI

CIRCULATION: 5000   FREQUENCY: Quarterly

JOURNAL TITLE: JOURNAL OF HIGHER EDUCATION

MANUSCRIPT ADDRESS: Robert J. Silverman, Editor
Ohio State University Press
2070 Neil Avenue
Columbus, OH 43210

TYPE OF ARTICLES: Research articles, theoretical articles, case studies, review articles, commentaries

MAJOR CONTENT AREAS: Administrative behavior, aging and aged, bureaucracy, economy and society, educational sociology, ethnic groups, human development, human organizations, law, sociology of science

TOPICS PREFERRED: Topics related to post-secondary education

INAPPROPRIATE TOPICS: Not given

NUMBER OF MANUSCRIPT COPIES: 3	PAGE CHARGES: No
REVIEW PERIOD: 8-10 wks.	STYLE REQUIREMENTS: Chicago Manuscript
PUBLICATION LAG TIME: 6-8 months	STYLE SHEET: Yes
EARLY PUBLICATION OPTION: No	REVISED THESES: No
ACCEPTANCE RATE: 8%	STUDENT PAPERS: Acceptable
AUTHORSHIP RESTRICTIONS: No	REPRINT POLICY: None

SUBSCRIPTION ADDRESS: Ohio State University Press
2070 Neil Avenue
Columbus, OH 43210

ANNUAL SUBSCRIPTION RATE: $12 individual, $14 institutional
INDEXED/ABSTRACTED IN: ASW, A:HL, CA, CSPA, EAA, HA, LLBA, PA, SEA, EI, CIJE, BI, BRI, URS

CIRCULATION: 5200   FREQUENCY: Bimonthly

JOURNAL TITLE: JOURNAL OF THE HISTORY OF THE
BEHAVIORAL SCIENCES
MANUSCRIPT ADDRESS: Barbara Ross, Editor
Psychology Department, College I
University of Massachusetts
Harbor Campus, Boston, MA   02125
TYPE OF ARTICLES: Research articles, case studies

MAJOR CONTENT AREAS: Anthropology, economy and society, general
sociology, law, organizations, religion

TOPICS PREFERRED: Historical aspects of the development of the
behavioral sciences

INAPPROPRIATE TOPICS: Not given

NUMBER OF MANUSCRIPT COPIES: 3   PAGE CHARGES: No
REVIEW PERIOD: 2 months   STYLE REQUIREMENTS: Chicago Manuscript
PUBLICATION LAG TIME: 12 months   STYLE SHEET: Yes
EARLY PUBLICATION OPTION: No   REVISED THESES: Yes
ACCEPTANCE RATE: 30%   STUDENT PAPERS: No
AUTHORSHIP RESTRICTIONS: No   REPRINT POLICY: None

SUBSCRIPTION ADDRESS: 4 Conant Square
Brandon VT 05733

ANNUAL SUBSCRIPTION RATE: $20 individual, $25 institutional
INDEXED/ABSTRACTED IN: Not given

CIRCULATION: 1000   FREQUENCY: Quarterly

JOURNAL TITLE: JOURNAL OF HOMOSEXUALITY

MANUSCRIPT ADDRESS: Professor John DeCecco
Department of Psychology
San Francisco State University
San Francisco, CA 94132
TYPE OF ARTICLES: Research articles, case studies, theoretical
articles, book review articles

MAJOR CONTENT AREAS: Sex roles, sexual behavior, sexual orientation,
social sex-role stereotypes

TOPICS PREFERRED: Human sexuality, sexual preference, masculinity,
femininity

INAPPROPRIATE TOPICS: Not given

NUMBER OF MANUSCRIPT COPIES: 3   PAGE CHARGES: No
REVIEW PERIOD: 1-2 mos.   STYLE REQUIREMENTS: APA
PUBLICATION LAG TIME: 8 months   STYLE SHEET: Yes
EARLY PUBLICATION OPTION: No   REVISED THESES: Yes
ACCEPTANCE RATE: 30%   STUDENT PAPERS: Yes
AUTHORSHIP RESTRICTIONS: No   REPRINT POLICY: 10

SUBSCRIPTION ADDRESS: The Haworth Press
149 Fifth Avenue
New York, NY 10010

ANNUAL SUBSCRIPTION RATE: $18 individual, $35 institutional
INDEXED/ABSTRACTED IN: PA, IM, SA, EM, CJA, ASW, BIOSIS, AA, CSPA

CIRCULATION: 1000   FREQUENCY: Quarterly

JOURNAL TITLE: THE JOURNAL OF HUMAN RESOURCES

MANUSCRIPT ADDRESS: 4315 Social Science Building
University of Wisconsin
1180 Observatory Drive
Madison, WI 53706

TYPE OF ARTICLES: Research articles

MAJOR CONTENT AREAS: Labor force, poverty, inequality, and policy

TOPICS PREFERRED: Empirical studies of the economics of education,
health economics, economics of poverty, human
resources, labor force, unemployment

INAPPROPRIATE TOPICS: Reviews of the literature, psychological studies

NUMBER OF MANUSCRIPT COPIES: 3		PAGE CHARGES: No	
REVIEW PERIOD: 3 months	STYLE REQUIREMENTS:	Chicago Manuscript	
PUBLICATION LAG TIME: 6-9 months	STYLE SHEET: Yes		
EARLY PUBLICATION OPTION: No	REVISED THESES: Not given		
ACCEPTANCE RATE: 10-15%	STUDENT PAPERS: Not given		
AUTHORSHIP RESTRICTIONS: No	REPRINT POLICY: 25		

SUBSCRIPTION ADDRESS: Journals Department
University of Wisconsin Press
PO Box 1379
Madison, WI 53701

ANNUAL SUBSCRIPTION RATE: $12 individual, $25 institutional

INDEXED/ABSTRACTED IN: JEL, PAIS

CIRCULATION: 2500   FREQUENCY: Quarterly

JOURNAL TITLE: JOURNAL OF INTERAMERICAN STUDIES AND
WORLD AFFAIRS

MANUSCRIPT ADDRESS: John P. Harrison, Editor
Box 24-8134
University of Miami
Coral Gables, FL 33124

TYPE OF ARTICLES: Research articles, theoretical articles, review
articles, case studies, commentaries

MAJOR CONTENT AREAS: Economy and society, general sociology, modernization, political sociology, poverty, inequality,
and policy, Latin American studies

TOPICS PREFERRED: Not given

INAPPROPRIATE TOPICS: Not given

NUMBER OF MANUSCRIPT COPIES: 3		PAGE CHARGES: No	
REVIEW PERIOD: Not given	STYLE REQUIREMENTS: Not given		
PUBLICATION LAG TIME: Not given	STYLE SHEET: Yes		
EARLY PUBLICATION OPTION: No	REVISED THESES: Not given		
ACCEPTANCE RATE: Not given	STUDENT PAPERS: No		
AUTHORSHIP RESTRICTIONS: No	REPRINT POLICY: 24		

SUBSCRIPTION ADDRESS: Sage Publications
275 S Beverly Drive
Beverly Hills, CA 90212

ANNUAL SUBSCRIPTION RATE: $13 individual, $22.50 institutional

INDEXED/ABSTRACTED IN: HA, IPSA, HRA, SUSA, ABC PS, SSCI, CC, PAIS,
SSI

CIRCULATION: Not given   FREQUENCY: Quarterly

JOURNAL TITLE: JOURNAL OF INTERGROUP RELATIONS

MANUSCRIPT ADDRESS: J. Griffin Crump
8924 Battery Road
Alexandria, Virginia   22308

TYPE OF ARTICLES: Those of interest to practitioners and theoreticians

MAJOR CONTENT AREAS: human rights; intergroup relations

TOPICS PREFERRED: Timely issues containing elements of interest to a
wide audience

INAPPROPRIATE TOPICS: Compilations of other authors' works

NUMBER OF MANUSCRIPT COPIES: 2   PAGE CHARGES: not given
REVIEW PERIOD: not given STYLE REQUIREMENTS: journal's own style
PUBLICATION LAG TIME: not given   STYLE SHEET: not given
EARLY PUBLICATION OPTION: not given   REVISED THESES: not given
ACCEPTANCE RATE: not given   STUDENT PAPERS: not given
AUTHORSHIP RESTRICTIONS: not given   REPRINT POLICY: not given

SUBSCRIPTION ADDRESS: Journal of Intergroup Relations
701 West Walnut Street
Louisville, Kentucky   40203

ANNUAL SUBSCRIPTION RATE: $11 one year; $20 two years; $29 three years
INDEXED/ABSTRACTED IN: Historical Abstracts; America: History & Life

CIRCULATION: not given   FREQUENCY: not given

JOURNAL TITLE: JOURNAL OF JEWISH COMMUNAL SERVICE

MANUSCRIPT ADDRESS: Mr. Sanford N. Sherman
15 E 26 Street
New York, NY 10010

TYPE OF ARTICLES: Research articles, review articles, case studies

MAJOR CONTENT AREAS: Not given

TOPICS PREFERRED: Not given

INAPPROPRIATE TOPICS: Not given

NUMBER OF MANUSCRIPT COPIES: 3   PAGE CHARGES: Not given
REVIEW PERIOD: Not given STYLE REQUIREMENTS: Not given
PUBLICATION LAG TIME: Not given   STYLE SHEET: Yes
EARLY PUBLICATION OPTION: Not given   REVISED THESES: Not given
ACCEPTANCE RATE: Not given   STUDENT PAPERS: Not given
AUTHORSHIP RESTRICTIONS: No   REPRINT POLICY: 1 journal

SUBSCRIPTION ADDRESS: 15 E 26 Street
New York, NY 10010

ANNUAL SUBSCRIPTION RATE: $9.50 individual, Not given - institutional
INDEXED/ABSTRACTED IN: Not given

CIRCULATION: 3300   FREQUENCY: Quarterly

JOURNAL TITLE: JOURNAL OF LEISURE RESEARCH

MANUSCRIPT ADDRESS: Dr. Arlin Epperson, Editor
College of Public & Community Services Ext. Div.
606 Clark Hall
Columbia, MO 65201

TYPE OF ARTICLES: Research articles, unsolicited book reviews

MAJOR CONTENT AREAS: Demography, population, transportation

TOPICS PREFERRED: Outdoor recreation, leisure, environmental planning,
policy related issues (management)

INAPPROPRIATE TOPICS: Not given

NUMBER OF MANUSCRIPT COPIES:	4	PAGE CHARGES:	No
REVIEW PERIOD:	2 months	STYLE REQUIREMENTS:	Not given
PUBLICATION LAG TIME:	9 months	STYLE SHEET:	Yes
EARLY PUBLICATION OPTION:	Yes	REVISED THESES:	Yes
ACCEPTANCE RATE:	Not given	STUDENT PAPERS:	No
AUTHORSHIP RESTRICTIONS:	No	REPRINT POLICY:	None

SUBSCRIPTION ADDRESS: National Recreation & Park Association
1601 N Kent Street
Arlington, VA 22209

ANNUAL SUBSCRIPTION RATE: $8 member, $10 nonmember
INDEXED/ABSTRACTED IN: Not given

CIRCULATION: 2500   FREQUENCY: Quarterly

JOURNAL TITLE: JOURNAL OF MARKETING RESEARCH

MANUSCRIPT ADDRESS: Harper Boyd, Editor
Dean, Graduate School of Business
Tulane University
New Orleans, LA 70118

TYPE OF ARTICLES: Research articles

MAJOR CONTENT AREAS: Mass communication, consumerism

TOPICS PREFERRED: Not given

INAPPROPRIATE TOPICS: Not given

NUMBER OF MANUSCRIPT COPIES:	3	PAGE CHARGES:	No
REVIEW PERIOD:	60 days	STYLE REQUIREMENTS:	JMR
PUBLICATION LAG TIME:	4-6 months	STYLE SHEET:	Yes
EARLY PUBLICATION OPTION:	No	REVISED THESES:	No
ACCEPTANCE RATE:	15%	STUDENT PAPERS:	No
AUTHORSHIP RESTRICTIONS:	No	REPRINT POLICY:	None

SUBSCRIPTION ADDRESS: American Marketing Association
222 S Riverside Plaza
Chicago, IL 60606

ANNUAL SUBSCRIPTION RATE: $18 individual, $30 institutional
INDEXED/ABSTRACTED IN: Not given

CIRCULATION: 12,000   FREQUENCY: Quarterly

JOURNAL TITLE: JOURNAL OF MARRIAGE AND THE FAMILY

MANUSCRIPT ADDRESS: Felix M. Berardo, Editor
Department of Sociology
University of Florida
Gainesville, FL 32611

TYPE OF ARTICLES: Research articles, theoretical articles, review articles, case studies, commentaries, unsolicited book reviews

MAJOR CONTENT AREAS: Aging and aged, communes, death & dying, demography, ethnic groups, family formation, family planning, marriage & divorce, sex roles, sexual behavior, values

TOPICS PREFERRED: Any topics which focus on marriage and family variables

INAPPROPRIATE TOPICS: Counseling articles, therapy articles, personal essays

NUMBER OF MANUSCRIPT COPIES: 3	PAGE CHARGES: No
REVIEW PERIOD: 2-4 mos.	STYLE REQUIREMENTS: APA
PUBLICATION LAG TIME: 4-6 months	STYLE SHEET: Yes
EARLY PUBLICATION OPTION: No	REVISED THESES: Acceptable
ACCEPTANCE RATE: 13%	STUDENT PAPERS: No
AUTHORSHIP RESTRICTIONS: No	REPRINT POLICY: None

SUBSCRIPTION ADDRESS: National Council on Family Relations
1219 University Avenue SE
Minneapolis, MN 55414

ANNUAL SUBSCRIPTION RATE: $20 individual, Not given - institutional
INDEXED/ABSTRACTED IN: SSI, CC, ECEA, BRI, ASW, CERDIC, S, PA, E, SA

CIRCULATION: 11,000   FREQUENCY: Quarterly

JOURNAL TITLE: JOURNAL OF MARRIAGE AND FAMILY COUNSELING

MANUSCRIPT ADDRESS: Florence Kaslow, Ph.D., Editor
Hahnemann Medical College
Department of Mental Health Services
230 N Broad Street, Philadelphia, PA 19102

TYPE OF ARTICLES: Theoretical articles illustrated with case materials, resumes on techniques utilized in marital and family therapy, case studies

MAJOR CONTENT AREAS: Adolescence, aging and aged, alcoholism & drug abuse, death & dying, family formation, family planning, law (family), marriage & divorce, sex roles, sexual behavior

TOPICS PREFERRED: General area of marriage & family therapy - theory & technique

INAPPROPRIATE TOPICS: Individual treatment, social planning

NUMBER OF MANUSCRIPT COPIES: 3	PAGE CHARGES: Yes
REVIEW PERIOD: 3-4 mos.	STYLE REQUIREMENTS: APA
PUBLICATION LAG TIME: 6-12 months	STYLE SHEET: Yes
EARLY PUBLICATION OPTION: No	REVISED THESES: Acceptable
ACCEPTANCE RATE: 25-30%	STUDENT PAPERS: No
AUTHORSHIP RESTRICTIONS: No	REPRINT POLICY: None

SUBSCRIPTION ADDRESS: Business Office
225 Yale Avenue
Claremont, CA 91711

ANNUAL SUBSCRIPTION RATE: $15 individual, $25 institutional
INDEXED/ABSTRACTED IN: Not given

CIRCULATION: 7000   FREQUENCY: Quarterly

JOURNAL TITLE: JOURNAL OF MATHEMATICAL PSYCHOLOGY

MANUSCRIPT ADDRESS: Dr. William H. Batchelder, Editor
School of Social Science
University of California at Irvine
Irvine, CA 92717

TYPE OF ARTICLES: Research articles, theoretical articles, technical notes, invited tutorials, invited book reviews

MAJOR CONTENT AREAS: Mathematical models

TOPICS PREFERRED: Mathematical models in psychology in psychophysics, learning, decision making devices, perception, measurement, memory, psychobiology

INAPPROPRIATE TOPICS: Mathematical papers without substantive concerns in psychology

NUMBER OF MANUSCRIPT COPIES: 3
REVIEW PERIOD: 3-4 mos.
PUBLICATION LAG TIME: 5-6 months
EARLY PUBLICATION OPTION: No
ACCEPTANCE RATE: 35-40%
AUTHORSHIP RESTRICTIONS: No

PAGE CHARGES: No
STYLE REQUIREMENTS: APA
STYLE SHEET: No
REVISED THESES: Acceptable
STUDENT PAPERS: No
REPRINT POLICY: 50

SUBSCRIPTION ADDRESS: Academic Press, Inc.
111 Fifth Avenue
New York, NY 10003

ANNUAL SUBSCRIPTION RATE: $32.50 individual, $65 institutional
INDEXED/ABSTRACTED IN: Not given

CIRCULATION: 1100

FREQUENCY: Bimonthly

JOURNAL TITLE: JOURNAL OF MATHEMATICAL SOCIOLOGY

MANUSCRIPT ADDRESS: Dr. Gordon H. Lewis
School of Urban and Public Affairs
Carnegie-Mellon University
Pittsburgh, PA 15213

TYPE OF ARTICLES: Theoretical articles, research articles, review articles

MAJOR CONTENT AREAS: Not given

TOPICS PREFERRED: Theoretical and applied social science involving significant use of mathematics or mathematical reasoning

INAPPROPRIATE TOPICS: "Statistical notes" and other contributions to statistics as such

NUMBER OF MANUSCRIPT COPIES: 3
REVIEW PERIOD: 3-4 mos.
PUBLICATION LAG TIME: 5-6 months
EARLY PUBLICATION OPTION: No
ACCEPTANCE RATE: 20%
AUTHORSHIP RESTRICTIONS: No

PAGE CHARGES: No
STYLE REQUIREMENTS: APA
STYLE SHEET: Yes
REVISED THESES: Not given
STUDENT PAPERS: Not given
REPRINT POLICY: 25

SUBSCRIPTION ADDRESS: Gordon & Breach Science Publishers
One Park Avenue
New York, NY 10016

ANNUAL SUBSCRIPTION RATE: $26 individual, $78 institutional
INDEXED/ABSTRACTED IN: Not given

CIRCULATION: Not given

FREQUENCY: Semiannually

JOURNAL TITLE: THE JOURNAL OF NEGRO EDUCATION

MANUSCRIPT ADDRESS: Bureau of Educational Research
Howard University
Washington, DC 20001

TYPE OF ARTICLES: Research articles, theoretical articles,
commentaries, review articles, case studies,
unsolicited book reviews

MAJOR CONTENT AREAS: Educational sociology, ethnic groups, family
formation, general sociology, human development,
human organizations, sociology of knowledge,
minorities, political sociology, race relations

TOPICS PREFERRED: The education of African-Americans and supporting
research data

INAPPROPRIATE TOPICS: Research comparing Blacks and Caucasians

NUMBER OF MANUSCRIPT COPIES: 2
REVIEW PERIOD: Not given
PUBLICATION LAG TIME: Not given
EARLY PUBLICATION OPTION: No
ACCEPTANCE RATE: 15%
AUTHORSHIP RESTRICTIONS: No

PAGE CHARGES: No
STYLE REQUIREMENTS: Chicago Manuscript
STYLE SHEET: Yes
REVISED THESES: Not given
STUDENT PAPERS: No
REPRINT POLICY: None

SUBSCRIPTION ADDRESS: Bureau of Educational Research
Howard University
Washington, DC 20001

ANNUAL SUBSCRIPTION RATE: $10 individual, Not given - institutional
INDEXED/ABSTRACTED IN: Not given

CIRCULATION: 3000   FREQUENCY: Quarterly

JOURNAL TITLE: JOURNAL OF PEASANT STUDIES

MANUSCRIPT ADDRESS: The Secretary
Frank Cass & Co. Ltd.
11 Gainsborough Road
London E11 1RS, England

TYPE OF ARTICLES: Research articles, theoretical articles, review
articles, case studies

MAJOR CONTENT AREAS: Administrative behavior, anthropology, communes,
economy and society, political sociology, poverty,
inequality, and policy, rural sociology, social
ideology, stratification, social theory

TOPICS PREFERRED: Not given

INAPPROPRIATE TOPICS: Not given

NUMBER OF MANUSCRIPT COPIES: 2
REVIEW PERIOD: 1 month
PUBLICATION LAG TIME: 6-9 months
EARLY PUBLICATION OPTION: No
ACCEPTANCE RATE: Not given
AUTHORSHIP RESTRICTIONS: No

PAGE CHARGES: No
STYLE REQUIREMENTS: Not given
STYLE SHEET: Yes
REVISED THESES: Acceptable
STUDENT PAPERS: No
REPRINT POLICY: 25

SUBSCRIPTION ADDRESS: Subscription Department
Frank Cass & Co. Ltd.
11 Gainsborough Road
London E11 1RS, England

ANNUAL SUBSCRIPTION RATE: $37.50 individual, $47.50 institutional
INDEXED/ABSTRACTED IN: Not given

CIRCULATION: 700   FREQUENCY: Quarterly

JOURNAL TITLE: JOURNAL OF PERSONALITY & SOCIAL PSYCHOLOGY

MANUSCRIPT ADDRESS: Anthony Greenwald
Ohio State University
404C West 17th Avenue
Columbus, OH 43210
TYPE OF ARTICLES: Not given

MAJOR CONTENT AREAS: Original reports of research, methodology, theory,
criticism, and literature review in the fields of
personality and social psychology of normal
processes and populations
TOPICS PREFERRED: Not given

INAPPROPRIATE TOPICS: Not given

NUMBER OF MANUSCRIPT COPIES: 4
REVIEW PERIOD: 2 months
PUBLICATION LAG TIME: 11 months
EARLY PUBLICATION OPTION: No
ACCEPTANCE RATE: 15-20%
AUTHORSHIP RESTRICTIONS: No

PAGE CHARGES: No
STYLE REQUIREMENTS: APA
STYLE SHEET: Yes
REVISED THESES: No
STUDENT PAPERS: No
REPRINT POLICY: 20

SUBSCRIPTION ADDRESS: APA, Subscription Section
1200 17th Street NW
Washington, DC 20036

ANNUAL SUBSCRIPTION RATE: $25 member, $60 nonmember
INDEXED/ABSTRACTED IN: PA

CIRCULATION: 6140   FREQUENCY: Monthly

JOURNAL TITLE: JOURNAL OF PERSONALITY ASSESSMENT

MANUSCRIPT ADDRESS: 7840 SW 51st
Portland, OR 97219

TYPE OF ARTICLES: Not given

MAJOR CONTENT AREAS: Personality assessment

TOPICS PREFERRED: Projective, objective, and other personality
assessment techniques

INAPPROPRIATE TOPICS: Not given

NUMBER OF MANUSCRIPT COPIES: 2
REVIEW PERIOD: 1 month
PUBLICATION LAG TIME: 6-8 months
EARLY PUBLICATION OPTION: No
ACCEPTANCE RATE: 60%
AUTHORSHIP RESTRICTIONS: No

PAGE CHARGES: Yes
STYLE REQUIREMENTS: APA
STYLE SHEET: No
REVISED THESES: Acceptable
STUDENT PAPERS: No
REPRINT POLICY: None

SUBSCRIPTION ADDRESS: 1070 E Angeleno Avenue
Burbank, CA 91501

ANNUAL SUBSCRIPTION RATE: $18 individual, Not given - institutional
INDEXED/ABSTRACTED IN: CC

CIRCULATION: 2700   FREQUENCY: Bimonthly

JOURNAL TITLE: JOURNAL OF POLITICAL AND MILITARY SOCIOLOGY

MANUSCRIPT ADDRESS: Department of Sociology
Northern Illinois University
DeKalb, IL 60115

TYPE OF ARTICLES: Research articles, theoretical articles, case
studies, commentaries, review articles, unsolicited book reviews, survey and review essays

MAJOR CONTENT AREAS: Leadership, sociology of peace, political
sociology, professions, social change, social
conflict, social ideology, social policy, social
structure, systems analysis, military sociology

TOPICS PREFERRED: Political socialization, political stratification,
political recruitment, military roles, political
movements, political violence

INAPPROPRIATE TOPICS: Historical, review essays, descriptive, technical
military

NUMBER OF MANUSCRIPT COPIES: 3	PAGE CHARGES: Yes	
REVIEW PERIOD: 10-12 wks	STYLE REQUIREMENTS: ASA	
PUBLICATION LAG TIME: 3 months	STYLE SHEET: Yes	
EARLY PUBLICATION OPTION: No	REVISED THESES: Yes	
ACCEPTANCE RATE: 15%	STUDENT PAPERS: Acceptable	
AUTHORSHIP RESTRICTIONS: No	REPRINT POLICY: 20	

SUBSCRIPTION ADDRESS: Department of Sociology
Northern Illinois University
DeKalb, IL 60115

ANNUAL SUBSCRIPTION RATE: $7.50 individual, $8.50 institutional
INDEXED/ABSTRACTED IN: SA, PAIS, IPSA, SSCI, HA, URS, A:HL

CIRCULATION: 1200   FREQUENCY: Semiannually

JOURNAL TITLE: JOURNAL OF POPULAR CULTURE

MANUSCRIPT ADDRESS: 100 University Hall
Bowling Green University
Bowling Green, OH 43403

TYPE OF ARTICLES: Popular culture articles, original observations,
mixture of English, sociology, anthropology,
communications theory, theoretical articles

MAJOR CONTENT AREAS: Aging and aged, communes, mass communication,
consumerism, educational sociology, groups,
industrial sociology, mass media, public opinion

TOPICS PREFERRED: Popular culture slant

INAPPROPRIATE TOPICS: "Pure" sociological theory

NUMBER OF MANUSCRIPT COPIES: 1	PAGE CHARGES: No	
REVIEW PERIOD: 3-6 mos.	STYLE REQUIREMENTS: MLA	
PUBLICATION LAG TIME: 3-12 months	STYLE SHEET: Yes	
EARLY PUBLICATION OPTION: No	REVISED THESES: No	
ACCEPTANCE RATE: 5-8%	STUDENT PAPERS: Yes	
AUTHORSHIP RESTRICTIONS: Yes	REPRINT POLICY: 20-25	

SUBSCRIPTION ADDRESS: Attn: Subscription Manager
100 University Hall
Bowling Green University
Bowling Green, OH 43403

ANNUAL SUBSCRIPTION RATE: $15 individual, $25 institutional
INDEXED/ABSTRACTED IN: BRI

CIRCULATION: 2500   FREQUENCY: Quarterly

JOURNAL TITLE: JOURNAL OF PSYCHIATRIC RESEARCH

MANUSCRIPT ADDRESS: Dr. Seymour Kety, Editor-in-Chief
Psychiatric Research Labs, R-4
Mass. General Hospital, Boston, MA 02114

TYPE OF ARTICLES: Research articles

MAJOR CONTENT AREAS: Psychiatric research

TOPICS PREFERRED: Clinical, biological, psychological and
sociological research on psychiatric issues

INAPPROPRIATE TOPICS: Not given

NUMBER OF MANUSCRIPT COPIES: Not given	PAGE CHARGES: Not given
REVIEW PERIOD: Not given	STYLE REQUIREMENTS: Not given
PUBLICATION LAG TIME: Not given	STYLE SHEET: Not given
EARLY PUBLICATION OPTION: Not given	REVISED THESES: Not given
ACCEPTANCE RATE: Not given	STUDENT PAPERS: Not given
AUTHORSHIP RESTRICTIONS: Not given	REPRINT POLICY: Not given

SUBSCRIPTION ADDRESS: Pergamon Press
Maxwell House, Fairview Park
Elmsford, NY 10523

ANNUAL SUBSCRIPTION RATE: $25 individual, $50 institutional
INDEXED/ABSTRACTED IN: BA, CA, HLI, IM, PA, SCI, SSCI

CIRCULATION: Not given   FREQUENCY: Not given

JOURNAL TITLE: JOURNAL OF PSYCHOHISTORY

MANUSCRIPT ADDRESS: 2315 Broadway
New York, NY 10024

TYPE OF ARTICLES: Research articles, review articles, unsolicited
book reviews, theoretical articles, commentaries,
case studies

MAJOR CONTENT AREAS: Adolescence,anthropology, collective behavior,
deviant behavior, family formation, human
development, mental health & illness, sexual
behavior, social conflict, social interaction

TOPICS PREFERRED: The impact of psychology on history, with parti-
cularly strong emphasis on the formation of historical character-types by methods of child-rearing

INAPPROPRIATE TOPICS: "Psychohistorical" studies that completely omit
any consideration of childhood

NUMBER OF MANUSCRIPT COPIES: 1	PAGE CHARGES: No
REVIEW PERIOD: 1 month	STYLE REQUIREMENTS: Chicago Manuscript
PUBLICATION LAG TIME: 6-9 months	STYLE SHEET: No
EARLY PUBLICATION OPTION: No	REVISED THESES: No
ACCEPTANCE RATE: 10%	STUDENT PAPERS: No
AUTHORSHIP RESTRICTIONS: No	REPRINT POLICY: 50

SUBSCRIPTION ADDRESS: 2315 Broadway
New York, NY 10024

ANNUAL SUBSCRIPTION RATE: $16 individual, $22 institutional
INDEXED/ABSTRACTED IN: PA, SA, CDAB, HA, A:HL

CIRCULATION: 2500   FREQUENCY: Quarterly

JOURNAL TITLE: THE JOURNAL OF PSYCHOLOGICAL ANTHROPOLOGY

MANUSCRIPT ADDRESS: SRA 89P Anchorage
Alaska   99507

TYPE OF ARTICLES: Research articles, theoretical articles, review
articles

MAJOR CONTENT AREAS: Anthropology, ethnic groups, human development,
sex roles, social theory, minorities, mental health
and illness, social change, socialization

TOPICS PREFERRED: General relationship of personality to culture

INAPPROPRIATE TOPICS: Polemics on race relations or sex role

NUMBER OF MANUSCRIPT COPIES:	3	PAGE CHARGES:	No
REVIEW PERIOD:	4 weeks	STYLE REQUIREMENTS:	Chicago Manuscript
PUBLICATION LAG TIME:	6 months	STYLE SHEET:	Yes
EARLY PUBLICATION OPTION:	Yes	REVISED THESES:	Yes
ACCEPTANCE RATE:	25%	STUDENT PAPERS:	Yes
AUTHORSHIP RESTRICTIONS:	No	REPRINT POLICY:	40

SUBSCRIPTION ADDRESS: 2315 Broadway
New York, NY 10024

ANNUAL SUBSCRIPTION RATE: $16 individual, $24 institutional
INDEXED/ABSTRACTED IN: Not given

CIRCULATION: 3000   FREQUENCY: Quarterly

JOURNAL TITLE: THE JOURNAL OF PSYCHOLOGY

MANUSCRIPT ADDRESS: Managing Editor
The Journal Press
Box 543, 2 Commercial Street
Provincetown, MA 02657

TYPE OF ARTICLES: Research articles, theoretical articles,
commentaries, review articles

MAJOR CONTENT AREAS: Adolescence,aging and aged, alcoholism & drug
abuse, collective behavior, social psychology,
physiological psychology, comparative psychology,
experimental psychology, race relations

TOPICS PREFERRED: Not given

INAPPROPRIATE TOPICS: Not given

NUMBER OF MANUSCRIPT COPIES:	2	PAGE CHARGES:	Yes
REVIEW PERIOD:	2-3 weeks	STYLE REQUIREMENTS:	Journal Press
PUBLICATION LAG TIME:	1-2 months	STYLE SHEET:	Yes
EARLY PUBLICATION OPTION:	Yes	REVISED THESES:	Not given
ACCEPTANCE RATE:	50%	STUDENT PAPERS:	Not given
AUTHORSHIP RESTRICTIONS:	Yes	REPRINT POLICY:	200

SUBSCRIPTION ADDRESS: Managing Editor
The Journal Press
Box 543, 2 Commercial Street
Provincetown, MA 02657

ANNUAL SUBSCRIPTION RATE: $45 individual, $45 institutional
INDEXED/ABSTRACTED IN: ASW, BA, BAMS, ECEA, EM, IM, PA, DSHA

CIRCULATION: 1700   FREQUENCY: Bimonthly

JOURNAL TITLE: JOURNAL OF REHABILITATION

MANUSCRIPT ADDRESS: 1522 K Street, NW
Washington, DC 20005

TYPE OF ARTICLES: Research articles, review articles, theoretical
articles, book reviews

MAJOR CONTENT AREAS: Community, counseling, mental retardation,
psychotherapy, social, rehabilitation

TOPICS PREFERRED: Rehabilitation in general, physiological and
psychological

INAPPROPRIATE TOPICS: Technical medical manuscripts dealing with
a specific disability

NUMBER OF MANUSCRIPT COPIES: Not given   PAGE CHARGES: Not given
REVIEW PERIOD: 6 months   STYLE REQUIREMENTS: Not given
PUBLICATION LAG TIME: 2 months   STYLE SHEET: Yes
EARLY PUBLICATION OPTION: No   REVISED THESES: Not given
ACCEPTANCE RATE: 20%   STUDENT PAPERS: Not given
AUTHORSHIP RESTRICTIONS: Not given   REPRINT POLICY: 5

SUBSCRIPTION ADDRESS: 1522 K Street, NW
Washington, DC 20005

ANNUAL SUBSCRIPTION RATE: $10 individual, $8 institutional
INDEXED/ABSTRACTED IN: PA, ASW, CCSBS, CIJE, DSHA, ERA, ECEA, GPE,
ILD, JHE, LLBA
CIRCULATION: 37,000   FREQUENCY: Not given

JOURNAL TITLE: JOURNAL OF RESEARCH IN CRIME & DELINQUENCY

MANUSCRIPT ADDRESS: Vincent O'Leary, Dean, School of Criminal Justice
State University of N.Y. at Albany
1400 Washington Avenue
Albany, NY 12222
TYPE OF ARTICLES: Research articles, review articles

MAJOR CONTENT AREAS: Alcoholism & drug abuse, criminology, delinquency
& crime, deviant behavior, law

TOPICS PREFERRED: Research in crime-delinquency

INAPPROPRIATE TOPICS: Replication studies

NUMBER OF MANUSCRIPT COPIES: 4   PAGE CHARGES: No
REVIEW PERIOD: 3-4 mos. STYLE REQUIREMENTS: APA
PUBLICATION LAG TIME: 6-12 months   STYLE SHEET: Yes
EARLY PUBLICATION OPTION: No   REVISED THESES: No
ACCEPTANCE RATE: 10-20%   STUDENT PAPERS: No
AUTHORSHIP RESTRICTIONS: No   REPRINT POLICY: None

SUBSCRIPTION ADDRESS: National Council on Crime and Delinquency
Continental Plaza
411 Hackensack Avenue
Hackensack, NJ 07601
ANNUAL SUBSCRIPTION RATE: $10 individual, $10 institutional
INDEXED/ABSTRACTED IN: UIPD, SPD

CIRCULATION: 1800   FREQUENCY: Semiannually

JOURNAL TITLE: JOURNAL OF SCHOOL HEALTH

MANUSCRIPT ADDRESS: American School Health Association
P O Box 708
Kent, OH 44240

TYPE OF ARTICLES: Practical application of new research and
knowledge, research articles

MAJOR CONTENT AREAS: Adolescence,alcoholism & drug abuse, death & dying,
health and illness, mental health & illness, sex-
roles, sexual behavior

TOPICS PREFERRED: Anything concerned with the health of school-age
children

INAPPROPRIATE TOPICS: Not given

NUMBER OF MANUSCRIPT COPIES: 3	PAGE CHARGES:	No
REVIEW PERIOD: 6-8 weeks	STYLE REQUIREMENTS:	AMA
PUBLICATION LAG TIME: 6 months	STYLE SHEET:	Yes
EARLY PUBLICATION OPTION: No	REVISED THESES:	No
ACCEPTANCE RATE: 25%	STUDENT PAPERS:	No
AUTHORSHIP RESTRICTIONS: No	REPRINT POLICY:	1

SUBSCRIPTION ADDRESS: American School Health Association
P O Box 708
Kent, OH 44240

ANNUAL SUBSCRIPTION RATE: $25 individual, $20 institutional
INDEXED/ABSTRACTED IN: IN, IM, HHW, IDL, EI, CINAHL, XMS,
ERIC
CIRCULATION: 11,000   FREQUENCY: Monthly

JOURNAL TITLE: JOURNAL OF SCHOOL PSYCHOLOGY

MANUSCRIPT ADDRESS: Beeman N. Phillips, Editor
Department of Educational Psychology
University of Texas
Austin, TX 78712
TYPE OF ARTICLES: Theoretical articles, articles on research,
opinions, and practice in school psychology

MAJOR CONTENT AREAS: Professional roles for school psychologists,
training issues and problems; mental health and
behavioral consultation, school related problems
of children; classroom behavior, learning
TOPICS PREFERRED: Not given

INAPPROPRIATE TOPICS: Not given

NUMBER OF MANUSCRIPT COPIES: 3	PAGE CHARGES:	No
REVIEW PERIOD: 2 months	STYLE REQUIREMENTS:	APA
PUBLICATION LAG TIME: 9-12 months	STYLE SHEET:	No
EARLY PUBLICATION OPTION: No	REVISED THESES:	Not given
ACCEPTANCE RATE: 25%	STUDENT PAPERS:	Not given
AUTHORSHIP RESTRICTIONS: No	REPRINT POLICY:	1 journal

SUBSCRIPTION ADDRESS: Human Sciences Press
72 Fifth Avenue
New York, NY 10011

ANNUAL SUBSCRIPTION RATE: $12.95 individual, $35 institutional
INDEXED/ABSTRACTED IN: PA, SSCI, ECEA, SSCA, CIJE, CC/BSES, EI

CIRCULATION: 3000   FREQUENCY: Quarterly

JOURNAL TITLE: JOURNAL OF SEX RESEARCH

MANUSCRIPT ADDRESS: Clive M. Davis, Ph.D., Editor
Department of Psychology
Syracuse University
Syracuse, NY 13210

TYPE OF ARTICLES: Research articles, review articles,
theoretical articles, case studies,
commentaries, unsolicited book reviews

MAJOR CONTENT AREAS: Marriage & divorce, sex roles, sexual
behavior

TOPICS PREFERRED: Human sexuality

INAPPROPRIATE TOPICS: Not given

NUMBER OF MANUSCRIPT COPIES: 3	PAGE CHARGES:	No
REVIEW PERIOD: 2-3 mos.	STYLE REQUIREMENTS:	APA
PUBLICATION LAG TIME: 9-12 months	STYLE SHEET:	Yes
EARLY PUBLICATION OPTION: No	REVISED THESES:	Not given
ACCEPTANCE RATE: 33%	STUDENT PAPERS:	No
AUTHORSHIP RESTRICTIONS: No	REPRINT POLICY:	1

SUBSCRIPTION ADDRESS: Mary B. Westervelt
208 Glen Burnie, MD 21061

ANNUAL SUBSCRIPTION RATE: $20 individual, $20 institutional
INDEXED/ABSTRACTED IN: Not given

CIRCULATION: 1200   FREQUENCY: Quarterly

JOURNAL TITLE: JOURNAL OF SOCIAL HISTORY

MANUSCRIPT ADDRESS: Editor
Journal of Social History
Carnegie-Mellon University
Pittsburgh, Pennsylvania 15213

TYPE OF ARTICLES: Not given

MAJOR CONTENT AREAS: Not given

TOPICS PREFERRED: Not given

INAPPROPRIATE TOPICS: Not given

NUMBER OF MANUSCRIPT COPIES: 1	PAGE CHARGES:	Not given
REVIEW PERIOD: Not given	STYLE REQUIREMENTS:	Chicago
PUBLICATION LAG TIME: Not given	STYLE SHEET:	Not given
EARLY PUBLICATION OPTION: Not given	REVISED THESES:	Not given
ACCEPTANCE RATE: Not given	STUDENT PAPERS:	Not given
AUTHORSHIP RESTRICTIONS: Not given	REPRINT POLICY:	Not given

SUBSCRIPTION ADDRESS: Journal of Social History
Carnegie-Mellon University
Pittsburgh, Pennsylvania 15213

ANNUAL SUBSCRIPTION RATE: $10 student, $15 individual, $20 institutional
INDEXED/ABSTRACTED IN: Not given

CIRCULATION: Not given   FREQUENCY: Quarterly

JOURNAL TITLE: JOURNAL OF SOCIAL ISSUES

MANUSCRIPT ADDRESS: Dr. Jacqueline D. Goodchilds
Department of Psychology
University of California
Los Angeles, CA 90024
TYPE OF ARTICLES: Solicited articles on issue themes

MAJOR CONTENT AREAS: Not given

TOPICS PREFERRED: Social issues

INAPPROPRIATE TOPICS: Not given

NUMBER OF MANUSCRIPT COPIES: 3   PAGE CHARGES: No
REVIEW PERIOD: Not given STYLE REQUIREMENTS: APA
PUBLICATION LAG TIME: 1 1/2 years   STYLE SHEET: No
EARLY PUBLICATION OPTION: No   REVISED THESES: No
ACCEPTANCE RATE: Not given   STUDENT PAPERS: Acceptable
AUTHORSHIP RESTRICTIONS: No   REPRINT POLICY: None

SUBSCRIPTION ADDRESS: Journal of Social Issues
P O Box 1248
Ann Arbor, MI 48106

ANNUAL SUBSCRIPTION RATE: $14 individual, $20 institutional
INDEXED/ABSTRACTED IN: Not given

CIRCULATION: 6500   FREQUENCY: Quarterly

JOURNAL TITLE: JOURNAL OF SOCIAL POLICY

MANUSCRIPT ADDRESS: The Editor
Department of Social & Psychological Studies
Chelsea College,
Manresa Road, London SW3 6LX, England
TYPE OF ARTICLES: Research articles, theoretical articles, review
articles, case studies, methodological, historical,
unsolicited book reviews, applied research
MAJOR CONTENT AREAS: Concerned with the historical and theoretical
analysis of social policy and with processes and
problems in the implementation of social policy
at both national and local levels
TOPICS PREFERRED: Not given

INAPPROPRIATE TOPICS: Not given

NUMBER OF MANUSCRIPT COPIES: 2   PAGE CHARGES: No
REVIEW PERIOD: 1-2 mos. STYLE REQUIREMENTS: Not given
PUBLICATION LAG TIME: 6 months   STYLE SHEET: Yes
EARLY PUBLICATION OPTION: No   REVISED THESES: Not given
ACCEPTANCE RATE: Not given   STUDENT PAPERS: Not given
AUTHORSHIP RESTRICTIONS: No   REPRINT POLICY: 25

SUBSCRIPTION ADDRESS: Cambridge University Press
32 East 57th Street
New York, NY 10022

ANNUAL SUBSCRIPTION RATE: $28.50 individual, $40 institutional
INDEXED/ABSTRACTED IN: PA, SEA, SA

CIRCULATION: 1250   FREQUENCY: Quarterly

JOURNAL TITLE: THE JOURNAL OF SOCIAL PSYCHOLOGY

MANUSCRIPT ADDRESS: The Managing Editor, The Journal Press
2 Commercial Street, PO Box 543
Provincetown, MA   02657

TYPE OF ARTICLES: Studies of persons in group settings and of
culture and personality

MAJOR CONTENT AREAS: Community, industrial/organizational, personality,
social, cross-cultural

TOPICS PREFERRED: Field research and cross-cultural research

INAPPROPRIATE TOPICS: Essays more suitable to popular magazines, those
not conforming to submission requirements

NUMBER OF MANUSCRIPT COPIES:	Not given	PAGE CHARGES:	Not given
REVIEW PERIOD:	1 month	STYLE REQUIREMENTS:	Not given
PUBLICATION LAG TIME:	15 months	STYLE SHEET:	Yes
EARLY PUBLICATION OPTION:	No	REVISED THESES:	Not given
ACCEPTANCE RATE:	40%	STUDENT PAPERS:	Not given
AUTHORSHIP RESTRICTIONS:	Not given	REPRINT POLICY:	100

SUBSCRIPTION ADDRESS: The Journal Press
2 Commercial Street, PO Box 543
Provincetown, MA   02657

ANNUAL SUBSCRIPTION RATE: $45 individual, Not given institutional
INDEXED/ABSTRACTED IN: PA, ASW, AA, BS, CSPA, CDL, CCSBS, CIJE,
DSHA, ECEA, IPAPL, IBSS, IPSA, JHE, LLBA
CIRCULATION: 2415   FREQUENCY: Not given

JOURNAL TITLE: JOURNAL OF SOCIAL RESEARCH

MANUSCRIPT ADDRESS: Department of Anthropology
Ranchi University
Ranchi-834001
Bihar, India

TYPE OF ARTICLES: Research articles, theoretical articles, review
articles, case studies

MAJOR CONTENT AREAS: Anthropology, demography, ecology, economy and
society, educational sociology, ethnic groups,
human development, marriage & divorce, migration,
sociology of peace, urban sociology

TOPICS PREFERRED: Theoretical interest or based on field work done
preferably in India

INAPPROPRIATE TOPICS: Not given

NUMBER OF MANUSCRIPT COPIES:	2	PAGE CHARGES:	Not given
REVIEW PERIOD:	2 months	STYLE REQUIREMENTS:	ASA
PUBLICATION LAG TIME:	6-12 months	STYLE SHEET:	Not given
EARLY PUBLICATION OPTION:	Not given	REVISED THESES:	Not given
ACCEPTANCE RATE:	33%	STUDENT PAPERS:	Not given
AUTHORSHIP RESTRICTIONS:	Not given	REPRINT POLICY:	25

SUBSCRIPTION ADDRESS: Department of Anthropology
Ranchi University
Ranchi-834001
Bihar, India

ANNUAL SUBSCRIPTION RATE: $4 individual, $4 institutional
INDEXED/ABSTRACTED IN: CAA, SA, UNESCOSA, ICSSR

CIRCULATION: 250   FREQUENCY: Semiannually

JOURNAL TITLE: JOURNAL OF SOCIO-ECONOMIC PLANNING SCIENCES

MANUSCRIPT ADDRESS: Sumner N. Levine, Editor
State University of New York
Stony Brook, NY 11790

TYPE OF ARTICLES: Theoretical and empirical studies

MAJOR CONTENT AREAS: Not given

TOPICS PREFERRED: Socio-economic planning

INAPPROPRIATE TOPICS: Not given

NUMBER OF MANUSCRIPT COPIES:	Not given	PAGE CHARGES:	Not given
REVIEW PERIOD:	2 months	STYLE REQUIREMENTS:	Not given
PUBLICATION LAG TIME:	6 months	STYLE SHEET:	Not given
EARLY PUBLICATION OPTION:	Not given	REVISED THESES:	Not given
ACCEPTANCE RATE:	Not given	STUDENT PAPERS:	Not given
AUTHORSHIP RESTRICTIONS:	Not given	REPRINT POLICY:	50

SUBSCRIPTION ADDRESS: Sumner N. Levine, Editor
State University of New York
Stony Brook, NY 11790

ANNUAL SUBSCRIPTION RATE: Not given
INDEXED/ABSTRACTED IN: Not given

CIRCULATION: 3000   FREQUENCY: Bimonthly

JOURNAL TITLE: JOURNAL OF SOCIOLOGY AND SOCIAL WELFARE

MANUSCRIPT ADDRESS: University of Connecticut
School of Social Work
West Hartford, CT 06117

TYPE OF ARTICLES: Research articles, theoretical articles, case
studies, commentaries

MAJOR CONTENT AREAS: Not given

TOPICS PREFERRED: Related to sociology and social welfare

INAPPROPRIATE TOPICS: Not given

NUMBER OF MANUSCRIPT COPIES:	3	PAGE CHARGES:	No
REVIEW PERIOD:	2-3 mos.	STYLE REQUIREMENTS:	ASA
PUBLICATION LAG TIME:	6 months	STYLE SHEET:	No
EARLY PUBLICATION OPTION:	Yes	REVISED THESES:	Yes
ACCEPTANCE RATE:	33%	STUDENT PAPERS:	Yes
AUTHORSHIP RESTRICTIONS:	No	REPRINT POLICY:	None

SUBSCRIPTION ADDRESS: University of Connecticut
School of Social Work
West Hartford, CT 06117

ANNUAL SUBSCRIPTION RATE: $8.50 individual, $12 institutional
INDEXED/ABSTRACTED IN: Not given

CIRCULATION: 600   FREQUENCY: Bimonthly

JOURNAL TITLE: JOURNAL OF STUDIES ON ALCOHOL

MANUSCRIPT ADDRESS: Editoral Office
Rutgers Center of Alcohol Studies
New Brunswick, NJ 08903

TYPE OF ARTICLES: Research articles, review articles, theoretical articles, book reviews

MAJOR CONTENT AREAS: All areas as related to alcohol problems

TOPICS PREFERRED: Alcohol and alcohol-related problems

INAPPROPRIATE TOPICS: Dissertations, descriptions of unevaluated treatment procedures

NUMBER OF MANUSCRIPT COPIES: Not given   PAGE CHARGES: Not given
REVIEW PERIOD: 4-6 months   STYLE REQUIREMENTS: Not given
PUBLICATION LAG TIME: 2-4 months   STYLE SHEET: Yes
EARLY PUBLICATION OPTION: No   REVISED THESES: Not given
ACCEPTANCE RATE: 35%   STUDENT PAPERS: Not given
AUTHORSHIP RESTRICTIONS: Not given   REPRINT POLICY: 25

SUBSCRIPTION ADDRESS: Publications Office, Rutgers Center of Alcohol Studies, Titsworth and Stone Roads
Piscataway, NJ 08854

ANNUAL SUBSCRIPTION RATE: $25 individual, $35 institutional
INDEXED/ABSTRACTED IN: PA, IM, EM, ASW, SA, ACP, BA, BS, CA, CCSBS, HA, PPA, PAISB, WAH
CIRCULATION: 3200   FREQUENCY: Not given

JOURNAL TITLE: JOURNAL OF THOUGHT

MANUSCRIPT ADDRESS: James J. Van Patten, Editor
University of Arkansas
434 Hawthorne Street
Fayetteville, AR 72701
TYPE OF ARTICLES: Not given

MAJOR CONTENT AREAS: Not given

TOPICS PREFERRED: Interdisciplinary communication

INAPPROPRIATE TOPICS: Not given

NUMBER OF MANUSCRIPT COPIES: Not given   PAGE CHARGES: Not given
REVIEW PERIOD: Not given   STYLE REQUIREMENTS: Not given
PUBLICATION LAG TIME: Not given   STYLE SHEET: Not given
EARLY PUBLICATION OPTION: Not given   REVISED THESES: Not given
ACCEPTANCE RATE: Not given   STUDENT PAPERS: Not given
AUTHORSHIP RESTRICTIONS: Not given   REPRINT POLICY: 1

SUBSCRIPTION ADDRESS: James J. Van Patten, Editor
University of Arkansas
434 Hawthorne Street
Fayetteville, AR 72701
ANNUAL SUBSCRIPTION RATE: $4 individual, $4 institutional
INDEXED/ABSTRACTED IN: Not given

CIRCULATION: 500   FREQUENCY: Quarterly

JOURNAL TITLE: JOURNAL OF YOUTH AND ADOLESCENCE

MANUSCRIPT ADDRESS: Daniel Offer, Dept. of Psychiatry
Michael Reese Hospital
University of Chicago
Chicago, Illinois

TYPE OF ARTICLES: Research articles, review articles, theoretical
articles

MAJOR CONTENT AREAS: Adolescence, deviant behavior, values, sex roles,
human development, family formation, mental health
and illness, social psychology

TOPICS PREFERRED: Research on development issues effecting youth

INAPPROPRIATE TOPICS: Case reports

NUMBER OF MANUSCRIPT COPIES:	3	PAGE CHARGES:	No
REVIEW PERIOD:	3 months	STYLE REQUIREMENTS:	Chicago Manuscript
PUBLICATION LAG TIME:	9 months	STYLE SHEET:	Yes
EARLY PUBLICATION OPTION:	No	REVISED THESES:	No
ACCEPTANCE RATE:	30%	STUDENT PAPERS:	No
AUTHORSHIP RESTRICTIONS:	No	REPRINT POLICY:	0

SUBSCRIPTION ADDRESS: Plenum Publishing Co., Inc.
227 West 17th Street
New York, New York 10011

ANNUAL SUBSCRIPTION RATE: $16 individual, $35 institutional
INDEXED/ABSTRACTED IN: IM, PA, SA, LHB

CIRCULATION: 1000   FREQUENCY: Quarterly

JOURNAL TITLE: KANSAS JOURNAL OF SOCIOLOGY

MANUSCRIPT ADDRESS: Articles Editor
Mid-American Review of Sociology
Department of Sociology
University of Kansas, Lawrence, KS 66045

TYPE OF ARTICLES: Research articles, theoretical articles, review
articles, case studies, commentaries

MAJOR CONTENT AREAS: Adolescence, aging and aged, bureaucracy, death &
dying, demography, ecology, ethnic groups, evolu-
tion, industrial sociology, leadership, marriage
& divorce, mass media, migration

TOPICS PREFERRED: Not given

INAPPROPRIATE TOPICS: Not given

NUMBER OF MANUSCRIPT COPIES:	3	PAGE CHARGES:	No
REVIEW PERIOD:	3 months	STYLE REQUIREMENTS:	ASA
PUBLICATION LAG TIME:	3 months	STYLE SHEET:	Yes
EARLY PUBLICATION OPTION:	No	REVISED THESES:	Yes
ACCEPTANCE RATE:	50%	STUDENT PAPERS:	Yes
AUTHORSHIP RESTRICTIONS:	Yes	REPRINT POLICY:	25

SUBSCRIPTION ADDRESS: Business Manager
Mid-American Review of Sociology
Department of Sociology
University of Kansas, Lawrence, KS 66045

ANNUAL SUBSCRIPTION RATE: $5 individual, $10 institutional
INDEXED/ABSTRACTED IN: SA

CIRCULATION: 150   FREQUENCY: Semiannually

JOURNAL TITLE: LAND REFORM, LAND SETTLEMENT AND COOPERATIVES

MANUSCRIPT ADDRESS: The Editor,
Human Resources Division, FAO
00100 Rome,Italy

TYPE OF ARTICLES: Case studies, research articles, commentaries,
review articles, theoretical articles

MAJOR CONTENT AREAS: Collective behavior, communes, community
development, economy and society, human
development, law, migration, poverty, inequality,
and policy, rural sociology, social change

TOPICS PREFERRED: Agrarian reform, land tenure, rural cooperation

INAPPROPRIATE TOPICS: Not given

NUMBER OF MANUSCRIPT COPIES: 2	PAGE CHARGES:	No
REVIEW PERIOD: 2 months	STYLE REQUIREMENTS:	FAO
PUBLICATION LAG TIME: 6 months	STYLE SHEET:	Yes
EARLY PUBLICATION OPTION: No	REVISED THESES:	No
ACCEPTANCE RATE: 80%	STUDENT PAPERS:	No
AUTHORSHIP RESTRICTIONS: No	REPRINT POLICY:	20

SUBSCRIPTION ADDRESS: Not given

ANNUAL SUBSCRIPTION RATE: No charge
INDEXED/ABSTRACTED IN: WAERSA

CIRCULATION: 3100   FREQUENCY: Semiannually

JOURNAL TITLE: LANGUAGE

MANUSCRIPT ADDRESS: Professor W.O. Bright, Editor
Department of Linguistics
UCLA
Los Angeles, CA 90024

TYPE OF ARTICLES: Research articles, theoretical articles, case
studies, commentaries, review articles,
unsolicited book reviews

MAJOR CONTENT AREAS: Sociology of language

TOPICS PREFERRED: General & Theoretical linguistics

INAPPROPRIATE TOPICS: Theories with no empirical support

NUMBER OF MANUSCRIPT COPIES: 3	PAGE CHARGES:	No
REVIEW PERIOD: 6 weeks	STYLE REQUIREMENTS:	LSA
PUBLICATION LAG TIME: 13 months	STYLE SHEET:	Yes
EARLY PUBLICATION OPTION: Not given	REVISED THESES:	No
ACCEPTANCE RATE: 25%	STUDENT PAPERS:	No
AUTHORSHIP RESTRICTIONS: No	REPRINT POLICY:	None

SUBSCRIPTION ADDRESS: LSA Subscription Services Office
428 E Preston Street
Baltimore, MD 21203

ANNUAL SUBSCRIPTION RATE: $25 individual, $40 institutional
INDEXED/ABSTRACTED IN: Not given

CIRCULATION: 7000   FREQUENCY: Quarterly

JOURNAL TITLE: LAW & CONTEMPORARY PROBLEMS

MANUSCRIPT ADDRESS: School of Law, Room 225
Duke University
Durham, NC 27706

TYPE OF ARTICLES: We solicit articles on specific topics for a
writing symposium

MAJOR CONTENT AREAS: Law

TOPICS PREFERRED: Not given

INAPPROPRIATE TOPICS: Unsolicited manuscripts

NUMBER OF MANUSCRIPT COPIES: Not given   PAGE CHARGES: No
REVIEW PERIOD: Not given STYLE REQUIREMENTS: Gov't. Prtg. Ofc.
PUBLICATION LAG TIME: 4-10 months   STYLE SHEET: No
EARLY PUBLICATION OPTION: No   REVISED THESES: No
ACCEPTANCE RATE: 90% solicited STUDENT PAPERS: No
AUTHORSHIP RESTRICTIONS: No   REPRINT POLICY: 100

SUBSCRIPTION ADDRESS: School of Law, Room 225
Duke University
Durham, NC 27706

ANNUAL SUBSCRIPTION RATE: $20 individual, $19 institutional
INDEXED/ABSTRACTED IN: Not given

CIRCULATION: 4000   FREQUENCY: Quarterly

JOURNAL TITLE: LAW & SOCIETY REVIEW

MANUSCRIPT ADDRESS: Professor Richard Abel
University of California School of Law
405 Hilgard
Los Angeles, CA 90024
TYPE OF ARTICLES: Research articles, theoretical articles, case
studies, review articles

MAJOR CONTENT AREAS: Society and legal process, law and behavioral
sciences

TOPICS PREFERRED: Articles and research notes to lawyers, social
scientists, and other scholars which bear upon the
relationship between society and legal process
INAPPROPRIATE TOPICS: Not given

NUMBER OF MANUSCRIPT COPIES: 3   PAGE CHARGES: No
REVIEW PERIOD: 3 weeks STYLE REQUIREMENTS: Not given
PUBLICATION LAG TIME: 6 months   STYLE SHEET: Yes
EARLY PUBLICATION OPTION: No   REVISED THESES: Acceptable
ACCEPTANCE RATE: 10%   STUDENT PAPERS: No
AUTHORSHIP RESTRICTIONS: No   REPRINT POLICY: 25

SUBSCRIPTION ADDRESS: Law and Society Association
University of Denver College of Law
200 W 14 Avenue
Denver, CO 80204
ANNUAL SUBSCRIPTION RATE: $15 individual, $20 institutional
INDEXED/ABSTRACTED IN: ABC PS, ACP, HA, A:HL, IBSS, PS, GPPS, SSI, SA

CIRCULATION: 2400   FREQUENCY: Quarterly

JOURNAL TITLE: MANPOWER

MANUSCRIPT ADDRESS: Ellis Rottman, Editor
601 D Street, NW
Washington, DC 20213

TYPE OF ARTICLES: Not given

MAJOR CONTENT AREAS: Not given

TOPICS PREFERRED: Programs, policies and issues involving
manpower training, poverty programs, education

INAPPROPRIATE TOPICS: Not given

NUMBER OF MANUSCRIPT COPIES: Not given	PAGE CHARGES: Not given
REVIEW PERIOD: 1-2 months	STYLE REQUIREMENTS: Not given
PUBLICATION LAG TIME: 3-5 months	STYLE SHEET: Not given
EARLY PUBLICATION OPTION: Not given	REVISED THESES: Not given
ACCEPTANCE RATE: Not given	STUDENT PAPERS: Not given
AUTHORSHIP RESTRICTIONS: Not given	REPRINT POLICY: 10

SUBSCRIPTION ADDRESS: Ellis Rottman, Editor
601 D Street, NW
Washington, DC 20213

ANNUAL SUBSCRIPTION RATE: $15.30 individual, $15.30 institutional
INDEXED/ABSTRACTED IN: Not given

CIRCULATION: 33,000   FREQUENCY: Monthly

JOURNAL TITLE: MARRIAGE GUIDANCE

MANUSCRIPT ADDRESS: Donald Godden
National Marriage Guidance Council
Publications Office, 7 Cedar Row
Shirehampton, Bristol BS11 OUJ England
TYPE OF ARTICLES: Theoretical articles, research articles,
commentaries

MAJOR CONTENT AREAS: Adolescence,alcoholism & drug abuse, counseling,
deviant behavior, family formation, family planning,
general sociology, human development, human
organizations, marriage & divorce, sex roles
TOPICS PREFERRED: Anything that affects marriage and family life

INAPPROPRIATE TOPICS: Not given

NUMBER OF MANUSCRIPT COPIES: 2	PAGE CHARGES: No
REVIEW PERIOD: 2 weeks	STYLE REQUIREMENTS: Not given
PUBLICATION LAG TIME: 6 months	STYLE SHEET: Yes
EARLY PUBLICATION OPTION: No	REVISED THESES: No
ACCEPTANCE RATE: 70%	STUDENT PAPERS: No
AUTHORSHIP RESTRICTIONS: No	REPRINT POLICY: 1-6

SUBSCRIPTION ADDRESS: Donald Godden
National Marriage Guidance Council
Publications Office, 7 Cedar Row
Shirehampton, Bristol BS11 OUJ England
ANNUAL SUBSCRIPTION RATE: $5 individual, $5 institutional
INDEXED/ABSTRACTED IN: Not given

CIRCULATION: 6000   FREQUENCY: Bimonthly

JOURNAL TITLE: MEDICAL ANTHROPOLOGY

MANUSCRIPT ADDRESS: Gretel and Pertti Pelto
Box U-58
University of Connecticut
Storrs, CT 06268

TYPE OF ARTICLES: Research articles, case studies, commentaries, review articles

MAJOR CONTENT AREAS: Anthropology, health and illness, medical sociology, mental health and illness, public health

TOPICS PREFERRED: Medical anthropology

INAPPROPRIATE TOPICS: Not given

NUMBER OF MANUSCRIPT COPIES: 1	PAGE CHARGES: No
REVIEW PERIOD: 6-8 weeks	STYLE REQUIREMENTS: Chicago Manuscript
PUBLICATION LAG TIME: 3 months	STYLE SHEET: Not given
EARLY PUBLICATION OPTION: No	REVISED THESES: Yes
ACCEPTANCE RATE: 50%	STUDENT PAPERS: Yes
AUTHORSHIP RESTRICTIONS: No	REPRINT POLICY: 2

SUBSCRIPTION ADDRESS: Redgrave Publishing Co.
430 Manville Road
Pleasantville, NY 10570

ANNUAL SUBSCRIPTION RATE: $17 individual, $25 Institutional
INDEXED/ABSTRACTED IN: Not given

CIRCULATION: 500   FREQUENCY: Quarterly

JOURNAL TITLE: MEMORY & COGNITION

MANUSCRIPT ADDRESS: Dr. Robert G. Crowder, Editor
Department of Psychology, Yale University
Box 11A Yale Station
New Haven, CT 06520

TYPE OF ARTICLES: Research articles, theoretical articles, review articles

MAJOR CONTENT AREAS: Social psychology, experimental psychology

TOPICS PREFERRED: Human memory, learning, perception, information processing, language, thought, general cognition

INAPPROPRIATE TOPICS: Not given

NUMBER OF MANUSCRIPT COPIES: 4	PAGE CHARGES: No
REVIEW PERIOD: 40 days	STYLE REQUIREMENTS: APA
PUBLICATION LAG TIME: 3-4 months	STYLE SHEET: Yes
EARLY PUBLICATION OPTION: Yes	REVISED THESES: Acceptable
ACCEPTANCE RATE: 20%	STUDENT PAPERS: Acceptable
AUTHORSHIP RESTRICTIONS: No	REPRINT POLICY: None

SUBSCRIPTION ADDRESS: Psychonomic Society, Inc.
1108 West 34th Street
Austin, TX 78705

ANNUAL SUBSCRIPTION RATE: $15 individual, $30 institutional
INDEXED/ABSTRACTED IN: PA

CIRCULATION: 1800   FREQUENCY: Bimonthly

JOURNAL TITLE: MENTAL RETARDATION

MANUSCRIPT ADDRESS: Sue Allen Warren, Ph.D.
765 Commonwealth Avenue
Boston, MA 02215

TYPE OF ARTICLES: Research articles, case studies, unsolicited
book reviews

MAJOR CONTENT AREAS: Not given

TOPICS PREFERRED: Not given

INAPPROPRIATE TOPICS: Not given

NUMBER OF MANUSCRIPT COPIES:	3	PAGE CHARGES:	No
REVIEW PERIOD:	3 months	STYLE REQUIREMENTS:	**APA**
PUBLICATION LAG TIME:	3 months	STYLE SHEET:	Yes
EARLY PUBLICATION OPTION:	Not given	REVISED THESES:	Yes
ACCEPTANCE RATE:	Not given	STUDENT PAPERS:	Yes
AUTHORSHIP RESTRICTIONS:	No	REPRINT POLICY:	None

SUBSCRIPTION ADDRESS: Not given

ANNUAL SUBSCRIPTION RATE: $22 individual, Not given-institutional
INDEXED/ABSTRACTED IN: ECEA

CIRCULATION: 12,000   FREQUENCY: Bimonthly

JOURNAL TITLE: MERRILL-PALMER QUARTERLY OF BEHAVIOR
AND DEVELOPMENT
MANUSCRIPT ADDRESS: Dr. Martin Hoffman, Editor
Department of Psychology
University of Michigan
Ann Arbor, MI 48109
TYPE OF ARTICLES: Research articles, theoretical articles, review
articles, case studies

MAJOR CONTENT AREAS: Adolescence, human development, sex roles,
socialization, infant & child behavior,
relations to parents, schools and peers

TOPICS PREFERRED: Not given

INAPPROPRIATE TOPICS: Not given

NUMBER OF MANUSCRIPT COPIES:	2	PAGE CHARGES:	No
REVIEW PERIOD:	3-6 mos.	STYLE REQUIREMENTS:	APA
PUBLICATION LAG TIME:	6-12 months	STYLE SHEET:	No
EARLY PUBLICATION OPTION:	No	REVISED THESES:	No
ACCEPTANCE RATE:	20%	STUDENT PAPERS:	No
AUTHORSHIP RESTRICTIONS:	No	REPRINT POLICY:	2

SUBSCRIPTION ADDRESS: Merrill-Palmer Quarterly
71 E Ferry
Detroit, MI 48202

ANNUAL SUBSCRIPTION RATE: $11 individual, $11 institutional
INDEXED/ABSTRACTED IN: ASW, CDAB, CIJE, LLBA, MRA, PA, SA, SEA

CIRCULATION: 1500   FREQUENCY: Quarterly

JOURNAL TITLE: METHODS OF INFORMATION IN MEDICINE

MANUSCRIPT ADDRESS: Hubert V. Pipberger, M.D.
Veterans Administration Hospital
50 Irving Street, N W
Washington, D C   20422

TYPE OF ARTICLES: Research articles, methodological articles, review articles

MAJOR CONTENT AREAS: Mass communication, epidemiology, modernization, population, public health, systems analysis

TOPICS PREFERRED: Methodology of medical data processing; information, documentation and statistics

INAPPROPRIATE TOPICS: Not given

NUMBER OF MANUSCRIPT COPIES:	3	PAGE CHARGES:	No
REVIEW PERIOD:	2-3 mos.	STYLE REQUIREMENTS:	Not given
PUBLICATION LAG TIME:	2-3 months	STYLE SHEET:	Yes
EARLY PUBLICATION OPTION:	No	REVISED THESES:	No
ACCEPTANCE RATE:	60%	STUDENT PAPERS:	No
AUTHORSHIP RESTRICTIONS:	No	REPRINT POLICY:	50

SUBSCRIPTION ADDRESS: F.K. Schattauer Verlag GmbH.
7 Stuttgart 1, Postfach 2945
Lenzhalde 3,
721886 fks, W. Germany

ANNUAL SUBSCRIPTION RATE: $38 individual, $38 institutional
INDEXED/ABSTRACTED IN: CC,ISA

CIRCULATION: 2500   FREQUENCY: Quarterly

JOURNAL TITLE: MILBANK MEMORIAL FUND QUARTERLY

MANUSCRIPT ADDRESS: Health & Society
Milbank Memorial Fund
40 Wall Street
New York, NY 10005

TYPE OF ARTICLES: Theoretical articles, commentaries, review articles, research articles

MAJOR CONTENT AREAS: Aging and aged, death & dying, demography, epidemiology, health and illness, medical sociology, social policy, population, poverty, inequality, and policy, public health

TOPICS PREFERRED: Health related

INAPPROPRIATE TOPICS: Econometrics

NUMBER OF MANUSCRIPT COPIES:	3	PAGE CHARGES:	No
REVIEW PERIOD:	6 weeks	STYLE REQUIREMENTS:	Chicago Manuscript
PUBLICATION LAG TIME:	4 months	STYLE SHEET:	Yes
EARLY PUBLICATION OPTION:	No	REVISED THESES:	No
ACCEPTANCE RATE:	5-10%	STUDENT PAPERS:	No
AUTHORSHIP RESTRICTIONS:	No	REPRINT POLICY:	100

SUBSCRIPTION ADDRESS: Prodist
156 5th Avenue
New York, NY 10010

ANNUAL SUBSCRIPTION RATE: $10 individual, $15 institutional
INDEXED/ABSTRACTED IN: CODEN

CIRCULATION: 3500   FREQUENCY: Quarterly

JOURNAL TITLE: MONOGRAPHS OF THE SOCIETY FOR RESEARCH IN
CHILD DEVELOPMENT

MANUSCRIPT ADDRESS: Frances Degen Horowitz, Editor
Department of Human Development
University of Kansas
Lawrence, KS 66045

TYPE OF ARTICLES: Research articles

MAJOR CONTENT AREAS: Adolescence, child development

TOPICS PREFERRED: Not given

INAPPROPRIATE TOPICS: Not given

NUMBER OF MANUSCRIPT COPIES: 3
REVIEW PERIOD: 3-4 mos.
PUBLICATION LAG TIME: 11-12 months
EARLY PUBLICATION OPTION: No
ACCEPTANCE RATE: 20%
AUTHORSHIP RESTRICTIONS: No

PAGE CHARGES: No
STYLE REQUIREMENTS: APA & Chicago
STYLE SHEET: Yes
REVISED THESES: No
STUDENT PAPERS: No
REPRINT POLICY: None

SUBSCRIPTION ADDRESS: University of Chicago Press
5801 S Ellis Avenue
Chicago, IL 60637

ANNUAL SUBSCRIPTION RATE: $18 individual, $18 institutional
INDEXED/ABSTRACTED IN: CDA, PA

CIRCULATION: 5000   FREQUENCY: 4-6 times per year

JOURNAL TITLE: MULTIVARIATE BEHAVIORAL RESEARCH

MANUSCRIPT ADDRESS: Editor, Department of Educational Psychology
University of Texas at Austin
Austin, TX 78712

TYPE OF ARTICLES: Research articles, theoretical articles

MAJOR CONTENT AREAS: Personality measurement and theory, factor
analysis and other multivariate analysis methods
and applications

TOPICS PREFERRED: Development and application of multivariate
analysis research methods

INAPPROPRIATE TOPICS: Psychological test development and statistical
analysis methods

NUMBER OF MANUSCRIPT COPIES: 3
REVIEW PERIOD: 3 months
PUBLICATION LAG TIME: 6 months
EARLY PUBLICATION OPTION: No
ACCEPTANCE RATE: 40%
AUTHORSHIP RESTRICTIONS: Yes

PAGE CHARGES: No
STYLE REQUIREMENTS: APA
STYLE SHEET: No
REVISED THESES: No
STUDENT PAPERS: No
REPRINT POLICY: None

SUBSCRIPTION ADDRESS: Business Manager of the Journal
Texas Christian University
Fort Worth, TX 76129

ANNUAL SUBSCRIPTION RATE: $15 individual, $24 institutional
INDEXED/ABSTRACTED IN: PA

CIRCULATION: 950   FREQUENCY: Quarterly

JOURNAL TITLE: NATURE

MANUSCRIPT ADDRESS: 4 Little Essex Street
London WC2, England

TYPE OF ARTICLES: Research articles, review articles

MAJOR CONTENT AREAS: Experimental

TOPICS PREFERRED: Experimental and observational science

INAPPROPRIATE TOPICS: Not given

NUMBER OF MANUSCRIPT COPIES:	Not given	PAGE CHARGES:	Not given
REVIEW PERIOD:	4 weeks	STYLE REQUIREMENTS:	Not given
PUBLICATION LAG TIME:	7 weeks	STYLE SHEET:	Yes
EARLY PUBLICATION OPTION:	No	REVISED THESES:	Not given
ACCEPTANCE RATE:	2%	STUDENT PAPERS:	Not given
AUTHORSHIP RESTRICTIONS:	Not given	REPRINT POLICY:	Not given

SUBSCRIPTION ADDRESS: 4 Little Essex Street
London WC2, England

ANNUAL SUBSCRIPTION RATE: $95 individual, Not given institutional
INDEXED/ABSTRACTED IN: AP, AA, AI, AATA, BAA, BEI, BS, CB, ISA,
LISA, PRAJ, WSA, WTA
CIRCULATION: 20,000   FREQUENCY: Not given

JOURNAL TITLE: NEW HUMAN SERVICES REVIEW

MANUSCRIPT ADDRESS: Alan Gartner
184 5th Avenue
New York, NY 10010

TYPE OF ARTICLES: Case studies, review articles, commentaries,
research articles, unsolicited book reviews

MAJOR CONTENT AREAS: Administrative behavior, aging and aged,
bureaucracy, community development, death & dying,
economy and society, human development, labor
force/labor relations, marriage & divorce
TOPICS PREFERRED: Human services practice, public policy

INAPPROPRIATE TOPICS: Not given

NUMBER OF MANUSCRIPT COPIES:	1	PAGE CHARGES:	No
REVIEW PERIOD:	2 weeks	STYLE REQUIREMENTS:	Not given
PUBLICATION LAG TIME:	2 months	STYLE SHEET:	Yes
EARLY PUBLICATION OPTION:	No	REVISED THESES:	No
ACCEPTANCE RATE:	Not given	STUDENT PAPERS:	No
AUTHORSHIP RESTRICTIONS:	No	REPRINT POLICY:	5

SUBSCRIPTION ADDRESS: Human Sciences Press
72 Fifth Avenue
New York, NY 10011

ANNUAL SUBSCRIPTION RATE: Not given
INDEXED/ABSTRACTED IN: HRA, AHMS

CIRCULATION: 2000   FREQUENCY: Bimonthly

JOURNAL TITLE: NEW SCHOLAR: STUDIES, ESSAYS, REVIEWS

MANUSCRIPT ADDRESS: University of California at
San Diego
La Jolla, CA 92093

TYPE OF ARTICLES: Research articles, case studies, review articles,
commentaries, theoretical articles, unsolicited
book reviews

MAJOR CONTENT AREAS: Administrative behavior, adolescence, anthropology,
criminology, ethnic groups, human development, law,
minorities, organizations, rural sociology, sex
roles, social change, social ideology

TOPICS PREFERRED: Not given

INAPPROPRIATE TOPICS: Not given

NUMBER OF MANUSCRIPT COPIES: 3	PAGE CHARGES: No	
REVIEW PERIOD: 6-8 weeks	STYLE REQUIREMENTS: Not given	
PUBLICATION LAG TIME: 3-12 months	STYLE SHEET: Yes	
EARLY PUBLICATION OPTION: Yes	REVISED THESES: Acceptable	
ACCEPTANCE RATE: 15%	STUDENT PAPERS: Yes	
AUTHORSHIP RESTRICTIONS: No	REPRINT POLICY: 10	

SUBSCRIPTION ADDRESS: University of California at San Diego
La Jolla, CA 92093

ANNUAL SUBSCRIPTION RATE: $7 individual, $10 institutional
INDEXED/ABSTRACTED IN: Not given

CIRCULATION: 1000   FREQUENCY: Semiannually

JOURNAL TITLE: NEW SOCIETY

MANUSCRIPT ADDRESS: Kings Reach Tower
Stamford Street
London S.E.1 England

TYPE OF ARTICLES: Research articles, case studies

MAJOR CONTENT AREAS: Not given

TOPICS PREFERRED: Social policy, social science

INAPPROPRIATE TOPICS: Not given

NUMBER OF MANUSCRIPT COPIES: 1	PAGE CHARGES: No	
REVIEW PERIOD: 1 month	STYLE REQUIREMENTS: Chicago Manuscript	
PUBLICATION LAG TIME: 1-12 months	STYLE SHEET: No	
EARLY PUBLICATION OPTION: No	REVISED THESES: Acceptable	
ACCEPTANCE RATE: 5%	STUDENT PAPERS: No	
AUTHORSHIP RESTRICTIONS: No	REPRINT POLICY: None	

SUBSCRIPTION ADDRESS: Paul Barker
New Science Publications
128 Long Acre
London, W.C. 2, England

ANNUAL SUBSCRIPTION RATE: $44 individual, $44 institutional
INDEXED/ABSTRACTED IN: Not given

CIRCULATION: 30,000   FREQUENCY: Weekly

JOURNAL TITLE: OFFENDER REHABILITATION

MANUSCRIPT ADDRESS: Sol Chaneles, Ph.D., Editor
333 West End Avenue
·New York, NY 10023

TYPE OF ARTICLES: Research articles, theoretical articles, case
studies, commentaries, life career experience
reports

MAJOR CONTENT AREAS: Administrative behavior, adolescence, aging and.
aged, counseling, delinquency & crime, law,human
development, mental health & illness, social
planning, professions, public health

TOPICS PREFERRED: Novel, challenging ways of looking at social
responses to the offender

INAPPROPRIATE TOPICS: Not given

NUMBER OF MANUSCRIPT COPIES:	3	PAGE CHARGES:	No
REVIEW PERIOD:	60 days	STYLE REQUIREMENTS:	Chicago Manuscript
PUBLICATION LAG TIME:	120 days	STYLE SHEET:	Yes
EARLY PUBLICATION OPTION:	Yes	REVISED THESES:	Yes
ACCEPTANCE RATE:	Not given	STUDENT PAPERS:	Yes
AUTHORSHIP RESTRICTIONS:	No	REPRINT POLICY:	50

SUBSCRIPTION ADDRESS: The Haworth Press
149 Fifth Avenue
New York, NY 10010

ANNUAL SUBSCRIPTION RATE: $16 individual, $30 institutional
INDEXED/ABSTRACTED IN: CJA, SA, ASW, PA, APC, JASA

CIRCULATION: 1000   FREQUENCY: Quarterly

JOURNAL TITLE: OPINION

MANUSCRIPT ADDRESS: James Kurtz, Editor
PO Box 688
Evanston, IL 60204

TYPE OF ARTICLES: Quality articles and essays

MAJOR CONTENT AREAS: Not given

TOPICS PREFERRED: Philosophy, sociology, theology

INAPPROPRIATE TOPICS: Not given

NUMBER OF MANUSCRIPT COPIES:	Not given	PAGE CHARGES:	Not given
REVIEW PERIOD:	1-2 months	STYLE REQUIREMENTS:	Not given
PUBLICATION LAG TIME:	3-6 months	STYLE SHEET:	Not given
EARLY PUBLICATION OPTION:	Not given	REVISED THESES:	Not given
ACCEPTANCE RATE:	35%	STUDENT PAPERS:	Yes
AUTHORSHIP RESTRICTIONS:	No	REPRINT POLICY:	5

SUBSCRIPTION ADDRESS: James Kurtz, Editor
PO Box 688
Evanston, IL 60204

ANNUAL SUBSCRIPTION RATE: $5 individual, $7.50 institutional
INDEXED/ABSTRACTED IN: Not given

CIRCULATION: 3700   FREQUENCY: Monthly

JOURNAL TITLE: PACIFIC SOCIOLOGICAL REVIEW

MANUSCRIPT ADDRESS: Aubrey Wendling, Editor
Department of Sociology
San Diego State University
San Diego, CA 92182

TYPE OF ARTICLES: Research articles, theoretical articles, case studies

MAJOR CONTENT AREAS: Administrative behavior, adolescence, bureaucracy, collective behavior, mass communication, criminology, demography, deviant behavior, ecology, educational sociology, ethnic groups

TOPICS PREFERRED: General sociology

INAPPROPRIATE TOPICS: Highly specialized, esoteric articles

NUMBER OF MANUSCRIPT COPIES: 2	PAGE CHARGES: No	
REVIEW PERIOD: 1-2 mos.	STYLE REQUIREMENTS: ASA	
PUBLICATION LAG TIME: 1 year	STYLE SHEET: Yes	
EARLY PUBLICATION OPTION: No	REVISED THESES: Acceptable	
ACCEPTANCE RATE: 8-11%	STUDENT PAPERS: No	
AUTHORSHIP RESTRICTIONS: No	REPRINT POLICY: 30	

SUBSCRIPTION ADDRESS: Ronald Hardert, Secretary-Treasurer
Department of Sociology
Arizona State University
Tempe, AZ 85281

ANNUAL SUBSCRIPTION RATE: $13.50 individual, $22.50 institutional
INDEXED/ABSTRACTED IN: Not given

CIRCULATION: 3000   FREQUENCY: Quarterly

JOURNAL TITLE: PEACE AND CHANGE, A JOURNAL OF PEACE RESEARCH

MANUSCRIPT ADDRESS: Berenice A. Carroll, Editor
Dept. of Political Science
University of Illinois
Urbana, IL

TYPE OF ARTICLES: Scholarly and interpretive articles

MAJOR CONTENT AREAS: Not given

TOPICS PREFERRED: Historical and humanistic dimensions of peace studies

INAPPROPRIATE TOPICS: Not given

NUMBER OF MANUSCRIPT COPIES: Not given	PAGE CHARGES: Not given	
REVIEW PERIOD: 3-6 months	STYLE REQUIREMENTS: Not given	
PUBLICATION LAG TIME: 4-6 months	STYLE SHEET: Not given	
EARLY PUBLICATION OPTION: Not given	REVISED THESES: Not given	
ACCEPTANCE RATE: Not given	STUDENT PAPERS: Yes	
AUTHORSHIP RESTRICTIONS: No	REPRINT POLICY: Not given	

SUBSCRIPTION ADDRESS: California State College, Sonoma
Rohnert Park, CA 94928

ANNUAL SUBSCRIPTION RATE: $7.50 individual, $10 institutional
INDEXED/ABSTRACTED IN: Not given

CIRCULATION: 500   FREQUENCY: Tri-yearly

JOURNAL TITLE: PERSONNEL

MANUSCRIPT ADDRESS: Frances Fore, Editor
135 West 50th Street
New York, NY 10020

TYPE OF ARTICLES: Not given

MAJOR CONTENT AREAS: Not given

TOPICS PREFERRED: New developments in personnel practices and
policies, industrial relations, pertinent
legislation
INAPPROPRIATE TOPICS: Not given

NUMBER OF MANUSCRIPT COPIES:	Not given	PAGE CHARGES:	Not given
REVIEW PERIOD:	2-4 weeks	STYLE REQUIREMENTS:	Not given
PUBLICATION LAG TIME:	2-4 months	STYLE SHEET:	Not given
EARLY PUBLICATION OPTION:	Not given	REVISED THESES:	Not given
ACCEPTANCE RATE:	25%	STUDENT PAPERS:	Not given
AUTHORSHIP RESTRICTIONS:	Not given	REPRINT POLICY:	200

SUBSCRIPTION ADDRESS: Frances Fore, Editor
135 West 50th Street
New York, NY 10020

ANNUAL SUBSCRIPTION RATE: $12 individual, Not given institutional
INDEXED/ABSTRACTED IN: Not given

CIRCULATION: 58,218   FREQUENCY: Bimonthly

JOURNAL TITLE: THE PERSONNEL ADMINISTRATOR

MANUSCRIPT ADDRESS: Editorial Offices
19 Church Street
Berea, OH 44017

TYPE OF ARTICLES: Research articles, case studies, theory in
practice

MAJOR CONTENT AREAS: Administrative behavior, alcoholism & drug abuse,
mass communication, counseling, human development,
human organizations, labor force/labor relations,
minorities, social change, social conflict
TOPICS PREFERRED: Emerging of women & minorities & related problems,
effect of legislation

INAPPROPRIATE TOPICS: Rehash of basic theory - no new perspectives

NUMBER OF MANUSCRIPT COPIES:	2	PAGE CHARGES:	No
REVIEW PERIOD:	2-3 mos.	STYLE REQUIREMENTS:	Chicago Manuscript
PUBLICATION LAG TIME:	3-4 months	STYLE SHEET:	Yes
EARLY PUBLICATION OPTION:	No	REVISED THESES:	No
ACCEPTANCE RATE:	20%	STUDENT PAPERS:	Yes
AUTHORSHIP RESTRICTIONS:	No	REPRINT POLICY:	2 journals

SUBSCRIPTION ADDRESS: Circulation Department
19 Church Street
Berea, OH 44017

ANNUAL SUBSCRIPTION RATE: $12 individual, $12 institutional
INDEXED/ABSTRACTED IN: Not given

CIRCULATION: 22,000   FREQUENCY: Monthly

JOURNAL TITLE: PERSONNEL AND GUIDANCE JOURNAL

MANUSCRIPT ADDRESS: 1607 New Hampshire Avenue, N W
Washington, D C   20009

TYPE OF ARTICLES: Review articles, theoretical articles, case
studies, commentaries, research articles,
unsolicited book reviews
MAJOR CONTENT AREAS: Counseling, deviant behavior, human development,
marriage & divorce, mental health & illness,
occupation & careers, society & institutions,
values, sociology of work
TOPICS PREFERRED: Counseling and guidance

INAPPROPRIATE TOPICS: Not given

NUMBER OF MANUSCRIPT COPIES:	3	PAGE CHARGES:	No
REVIEW PERIOD:	2 months	STYLE REQUIREMENTS:	APA & Chicago
PUBLICATION LAG TIME:	8-9 months	STYLE SHEET:	Yes
EARLY PUBLICATION OPTION:	Yes	REVISED THESES:	No
ACCEPTANCE RATE:	15%	STUDENT PAPERS:	Yes
AUTHORSHIP RESTRICTIONS:	No	REPRINT POLICY:	5

SUBSCRIPTION ADDRESS: 1607 Hampshire Avenue, N W
Washington, D C   20009

ANNUAL SUBSCRIPTION RATE: $20 individual, Not given-institutional
INDEXED/ABSTRACTED IN: Not given

CIRCULATION: 47,000   FREQUENCY: 10 times per year

JOURNAL TITLE: PHILIPPINE SOCIOLOGICAL REVIEW

MANUSCRIPT ADDRESS: Frank Lynch, Editor
Box 655 Greenhills
Rizal D-738, Philippines

TYPE OF ARTICLES: Not given

MAJOR CONTENT AREAS: Not given

TOPICS PREFERRED: Philippine sociology and anthropology

INAPPROPRIATE TOPICS: Not given

NUMBER OF MANUSCRIPT COPIES:	Not given	PAGE CHARGES:	Not given
REVIEW PERIOD:	1-2 months	STYLE REQUIREMENTS:	Not given
PUBLICATION LAG TIME:	4-12 months	STYLE SHEET:	Not given
EARLY PUBLICATION OPTION:	Not given	REVISED THESES:	Not given
ACCEPTANCE RATE:	50%	STUDENT PAPERS:	Not given
AUTHORSHIP RESTRICTIONS:	Not given	REPRINT POLICY:	10

SUBSCRIPTION ADDRESS: Frank Lynch, Editor
Box 655 Greenhills
Rizal D-738, Philippines

ANNUAL SUBSCRIPTION RATE: $8.50 individual, $8.50 institutional
INDEXED/ABSTRACTED IN: Not given

CIRCULATION: 1000   FREQUENCY: Quarterly

JOURNAL TITLE: PHYLON

MANUSCRIPT ADDRESS: Editor, Atlanta University
223 Chestnut Street, S W
Atlanta, GA 30314

TYPE OF ARTICLES: Research articles, theoretical articles,
commentaries, case studies

MAJOR CONTENT AREAS: Anthropology, demography, educational sociology,
ethnic groups, human development, mental health &
illness, migration, minorities, political
sociology, population, sex roles, social change
TOPICS PREFERRED: Research studies, literary critiques, theoretical
discussions that relate to minority groups

INAPPROPRIATE TOPICS: Short stories, poetry, non-scientific material

NUMBER OF MANUSCRIPT COPIES:	3	PAGE CHARGES:	No
REVIEW PERIOD:	3-12 mos.	STYLE REQUIREMENTS:	Chicago Manuscript
PUBLICATION LAG TIME:	Not given	STYLE SHEET:	Yes
EARLY PUBLICATION OPTION:	No	REVISED THESES:	Acceptable
ACCEPTANCE RATE:	50%	STUDENT PAPERS:	No
AUTHORSHIP RESTRICTIONS:	No	REPRINT POLICY:	25

SUBSCRIPTION ADDRESS: Subscription Secretary, Phylon
Atlanta University
223 Chestnut Street S W
Atlanta, GA 30314
ANNUAL SUBSCRIPTION RATE: $7 individual , $7 institutional
INDEXED/ABSTRACTED IN: Not given

CIRCULATION: 300-4000   FREQUENCY: Quarterly

JOURNAL TITLE: POLICY SCIENCES

MANUSCRIPT ADDRESS: Dr. Thomas J. Anton
Institute of Public Policy Studies
The University of Michigan
1516 Rackham Building, Ann Arbor, MI 48109
TYPE OF ARTICLES: Research articles, case studies, review articles,
book reviews

MAJOR CONTENT AREAS: Administrative behavior, economy and society,
organizations, social planning, social issues,
social policy, social structure, society &
institutions, policy studies
TOPICS PREFERRED: Not given

INAPPROPRIATE TOPICS: Not given

NUMBER OF MANUSCRIPT COPIES:	3	PAGE CHARGES:	No
REVIEW PERIOD:	Not given	STYLE REQUIREMENTS:	Chicago Manuscript
PUBLICATION LAG TIME:	6 months	STYLE SHEET:	Yes
EARLY PUBLICATION OPTION:	Not given	REVISED THESES:	Acceptable
ACCEPTANCE RATE:	Not given	STUDENT PAPERS:	No
AUTHORSHIP RESTRICTIONS:	No	REPRINT POLICY:	50

SUBSCRIPTION ADDRESS: Elsevier
PO Box 211
Amsterdam
The Netherlands
ANNUAL SUBSCRIPTION RATE: $70.20 individual, Not given-institutional
INDEXED/ABSTRACTED IN: ABC PS, CC/SBS, CCM, EA, EAA, HRA, IEA, ISA,
IAOR, IPSA, RZ:EP, SPAA, SUSA, SA, SICC, URS, UAA
CIRCULATION: 1500   FREQUENCY: Quarterly

JOURNAL TITLE: POLITICAL SCIENCE QUARTERLY

MANUSCRIPT ADDRESS: 2852 Broadway
New York, NY 10025

TYPE OF ARTICLES: Research articles, case studies,review
articles, commentaries,theoretical articles

MAJOR CONTENT AREAS: Bureaucracy, community development, ethnic
groups, housing and renewal, law, political
sociology, poverty, inequality, and policy,
public opinion, race relations, social policy

TOPICS PREFERRED: Politics, public affairs

INAPPROPRIATE TOPICS: Not given

NUMBER OF MANUSCRIPT COPIES: 2	PAGE CHARGES:	No
REVIEW PERIOD: 4-6 weeks	STYLE REQUIREMENTS:	Chicago Manuscript
PUBLICATION LAG TIME: 3-6 months	STYLE SHEET:	Yes
EARLY PUBLICATION OPTION: Yes	REVISED THESES:	Yes
ACCEPTANCE RATE: 12%	STUDENT PAPERS:	No
AUTHORSHIP RESTRICTIONS: No	REPRINT POLICY:	50

SUBSCRIPTION ADDRESS: Academy of Political Science
2852 Broadway
New York, NY 10025

ANNUAL SUBSCRIPTION RATE: $16 individual, $22 institutional
INDEXED/ABSTRACTED IN: RG, SSI, ABC PS, IBPS, IPSA, HA

CIRCULATION: 10,500   FREQUENCY: Quarterly

JOURNAL TITLE: POLITICAL THEORY

MANUSCRIPT ADDRESS: Benjamin Barber
Department of Political Science
Columbia University
New York, NY 10027

TYPE OF ARTICLES: Research articles, theoretical articles,
review articles,commentaries

MAJOR CONTENT AREAS: Social theory

TOPICS PREFERRED: Not given

INAPPROPRIATE TOPICS: Not given

NUMBER OF MANUSCRIPT COPIES: 2	PAGE CHARGES:	No
REVIEW PERIOD: Not given	STYLE REQUIREMENTS:	Not given
PUBLICATION LAG TIME: Not given	STYLE SHEET:	Yes
EARLY PUBLICATION OPTION: No	REVISED THESES:	Not given
ACCEPTANCE RATE: Not given	STUDENT PAPERS:	No
AUTHORSHIP RESTRICTIONS: No	REPRINT POLICY:	24

SUBSCRIPTION ADDRESS: Sage Publications
275 S Beverly Drive
Beverly Hills, CA 90212

ANNUAL SUBSCRIPTION RATE: $14.40 individual, $24 institutional
INDEXED/ABSTRACTED IN: IPSA, HRA, SUSA, ABC PS, CC, SSCI, PAII, PI

CIRCULATION: Not given   FREQUENCY: Quarterly

JOURNAL TITLE: POPULATION REVIEW

MANUSCRIPT ADDRESS: Dr. S. Chandrasekhar, Editor
Annamalai University
Chidambaram, South India

TYPE OF ARTICLES: Research articles, case studies, review
articles, unsolicited book reviews

MAJOR CONTENT AREAS: Aging and aged, anthropology, community
development, law, urban sociology, stratification, marriage & divorce, population, race
relations, family planning
TOPICS PREFERRED: Population problems and policies, and family
planning in developing countries

INAPPROPRIATE TOPICS: Not given

NUMBER OF MANUSCRIPT COPIES: 2	PAGE CHARGES: No	
REVIEW PERIOD: 4 months	STYLE REQUIREMENTS: Not given	
PUBLICATION LAG TIME: 6 months	STYLE SHEET: Yes	
EARLY PUBLICATION OPTION: No	REVISED THESES: Yes	
ACCEPTANCE RATE: 50%	STUDENT PAPERS: No	
AUTHORSHIP RESTRICTIONS: No	REPRINT POLICY: 2	

SUBSCRIPTION ADDRESS: Secretary, Population Review
Annamalai University
Chidambaram, South India

ANNUAL SUBSCRIPTION RATE: $10 individual, $10 institutional
INDEXED/ABSTRACTED IN: Not given

CIRCULATION: 4000   FREQUENCY: Semiannually

JOURNAL TITLE: POPULATION STUDIES

MANUSCRIPT ADDRESS: Population Investigation Committee
London School of Economics
Houghton Street
London WC2A 2AE, England
TYPE OF ARTICLES: Research articles, theoretical articles, case
studies, review articles

MAJOR CONTENT AREAS: Demography, family formation, family planning,
health and illness, marriage & divorce, migration,
minorities, population, public health, social
change, social mobility, suicide
TOPICS PREFERRED: Marriage, fertility (including fertility
control) and mortality

INAPPROPRIATE TOPICS: Econometric analyses

NUMBER OF MANUSCRIPT COPIES: 2-3	PAGE CHARGES: No	
REVIEW PERIOD: 3-4 mos.	STYLE REQUIREMENTS: Oxford	
PUBLICATION LAG TIME: 6-12 months	STYLE SHEET: Yes	
EARLY PUBLICATION OPTION: Not given	REVISED THESES: Yes	
ACCEPTANCE RATE: 20%	STUDENT PAPERS: No	
AUTHORSHIP RESTRICTIONS: Not given	REPRINT POLICY: 25	

SUBSCRIPTION ADDRESS: London School of Economics
Houghton Street, Aldwych
London WC2A 2AE, England

ANNUAL SUBSCRIPTION RATE: $30 individual, $30 institutional
INDEXED/ABSTRACTED IN: CC, EM, C, PI

CIRCULATION: 3100   FREQUENCY: Tri-yearly

JOURNAL TITLE: THE PRISON JOURNAL

MANUSCRIPT ADDRESS: 311 S Juniper
Philadelphia, PA 19107

TYPE OF ARTICLES: Commentaries, review articles, case studies

MAJOR CONTENT AREAS: Criminology, delinquency & crime, rehabilitation

TOPICS PREFERRED: Criminal justice reform

INAPPROPRIATE TOPICS: Not given

NUMBER OF MANUSCRIPT COPIES:	1	PAGE CHARGES:	No
REVIEW PERIOD:	3 weeks	STYLE REQUIREMENTS:	ASA
PUBLICATION LAG TIME:	6 months	STYLE SHEET:	Yes
EARLY PUBLICATION OPTION:	No	REVISED THESES:	No
ACCEPTANCE RATE:	20%	STUDENT PAPERS:	No
AUTHORSHIP RESTRICTIONS:	No	REPRINT POLICY:	10 journals

SUBSCRIPTION ADDRESS: 311 S Juniper
Philadelphia, PA 19107

ANNUAL SUBSCRIPTION RATE: $2 individual, $2 institutional
INDEXED/ABSTRACTED IN: Not given

CIRCULATION: 1300   FREQUENCY: Semiannually

JOURNAL TITLE: PSYCHIATRIC JOURNAL OF UNIVERSITY OF OTTAWA

MANUSCRIPT ADDRESS: Wayne Quan, M.D., Managing Editor
197 Cumberland
Ottawa, Ontario, K1B 3XF
Canada

TYPE OF ARTICLES: Research articles, theoretical articles, review
articles, case studies, commentaries, unsolicited
book reviews

MAJOR CONTENT AREAS: Alcoholism & drug abuse, death & dying, health &
illness, medical sociology, mental health &
illness, suicide

TOPICS PREFERRED: Research aspects of psychiatry

INAPPROPRIATE TOPICS: Not given

NUMBER OF MANUSCRIPT COPIES:	2	PAGE CHARGES:	No
REVIEW PERIOD:	1-2 months	STYLE REQUIREMENTS:	Index Medicus
PUBLICATION LAG TIME:	2 months	STYLE SHEET:	No
EARLY PUBLICATION OPTION:	No	REVISED THESES:	No
ACCEPTANCE RATE:	40%	STUDENT PAPERS:	No
AUTHORSHIP RESTRICTIONS:	No	REPRINT POLICY:	0

SUBSCRIPTION ADDRESS: Wayne Quan, M.D. , Managing Editor
197 Cumberland
Ottawa, Ontario, K1B 3XF
Canada

ANNUAL SUBSCRIPTION RATE: $25 individual, $25 institutional
INDEXED/ABSTRACTED IN: EM, PA, CDA

CIRCULATION: 5000   FREQUENCY: Quarterly

JOURNAL TITLE: PSYCHIATRY: JOURNAL FOR THE STUDY OF INTER-
PERSONAL PROCESSES

MANUSCRIPT ADDRESS: 1610 New Hampshire Avenue, NW
Washington, DC 20009

TYPE OF ARTICLES: Research articles, theoretical articles, review
articles, case studies, commentaries, unsolicited
book reviews

MAJOR CONTENT AREAS: Mental health & illness, social psychology

TOPICS PREFERRED: Interdisciplinary and cross-cultural works
in the field of human behavior

INAPPROPRIATE TOPICS: Not given

NUMBER OF MANUSCRIPT COPIES:	2	PAGE CHARGES:	No
REVIEW PERIOD:	2-4 mos.	STYLE REQUIREMENTS:	Not given
PUBLICATION LAG TIME:	10-12 months	STYLE SHEET:	Yes
EARLY PUBLICATION OPTION:	No	REVISED THESES:	Acceptable
ACCEPTANCE RATE:	15%	STUDENT PAPERS:	No
AUTHORSHIP RESTRICTIONS:	No	REPRINT POLICY:	None

SUBSCRIPTION ADDRESS: 1610 New Hampshire Avenue, NW
Washington, DC 20009

ANNUAL SUBSCRIPTION RATE: $15 individual, $ 24 institutional
INDEXED/ABSTRACTED IN: IM, PA, SA, EM

CIRCULATION: 3300   FREQUENCY: Quarterly

JOURNAL TITLE: THE PSYCHOANALYTIC QUARTERLY

MANUSCRIPT ADDRESS: 57 W 57th Street
New York, NY 10019

TYPE OF ARTICLES: Case studies, theoretical articles, research
articles

MAJOR CONTENT AREAS: Not given

TOPICS PREFERRED: Psychoanalysis, psychology, psychiatry and
related disciplines

INAPPROPRIATE TOPICS: Not given

NUMBER OF MANUSCRIPT COPIES:	2	PAGE CHARGES:	No
REVIEW PERIOD:	3-4 mos.	STYLE REQUIREMENTS:	Not given
PUBLICATION LAG TIME:	1 year	STYLE SHEET:	No
EARLY PUBLICATION OPTION:	Yes	REVISED THESES:	No
ACCEPTANCE RATE:	18%	STUDENT PAPERS:	No
AUTHORSHIP RESTRICTIONS:	No	REPRINT POLICY:	None

SUBSCRIPTION ADDRESS: 57 W 57th Street
New York, NY 10019

ANNUAL SUBSCRIPTION RATE: $25 individual, $25 institutional
INDEXED/ABSTRACTED IN: A,IM, EM, PA, ASW, G, CPLI

CIRCULATION: 4000   FREQUENCY: Quarterly

JOURNAL TITLE: THE PSYCHOANALYTIC REVIEW

MANUSCRIPT ADDRESS: 150 West 13 Street
New York, NY 10011

TYPE OF ARTICLES: Clinical material, theoretical articles,
research articles, case studies

MAJOR CONTENT AREAS: Psychoanalysis, humanities

TOPICS PREFERRED: Psychoanalysis

INAPPROPRIATE TOPICS: Not given

NUMBER OF MANUSCRIPT COPIES: 3   PAGE CHARGES: Not given
REVIEW PERIOD: 4 months STYLE REQUIREMENTS: Not given
PUBLICATION LAG TIME: 24-36 months   STYLE SHEET: Yes
EARLY PUBLICATION OPTION: Yes   REVISED THESES: Yes
ACCEPTANCE RATE: 40-50%   STUDENT PAPERS: Not given
AUTHORSHIP RESTRICTIONS: No   REPRINT POLICY: Not given

SUBSCRIPTION ADDRESS: Human Sciences Press
72 Fifth Avenue
New York, NY 10011

ANNUAL SUBSCRIPTION RATE: $16 individual, $32 institutional
INDEXED/ABSTRACTED IN: IM, PA, ASW, EM

CIRCULATION: 2200   FREQUENCY: Quarterly

JOURNAL TITLE: PSYCHODRAMA, GROUP PSYCHOTHERAPY & SOCIOMETRY

MANUSCRIPT ADDRESS: PO Box 311
Beacon, NY 12508

TYPE OF ARTICLES: Case studies, research articles

MAJOR CONTENT AREAS: Sex roles, sexual behavior, social change,
social conflict, social ideology, social
institutions, social interaction, social
movements, social policy, social structure
TOPICS PREFERRED: Helping professions

INAPPROPRIATE TOPICS: Not given

NUMBER OF MANUSCRIPT COPIES: 2   PAGE CHARGES: Not given
REVIEW PERIOD: Not given STYLE REQUIREMENTS: APA
PUBLICATION LAG TIME: 6 months   STYLE SHEET: Yes
EARLY PUBLICATION OPTION: No   REVISED THESES: Yes
ACCEPTANCE RATE: 75%   STUDENT PAPERS: Yes
AUTHORSHIP RESTRICTIONS: No   REPRINT POLICY: None

SUBSCRIPTION ADDRESS: PO Box 311
Beacon, NY 12508

ANNUAL SUBSCRIPTION RATE: $14 individual, $14 institutional
INDEXED/ABSTRACTED IN: Not given

CIRCULATION: 1500   FREQUENCY: Annually

JOURNAL TITLE: PSYCHOLOGICAL BULLETIN

MANUSCRIPT ADDRESS: R.J. Herrnstein
Harvard University
33 Kirkland Street
Cambridge, MA 02138
TYPE OF ARTICLES: Not given

MAJOR CONTENT AREAS: Not given

TOPICS PREFERRED: Not given

INAPPROPRIATE TOPICS: Not given

NUMBER OF MANUSCRIPT COPIES: 2   PAGE CHARGES: No
REVIEW PERIOD: 3 months STYLE REQUIREMENTS: APA
PUBLICATION LAG TIME: 16 months   STYLE SHEET: Yes
EARLY PUBLICATION OPTION: No   REVISED THESES: No
ACCEPTANCE RATE: 14%   STUDENT PAPERS: No
AUTHORSHIP RESTRICTIONS: No   REPRINT POLICY: 20

SUBSCRIPTION ADDRESS: APA Subscription Section
1200 17th Street NW
Washington, DC 20036

ANNUAL SUBSCRIPTION RATE: $15 member, $35 nonmember
INDEXED/ABSTRACTED IN: PA

CIRCULATION: 9900   FREQUENCY: Bimonthly

JOURNAL TITLE: THE PSYCHOLOGICAL RECORD

MANUSCRIPT ADDRESS: Kenyon College
Gambier, OH 43022

TYPE OF ARTICLES: Research article, theoretical articles

MAJOR CONTENT AREAS: Human development, mental health & illness,
socialization, social psychology, sociobiology

TOPICS PREFERRED: Psychological research and theory

INAPPROPRIATE TOPICS: Not given

NUMBER OF MANUSCRIPT COPIES: 2   PAGE CHARGES: Yes
REVIEW PERIOD: 2 months STYLE REQUIREMENTS: APA
PUBLICATION LAG TIME: 2 months   STYLE SHEET: Yes
EARLY PUBLICATION OPTION: No   REVISED THESES: No
ACCEPTANCE RATE: 60%   STUDENT PAPERS: No
AUTHORSHIP RESTRICTIONS: No   REPRINT POLICY: Not given

SUBSCRIPTION ADDRESS: Kenyon College
Gambier, OH 43022

ANNUAL SUBSCRIPTION RATE: $6 individual, $10 institutional
INDEXED/ABSTRACTED IN: ISI, SA, PA, EM, ACP, AB, KSTIC

CIRCULATION: 2000   FREQUENCY: Quarterly

JOURNAL TITLE: PSYCHOLOGICAL REVIEW

MANUSCRIPT ADDRESS: William K. Estes
Rockefeller University
New York, NY 10021

TYPE OF ARTICLES: Not given

MAJOR CONTENT AREAS: Not given

TOPICS PREFERRED: Not given

INAPPROPRIATE TOPICS: Not given

NUMBER OF MANUSCRIPT COPIES:	3	PAGE CHARGES:	No
REVIEW PERIOD:	5 weeks	STYLE REQUIREMENTS:	APA
PUBLICATION LAG TIME:	8 months	STYLE SHEET:	Yes
EARLY PUBLICATION OPTION:	No	REVISED THESES:	No
ACCEPTANCE RATE:	10%	STUDENT PAPERS:	No
AUTHORSHIP RESTRICTIONS:	No	REPRINT POLICY:	20

SUBSCRIPTION ADDRESS: APA, Subscription Section
1200 17th Street NW
Washington, DC 20036

ANNUAL SUBSCRIPTION RATE: $8 member, $20 nonmember
INDEXED/ABSTRACTED IN: PA

CIRCULATION: 8350   FREQUENCY: Bimonthly

JOURNAL TITLE: PSYCHOLOGY - A JOURNAL OF HUMAN BEHAVIOR

MANUSCRIPT ADDRESS: PO Box 6495
Savannah, GA 31405

TYPE OF ARTICLES: Research articles, case studies, theoretical
articles, commentaries, review articles,
unsolicited book reviews
MAJOR CONTENT AREAS: Adolescence, aging and aged, alcoholism & drug
abuse, anthropology, counseling, criminology,
death & dying, delinquency & crime, deviant
behavior, family formation, family planning
TOPICS PREFERRED: Not given

INAPPROPRIATE TOPICS: Not given

NUMBER OF MANUSCRIPT COPIES:	2	PAGE CHARGES:	Yes
REVIEW PERIOD:	10 days	STYLE REQUIREMENTS:	ASA, APA
PUBLICATION LAG TIME:	3 months	STYLE SHEET:	Yes
EARLY PUBLICATION OPTION:	No	REVISED THESES:	Yes
ACCEPTANCE RATE:	50%	STUDENT PAPERS:	No
AUTHORSHIP RESTRICTIONS:	No	REPRINT POLICY:	None

SUBSCRIPTION ADDRESS: PO Box 6495
Savannah, GA 31405

ANNUAL SUBSCRIPTION RATE: $7 individual, $7 institutional
INDEXED/ABSTRACTED IN: PA

CIRCULATION: 4000   FREQUENCY: Quarterly

JOURNAL TITLE: PSYCHOLOGY TODAY

MANUSCRIPT ADDRESS: One Park Avenue
New York, NY 10016

TYPE OF ARTICLES: Popular pieces based on research

MAJOR CONTENT AREAS: Psychology

TOPICS PREFERRED: Current issues in behavioral sciences

INAPPROPRIATE TOPICS: Not given

NUMBER OF MANUSCRIPT COPIES: 1   PAGE CHARGES: No
REVIEW PERIOD: 2-4 weeks STYLE REQUIREMENTS: Chicago Manuscript
PUBLICATION LAG TIME: 3 months   STYLE SHEET: Yes
EARLY PUBLICATION OPTION: Yes   REVISED THESES: No
ACCEPTANCE RATE: 10%   STUDENT PAPERS: No
AUTHORSHIP RESTRICTIONS: No   REPRINT POLICY: 10 journals

SUBSCRIPTION ADDRESS: PO Box 2990
Boulder, CO 80323

ANNUAL SUBSCRIPTION RATE: $12 individual, $12 institutional
INDEXED/ABSTRACTED IN: RGPL

CIRCULATION: 1.2 million   FREQUENCY: Monthly

JOURNAL TITLE: PSYCHOPHYSIOLOGY

MANUSCRIPT ADDRESS: William F. Prokasy, Editor
205 Spencer Hall
University of Utah
Salt Lake City, UT 84112
TYPE OF ARTICLES: Research articles, theoretical articles, review
articles, case studies

MAJOR CONTENT AREAS: Human development, mental health & illness,
sexual behavior, conditioning, sleep, bio-
feedback, psychosomatic medicine

TOPICS PREFERRED: Relationships between overt human behavior
and autonomic and central nervous system
behavior; animal behavior relationships
INAPPROPRIATE TOPICS: Not given

NUMBER OF MANUSCRIPT COPIES: 4   PAGE CHARGES: No
REVIEW PERIOD: 40 days   STYLE REQUIREMENTS: APA
PUBLICATION LAG TIME: 4-6 months   STYLE SHEET: Yes
EARLY PUBLICATION OPTION: No   REVISED THESES: Yes
ACCEPTANCE RATE: 60%   STUDENT PAPERS: No
AUTHORSHIP RESTRICTIONS: No   REPRINT POLICY: None

SUBSCRIPTION ADDRESS: PO Box 1481
Baltimore, MD 21203

ANNUAL SUBSCRIPTION RATE: $22 individual, $30 institutional
INDEXED/ABSTRACTED IN: IM, PA

CIRCULATION: 2000   FREQUENCY: Bimonthly

JOURNAL TITLE: PSYCHOSOMATIC MEDICINE

MANUSCRIPT ADDRESS: American Elsevier
52 Vanderbilt Avenue
New York, NY 10017

TYPE OF ARTICLES: Not given

MAJOR CONTENT AREAS: Health and illness, public health

TOPICS PREFERRED: Not given

INAPPROPRIATE TOPICS: Not given

NUMBER OF MANUSCRIPT COPIES:	Not given	PAGE CHARGES: Yes
REVIEW PERIOD:	Not given	STYLE REQUIREMENTS: Not given
PUBLICATION LAG TIME:	4-6 months	STYLE SHEET: Yes
EARLY PUBLICATION OPTION:	Not given	REVISED THESES: Not given
ACCEPTANCE RATE:	Not given	STUDENT PAPERS: Not given
AUTHORSHIP RESTRICTIONS:	Not given	REPRINT POLICY: None

SUBSCRIPTION ADDRESS: American Elsevier
52 Vanderbilt Avenue
New York, NY 10017

ANNUAL SUBSCRIPTION RATE: Not given
INDEXED/ABSTRACTED IN: Not given

CIRCULATION: 3000   FREQUENCY: Not given

JOURNAL TITLE: PUBLIC ADMINISTRATION REVIEW

MANUSCRIPT ADDRESS: ASPA
Suite 300
1225 Connecticut Avenue
Washington, DC 20036
TYPE OF ARTICLES: Research articles, theoretical articles

MAJOR CONTENT AREAS: Administrative behavior, community development,
labor force/labor relations, poverty, inequal-
ity, and policy, public administration

TOPICS PREFERRED: Public administration

INAPPROPRIATE TOPICS: Political science

NUMBER OF MANUSCRIPT COPIES:	3	PAGE CHARGES: No
REVIEW PERIOD:	3 months	STYLE REQUIREMENTS: Turabian
PUBLICATION LAG TIME:	1 year	STYLE SHEET: Yes
EARLY PUBLICATION OPTION:	Yes	REVISED THESES: No
ACCEPTANCE RATE:	10%	STUDENT PAPERS: No
AUTHORSHIP RESTRICTIONS:	No	REPRINT POLICY: 3 journals

SUBSCRIPTION ADDRESS: ASPA
Suite 300
1225 Connecticut Avenue, NW
Washington, DC 20036
ANNUAL SUBSCRIPTION RATE: $30 individual, $25 institutional
INDEXED/ABSTRACTED IN: PAIS, SSI, BRI

CIRCULATION: 22,000   FREQUENCY: Bimonthly

JOURNAL TITLE: THE PUBLIC OPINION QUARTERLY

MANUSCRIPT ADDRESS: Journalism Bldg.
Columbia University
116th St. and Broadway
New York, NY 10027

TYPE OF ARTICLES: Research articles, theoretical articles,
commentaries, unsolicited book reviews

MAJOR CONTENT AREAS: Mass communication, mass media, public
opinion, reference groups, social ideology

TOPICS PREFERRED: Public opinion, mass communication, public
relations, market research

INAPPROPRIATE TOPICS: Not given

NUMBER OF MANUSCRIPT COPIES:	2	PAGE CHARGES:	No
REVIEW PERIOD:	3-4 mos.	STYLE REQUIREMENTS:	ASA
PUBLICATION LAG TIME:	2-3 months	STYLE SHEET:	Yes
EARLY PUBLICATION OPTION:	No	REVISED THESES:	Acceptable
ACCEPTANCE RATE:	10-15%	STUDENT PAPERS:	Yes
AUTHORSHIP RESTRICTIONS:	No	REPRINT POLICY:	5 journals

SUBSCRIPTION ADDRESS: Columbia University Press
136 South Broadway
Irvington-on-Hudson, NY 10533

ANNUAL SUBSCRIPTION RATE: $12 individual, $12 institutional
INDEXED/ABSTRACTED IN: PAIS, SSI, USPSD, CRIS

CIRCULATION: 5200   FREQUENCY: Quarterly

JOURNAL TITLE: PUBLIC TELECOMMUNICATIONS REVIEW

MANUSCRIPT ADDRESS: NAEB/PTR
1346 Connecticut Avenue NW
Washington, DC 20036

TYPE OF ARTICLES: Research articles, case studies, theoretical
articles, commentaries

MAJOR CONTENT AREAS: Administrative behavior, mass communication,
educational sociology, mass media

TOPICS PREFERRED: Public telecommunications

INAPPROPRIATE TOPICS: Not given

NUMBER OF MANUSCRIPT COPIES:	2	PAGE CHARGES:	Not given
REVIEW PERIOD:	2-8 weeks	STYLE REQUIREMENTS:	Not given
PUBLICATION LAG TIME:	2 months	STYLE SHEET:	Yes
EARLY PUBLICATION OPTION:	No	REVISED THESES:	Yes
ACCEPTANCE RATE:	20%	STUDENT PAPERS:	No
AUTHORSHIP RESTRICTIONS:	No	REPRINT POLICY:	3

SUBSCRIPTION ADDRESS: NAEB/PTR
1346 Connecticut Avenue NW
Washington, DC 20036

ANNUAL SUBSCRIPTION RATE: $18 individual, $18 institutional
INDEXED/ABSTRACTED IN: Not given

CIRCULATION: 5000   FREQUENCY: Bimonthly

JOURNAL TITLE: PUBLIC WELFARE

MANUSCRIPT ADDRESS: Johnny Doherty, Editor
1155 16th Street, NW, Suite 201
Washington, DC   20036

TYPE OF ARTICLES: National social welfare policy and issues, child
welfare, health care, welfare staff training programs, case studies, commentaries

MAJOR CONTENT AREAS: Economy and society, educational sociology, health
and illness, housing and renewal, social planning,
poverty, inequality and policy, rural sociology,
social issues, social policy

TOPICS PREFERRED: Not given

INAPPROPRIATE TOPICS: Anecdotal caseworker pieces

NUMBER OF MANUSCRIPT COPIES:	3	PAGE CHARGES:	No
REVIEW PERIOD:	2 months	STYLE REQUIREMENTS:	Chicago Manuscript
PUBLICATION LAG TIME:	2 months	STYLE SHEET:	Yes
EARLY PUBLICATION OPTION:	No	REVISED THESES:	Acceptable
ACCEPTANCE RATE:	20%	STUDENT PAPERS:	No
AUTHORSHIP RESTRICTIONS:	No	REPRINT POLICY:	2 journals

SUBSCRIPTION ADDRESS: Ms. Martha Nash
1155 16th Street, NW, Suite 201
Washington, DC   20036

ANNUAL SUBSCRIPTION RATE: $8 individual, $8 institutional
INDEXED/ABSTRACTED IN: Not given

CIRCULATION: 13,000   FREQUENCY: Quarterly

JOURNAL TITLE: QUADERNI DI SOCIOLOGIA

MANUSCRIPT ADDRESS: Casa Editrice Taylor
Corso Stati Uniti 53
10129 Turin, Italy

TYPE OF ARTICLES: Research articles, theoretical articles, case
studies, commentaries, review articles,
unsolicited book reviews

MAJOR CONTENT AREAS: Mass communication, deviant behavior, educational
sociology, leadership, modernization, organiza-
tions, public opinion, rural sociology, social
change, social mobility, social theory

TOPICS PREFERRED: Not given

INAPPROPRIATE TOPICS: Not given

NUMBER OF MANUSCRIPT COPIES:	2	PAGE CHARGES:	Not given
REVIEW PERIOD:	30-40 days	STYLE REQUIREMENTS:	ASA
PUBLICATION LAG TIME:	40-60 days	STYLE SHEET:	Yes
EARLY PUBLICATION OPTION:	No	REVISED THESES:	Yes
ACCEPTANCE RATE:	80%	STUDENT PAPERS:	No
AUTHORSHIP RESTRICTIONS:	No	REPRINT POLICY:	25

SUBSCRIPTION ADDRESS: Casa Editrice Taylor
Corso Stati Uniti 53
10129 Turin, Italy

ANNUAL SUBSCRIPTION RATE: $17.50 individual, $17.50 institutional
INDEXED/ABSTRACTED IN: Not given

CIRCULATION: 1000   FREQUENCY: Quarterly

JOURNAL TITLE: QUARTERLY JOURNAL OF ECONOMICS

MANUSCRIPT ADDRESS: Littauer 227
Harvard University
Cambridge, MA 02138

TYPE OF ARTICLES: Research articles, theoretical articles

MAJOR CONTENT AREAS: Economy and society, transportation

TOPICS PREFERRED: Economics

INAPPROPRIATE TOPICS: Not given

NUMBER OF MANUSCRIPT COPIES: 2   PAGE CHARGES: No
REVIEW PERIOD: 8 months   STYLE REQUIREMENTS: Chicago Manuscript
PUBLICATION LAG TIME: 12 months   STYLE SHEET: Yes
EARLY PUBLICATION OPTION: No   REVISED THESES: Acceptable
ACCEPTANCE RATE: 9%   STUDENT PAPERS: No
AUTHORSHIP RESTRICTIONS: No   REPRINT POLICY: 25

SUBSCRIPTION ADDRESS: Subscriptions
John Wiley & Sons
605 Third Avenue
New York, NY 10016
ANNUAL SUBSCRIPTION RATE: $20 individual, $20 institutional
INDEXED/ABSTRACTED IN: JEL

CIRCULATION: 5500   FREQUENCY: Quarterly

JOURNAL TITLE: QUARTERLY JOURNAL OF EXPERIMENTAL PSYCHOLOGY

MANUSCRIPT ADDRESS: Professor R. Davis, Dept. of Psychology
The University of Reading, Earley Gate,
Whiteknights
Reading RG6 2AL, U.K.
TYPE OF ARTICLES: Experimental work in all branches of human
and animal psychology, short notes on
experimental apparatus
MAJOR CONTENT AREAS: Experimental, learning, perception, physiological

TOPICS PREFERRED: Mechanisms underlying behavior

INAPPROPRIATE TOPICS: Not given

NUMBER OF MANUSCRIPT COPIES: Not given   PAGE CHARGES: Not given
REVIEW PERIOD: 1-3 mos.   STYLE REQUIREMENTS: Not given
PUBLICATION LAG TIME: 6-9 months   STYLE SHEET: No
EARLY PUBLICATION OPTION: No   REVISED THESES: Not given
ACCEPTANCE RATE: 60%   STUDENT PAPERS: Not given
AUTHORSHIP RESTRICTIONS: Not given   REPRINT POLICY: 25

SUBSCRIPTION ADDRESS: Academic Press, Inc.
111 Fifth Avenue
New York, NY 10003

ANNUAL SUBSCRIPTION RATE: $31 individual, Not given institutional
INDEXED/ABSTRACTED IN: PA, CCSBS, PRG

CIRCULATION: 1650   FREQUENCY: Not given

JOURNAL TITLE: QUARTERLY JOURNAL OF SPEECH

MANUSCRIPT ADDRESS: Robert P. Friedman, Editor
Department of Speech
University of Oregon
Eugene, OR 97403

TYPE OF ARTICLES: Research articles, theoretical articles

MAJOR CONTENT AREAS: Administrative behavior, bureaucracy, mass
communication, ethnic groups, human development,
law, popular culture, race relations, sex roles,
social change, social ideology, social interaction

TOPICS PREFERRED: Not given

INAPPROPRIATE TOPICS: Not given

NUMBER OF MANUSCRIPT COPIES: 3	PAGE CHARGES: No	
REVIEW PERIOD: 2 months	STYLE REQUIREMENTS: MLA	
PUBLICATION LAG TIME: 6-12 months	STYLE SHEET: Not given	
EARLY PUBLICATION OPTION: No	REVISED THESES: Acceptable	
ACCEPTANCE RATE: 15%	STUDENT PAPERS: No	
AUTHORSHIP RESTRICTIONS: No	REPRINT POLICY: 20-25	

SUBSCRIPTION ADDRESS: Speech Communication Association
5205 Leesburg Pike
Falls Church, VA 22041

ANNUAL SUBSCRIPTION RATE: $25 individual, $20 institutional
INDEXED/ABSTRACTED IN: QJS, EI, RGPL, ERIC, CIJE

CIRCULATION: 6800   FREQUENCY: Quarterly

JOURNAL TITLE: RACE & CLASS (formerly RACE)

MANUSCRIPT ADDRESS: Editor
Institute of Race Relations
247-9 Pentonville Road
London N1, England

TYPE OF ARTICLES: Short, clear, free of jargon

MAJOR CONTENT AREAS: Race relations and transnational studies

TOPICS PREFERRED: Third World problems and realities

INAPPROPRIATE TOPICS: Not given

NUMBER OF MANUSCRIPT COPIES: Not given	PAGE CHARGES: Not given	
REVIEW PERIOD: Not given	STYLE REQUIREMENTS:	
PUBLICATION LAG TIME: Not given	STYLE SHEET: Not given	
EARLY PUBLICATION OPTION: Not given	REVISED THESES: Not given	
ACCEPTANCE RATE: Not given	STUDENT PAPERS: Not given	
AUTHORSHIP RESTRICTIONS: Not given	REPRINT POLICY: Not given	

SUBSCRIPTION ADDRESS: Institute of Race Relations
247-9 Pentonville Road
London N1, England

ANNUAL SUBSCRIPTION RATE: $15 for four issues
INDEXED/ABSTRACTED IN: Not given

CIRCULATION: Not given   FREQUENCY: Quarterly

JOURNAL TITLE: RECHERCHES SOCIOGRAPHIQUES

MANUSCRIPT ADDRESS: Departement de sociologie
Faculté des sciences sociales
Université Laval
Québec Qué GIK 7P4 Canada
TYPE OF ARTICLES: Research articles, case studies, review
articles, commentaries

MAJOR CONTENT AREAS: Anthropology, mass communication, demography,
groups, occupations & careers, social planning,
professions, religion, sociology of science,
social change, social issues, social structure
TOPICS PREFERRED: Social problems of Québec, past and present

INAPPROPRIATE TOPICS: Not given

NUMBER OF MANUSCRIPT COPIES: 1   PAGE CHARGES: No
REVIEW PERIOD: 1-2 weeks STYLE REQUIREMENTS: Chicago Manuscript
PUBLICATION LAG TIME: 2-3 months   STYLE SHEET: No
EARLY PUBLICATION OPTION: Yes   REVISED THESES: Yes
ACCEPTANCE RATE: 80%   STUDENT PAPERS: Yes
AUTHORSHIP RESTRICTIONS: No   REPRINT POLICY: 20

SUBSCRIPTION ADDRESS: Les Presses de l'Université Laval
Université Laval
Québec Qué GIK 7P4
Canada
ANNUAL SUBSCRIPTION RATE: $10 individual, $20 institutional
INDEXED/ABSTRACTED IN: SA

CIRCULATION: 1250   FREQUENCY: Tri-yearly

JOURNAL TITLE: RELIGIOUS HUMANISM

MANUSCRIPT ADDRESS: J. Harold Hadley, Editor
PO Box 278
Yellow Springs, OH 45387

TYPE OF ARTICLES: Religious articles, theoretical articles,
research articles, case studies, review articles,
unsolicited book reviews, commentaries
MAJOR CONTENT AREAS: Death & dying, human development, religion, social
change, social ideology

TOPICS PREFERRED: Religious, ethical, philosophical, humanistic

INAPPROPRIATE TOPICS: Conservative or fundamentalist religious approaches

NUMBER OF MANUSCRIPT COPIES: 2   PAGE CHARGES: No
REVIEW PERIOD: 4 weeks STYLE REQUIREMENTS: Chicago Manuscript
PUBLICATION LAG TIME: 3 months   STYLE SHEET: Yes
EARLY PUBLICATION OPTION: No   REVISED THESES: No
ACCEPTANCE RATE: Not given   STUDENT PAPERS: Yes
AUTHORSHIP RESTRICTIONS: No   REPRINT POLICY: 4 journals

SUBSCRIPTION ADDRESS: PO Box 278
Yellow Springs, OH 45387

ANNUAL SUBSCRIPTION RATE: $5 individual , $5 institutional
INDEXED/ABSTRACTED IN: XUM, RTA

CIRCULATION: 1000   FREQUENCY: Quarterly

JOURNAL TITLE: RESEARCH ON CONSUMER BEHAVIOR

MANUSCRIPT ADDRESS: Robert Ferber, Editor
University of Illinois at Chicago Circle
PO Box 6905
Chicago, IL 60680

TYPE OF ARTICLES: Research articles, theoretical articles, review articles, commentaries, case studies, unsolicited book reviews

MAJOR CONTENT AREAS: Administrative behavior, collective behavior, ecology, health and illness, human organizations, population, race relations, rural sociology, sex roles, social psychology

TOPICS PREFERRED: Interdisciplinary aspects of consumer behavior

INAPPROPRIATE TOPICS: Overly technical manuscripts

NUMBER OF MANUSCRIPT COPIES:	4	PAGE CHARGES:	No
REVIEW PERIOD:	3 months	STYLE REQUIREMENTS:	JCR
PUBLICATION LAG TIME:	3-6 months	STYLE SHEET:	Yes
EARLY PUBLICATION OPTION:	No	REVISED THESES:	Yes
ACCEPTANCE RATE:	15%	STUDENT PAPERS:	No
AUTHORSHIP RESTRICTIONS:	No	REPRINT POLICY:	None

SUBSCRIPTION ADDRESS: Journal of Consumer Research
222 S Riverside Plaza
Chicago, IL 60606

ANNUAL SUBSCRIPTION RATE: $14.50 member , $29 nonmember
INDEXED/ABSTRACTED IN: MRA, MIG, CC, SSCI, MC, CUND, SA

CIRCULATION: 4000   FREQUENCY: Quarterly

JOURNAL TITLE: REVIEW OF PUBLIC DATA USE

MANUSCRIPT ADDRESS: Managing Editor
1601 N Kent Street
Suite 900
Arlington, VA 22209

TYPE OF ARTICLES: Research articles, theoretical articles, case studies

MAJOR CONTENT AREAS: Community development, criminology, demography, family planning, migration, minorities, public health, rural sociology, social policy, social structure, sociometry

TOPICS PREFERRED: Social science research and methodology

INAPPROPRIATE TOPICS: Not given

NUMBER OF MANUSCRIPT COPIES:	3	PAGE CHARGES:	No
REVIEW PERIOD:	2-4 mos.	STYLE REQUIREMENTS:	ASA
PUBLICATION LAG TIME:	2-4 months	STYLE SHEET:	Yes
EARLY PUBLICATION OPTION:	No	REVISED THESES:	Yes
ACCEPTANCE RATE:	Not given	STUDENT PAPERS:	No
AUTHORSHIP RESTRICTIONS:	No	REPRINT POLICY:	5

SUBSCRIPTION ADDRESS: Subscription Department
National Technical Information Service
5285 Port Royal Road
Springfield, VA 22616

ANNUAL SUBSCRIPTION RATE: $60 individual, $60 institutional
INDEXED/ABSTRACTED IN: CC (SBS), SSCI, ASA, UAA

CIRCULATION: 600   FREQUENCY: Bimonthly

JOURNAL TITLE: REVIEW OF RELIGIOUS RESEARCH

MANUSCRIPT ADDRESS: Dr. James D. Davidson
Purdue University
Department of Sociology
West Lafayette, IN 47906

TYPE OF ARTICLES: Research articles, review articles, theoretical articles

MAJOR CONTENT AREAS: Adolescence, collective behavior, death & dying,
general sociology, marriage & divorce, mental
health & illness, peace, sociology, religion,
rural sociology, social ideology, suicide, values

TOPICS PREFERRED: Sociology of religion

INAPPROPRIATE TOPICS: Not given

NUMBER OF MANUSCRIPT COPIES: 2   PAGE CHARGES: No
REVIEW PERIOD: 3 months   STYLE REQUIREMENTS: ASA
PUBLICATION LAG TIME: 6-12 months   STYLE SHEET: Yes
EARLY PUBLICATION OPTION: No   REVISED THESES: No
ACCEPTANCE RATE: 30%   STUDENT PAPERS: No
AUTHORSHIP RESTRICTIONS: No   REPRINT POLICY: 5

SUBSCRIPTION ADDRESS: Religious Research Association
PO Box 228
Cathedral Station
New York, NY 10025

ANNUAL SUBSCRIPTION RATE: $12 individual, $12 institutional
INDEXED/ABSTRACTED IN: TL, SSCR, SA, IRPL, RTA, CC/BSES,
CERDIC

CIRCULATION: 1000   FREQUENCY: Tri-yearly

JOURNAL TITLE: THE REVIEW OF SOCIAL THEORY

MANUSCRIPT ADDRESS: Robert Hagan, Editor
Department of Sociology
University of Missouri
Columbia, MO 65207

TYPE OF ARTICLES: Not given

MAJOR CONTENT AREAS: Not given

TOPICS PREFERRED: Philosophy of science; cross-disciplinary
theoretical and methodological implications

INAPPROPRIATE TOPICS: Not given

NUMBER OF MANUSCRIPT COPIES: Not given   PAGE CHARGES: Not given
REVIEW PERIOD: 1-10 mos. STYLE REQUIREMENTS: Not given
PUBLICATION LAG TIME: 6 months   STYLE SHEET: Not given
EARLY PUBLICATION OPTION: Not given   REVISED THESES: Not given
ACCEPTANCE RATE: Not given   STUDENT PAPERS: Not given
AUTHORSHIP RESTRICTIONS: Not given   REPRINT POLICY: 3

SUBSCRIPTION ADDRESS: Robert Hagan, Editor
Department of Sociology
University of Missouri
Columbia, MO 65207

ANNUAL SUBSCRIPTION RATE: $3 individual, $5 institutional
INDEXED/ABSTRACTED IN: Not given

CIRCULATION: 100   FREQUENCY: Semiannually

JOURNAL TITLE: REVIEW ON EDUCATIONAL RESEARCH

MANUSCRIPT ADDRESS: Dr. Samuel Messick, Editor
Box 2604
Educational Testing Service
Princeton, NJ 08540
TYPE OF ARTICLES: Integrative review articles

MAJOR CONTENT AREAS: Educational sociology

TOPICS PREFERRED: Educational research

INAPPROPRIATE TOPICS: Not given

NUMBER OF MANUSCRIPT COPIES: 3	PAGE CHARGES: No	
REVIEW PERIOD: 6 months	STYLE REQUIREMENTS: APA	
PUBLICATION LAG TIME: 6 months	STYLE SHEET: No	
EARLY PUBLICATION OPTION: No	REVISED THESES: No	
ACCEPTANCE RATE: 20%	STUDENT PAPERS: No	
AUTHORSHIP RESTRICTIONS: No	REPRINT POLICY: 50	

SUBSCRIPTION ADDRESS: AERA
1126 16th Street NW
Washington, DC 20036

ANNUAL SUBSCRIPTION RATE: $12 individual, $14 institutional
INDEXED/ABSTRACTED IN: UIPD, LH, EMY, SPD, EAA, LM, EY, CGCI, DA, PA,
SPD, ED
CIRCULATION: 16,500   FREQUENCY: Quarterly

JOURNAL TITLE: REVUE FRANCAISE DES AFFAIRES SOCIALES

MANUSCRIPT ADDRESS: Place de Fontenoy
75 Paris, France

TYPE OF ARTICLES: Research articles, commentaries, case studies,
theoretical articles

MAJOR CONTENT AREAS: Aging & aged, alcoholism & drug abuse, family
formation, labor force/labor relations, poverty,
inequality, and policy, social conflict, social
institutions, social theory, systems analysis
TOPICS PREFERRED: Social issues

INAPPROPRIATE TOPICS: Not given

NUMBER OF MANUSCRIPT COPIES: 1	PAGE CHARGES: Not given	
REVIEW PERIOD: 15 days	STYLE REQUIREMENTS: Not given	
PUBLICATION LAG TIME: 2 months	STYLE SHEET: Yes	
EARLY PUBLICATION OPTION: Not given	REVISED THESES: Not given	
ACCEPTANCE RATE: 90%	STUDENT PAPERS: Yes	
AUTHORSHIP RESTRICTIONS: No	REPRINT POLICY: 50	

SUBSCRIPTION ADDRESS: Documentation Francaise
29-31 Quoi Voltaire
75SHD Paris Cedex 07
France
ANNUAL SUBSCRIPTION RATE: Not given
INDEXED/ABSTRACTED IN: Not given

CIRCULATION: 20,000   FREQUENCY: Quarterly

JOURNAL TITLE: RURAL SOCIOLOGY

MANUSCRIPT ADDRESS: James H. Copp, Editor
317 Agriculture Building,Texas A&M University
College Station, TX 77843

TYPE OF ARTICLES: Research articles, theoretical articles, review
articles

MAJOR CONTENT AREAS: Community development, ecology, migration, population, race relations, rural sociology, social
change, social conflict, social institutions,
social mobility, poverty,inequality, and policy

TOPICS PREFERRED: Rural life

INAPPROPRIATE TOPICS: Rural-urban comparisons on attitudes and values

NUMBER OF MANUSCRIPT COPIES: 4	PAGE CHARGES: No	
REVIEW PERIOD: 3 months	STYLE REQUIREMENTS: ASA	
PUBLICATION LAG TIME: 6 months	STYLE SHEET: No	
EARLY PUBLICATION OPTION: No	REVISED THESES: No	
ACCEPTANCE RATE: 13%	STUDENT PAPERS: No	
AUTHORSHIP RESTRICTIONS: No	REPRINT POLICY: None	

SUBSCRIPTION ADDRESS: Dr. John E. Dunkelberger
Department of Agricultural Economics & Rural Soc.
Auburn University
Auburn, AL 36830

ANNUAL SUBSCRIPTION RATE: $20 individual, $24 institutional

INDEXED/ABSTRACTED IN: AI, BA, CIJE, GRBHA, SCI, PAIS, SA, CS,
PHRA, ASW, HA, WAERSA

CIRCULATION: 2800   FREQUENCY: Quarterly

JOURNAL TITLE: S.A.M. ADVANCED MANAGEMENT JOURNAL

MANUSCRIPT ADDRESS: 135 West 50th Street
New York, NY 10020

TYPE OF ARTICLES: Case studies, research articles, theoretical
articles

MAJOR CONTENT AREAS: Consumerism, human development, human organizations, industrial sociology, labor force/
labor relations, mass media, occupations &
careers, organizations, systems analysis

TOPICS PREFERRED: Management

INAPPROPRIATE TOPICS: Technical manuscripts

NUMBER OF MANUSCRIPT COPIES: 1	PAGE CHARGES: Yes	
REVIEW PERIOD: 2 weeks	STYLE REQUIREMENTS: Chicago Manuscript	
PUBLICATION LAG TIME: 3-6 months	STYLE SHEET: Yes	
EARLY PUBLICATION OPTION: No	REVISED THESES: No	
ACCEPTANCE RATE: 30%	STUDENT PAPERS: No	
AUTHORSHIP RESTRICTIONS: No	REPRINT POLICY: 100	

SUBSCRIPTION ADDRESS: American Management Associations
Fulfillment Department
Saranac Lake, NY 12983

ANNUAL SUBSCRIPTION RATE: $13 individual, Not given - institutional

INDEXED/ABSTRACTED IN: Not given

CIRCULATION: 11,000   FREQUENCY: Quarterly

JOURNAL TITLE: SCHOOL REVIEW

MANUSCRIPT ADDRESS: 5835 S Kemiark
Chicago, IL   60637

TYPE OF ARTICLES: Research articles, case studies, theoretical
articles, commentaries, review articles

MAJOR CONTENT AREAS: Bureaucracy, mass communication, deviant behavior,
educational sociology, mass media, minorities,
organizations, public opinion, race relations, sex
roles, social change, social policy, socialization

TOPICS PREFERRED: Educational policy and theory

INAPPROPRIATE TOPICS: Educational practice

NUMBER OF MANUSCRIPT COPIES:	2	PAGE CHARGES:	No
REVIEW PERIOD:	1-6 mos.	STYLE REQUIREMENTS:	Chicago Manuscript
PUBLICATION LAG TIME:	1 year	STYLE SHEET:	Yes
EARLY PUBLICATION OPTION:	Yes	REVISED THESES:	No
ACCEPTANCE RATE:	8%	STUDENT PAPERS:	No
AUTHORSHIP RESTRICTIONS:	No	REPRINT POLICY:	25

SUBSCRIPTION ADDRESS: 5801 S Ellis Avenue
Chicago, IL   60637

ANNUAL SUBSCRIPTION RATE: $15 individual, $20 institutional
INDEXED/ABSTRACTED IN: EI, SA, PA

CIRCULATION: 4000   FREQUENCY: Quarterly

JOURNAL TITLE: SCIENCE

MANUSCRIPT ADDRESS: 1515 Massachusetts Avenue, NW
Washington, DC   20005

TYPE OF ARTICLES: Research articles, review articles, theoretical
articles

MAJOR CONTENT AREAS: Experimental

TOPICS PREFERRED: Those of interdisciplinary import

INAPPROPRIATE TOPICS: Not given

NUMBER OF MANUSCRIPT COPIES:	Not given	PAGE CHARGES:	Not given
REVIEW PERIOD:	4-8 weeks	STYLE REQUIREMENTS:	Not given
PUBLICATION LAG TIME:	4-10 weeks	STYLE SHEET:	Yes
EARLY PUBLICATION OPTION:	No	REVISED THESES:	Not given
ACCEPTANCE RATE:	20-25%	STUDENT PAPERS:	Not given
AUTHORSHIP RESTRICTIONS:	Not given	REPRINT POLICY:	Not given

SUBSCRIPTION ADDRESS: 1515 Massachusetts Avenue, NW
Washington, DC   20005

ANNUAL SUBSCRIPTION RATE: $25 individual, $50 institutional
INDEXED/ABSTRACTED IN: PA, SA, ARGPL, AA, AATA, BRD, BRI, BAA, BS,
CSPA, CB, CIJE, DSHA, GAA, IPAPL, IPARL, ISA
CIRCULATION: 145,000   FREQUENCY: Not given

JOURNAL TITLE: THE SCIENCES

MANUSCRIPT ADDRESS: The New York Academy of Sciences
2 East 63rd Street
New York, NY 10021

TYPE OF ARTICLES: Review articles, commentaries, advanced research

MAJOR CONTENT AREAS: Physical science, biological science, chemical science, behavioral science, mathematics, technology, medicine

TOPICS PREFERRED: Not given

INAPPROPRIATE TOPICS: Specialized papers designed for publication in peer-reviewed journals

NUMBER OF MANUSCRIPT COPIES: 2   PAGE CHARGES: No
REVIEW PERIOD: 2 weeks   STYLE REQUIREMENTS: New York Times
PUBLICATION LAG TIME: 4-6 months   STYLE SHEET: Yes
EARLY PUBLICATION OPTION: No   REVISED THESES: No
ACCEPTANCE RATE: Not given   STUDENT PAPERS: No
AUTHORSHIP RESTRICTIONS: No   REPRINT POLICY: None

SUBSCRIPTION ADDRESS: The New York Academy of Sciences
2 East 63rd Street
New York, NY 10021

ANNUAL SUBSCRIPTION RATE: $5 individual, $5 institutional
INDEXED/ABSTRACTED IN: CC, RGPL

CIRCULATION: 35,000   FREQUENCY: 8 times per year

JOURNAL TITLE: SEXUALITY AND DISABILITY

MANUSCRIPT ADDRESS: Ami Shaked, Editor
Purdue University School of Science
1201 E 38th Street
Indianapolis, IN 46205

TYPE OF ARTICLES: Research articles, case studies, review articles, theoretical articles, commentaries

MAJOR CONTENT AREAS: Adolescence, aging and aged, alcoholism & drug abuse, counseling, health and illness, mental health and illness, rehabilitation, sex roles, sexual behavior, marriage & divorce

TOPICS PREFERRED: Sexual behavior and function in relation to medical and mental illness or disability, sex education and the disabled

INAPPROPRIATE TOPICS: Topics dealing with sexuality but not in relation to physical or mental illness or disability

NUMBER OF MANUSCRIPT COPIES: 3   PAGE CHARGES: Yes
REVIEW PERIOD: 3-4 mos. STYLE REQUIREMENTS: Index Medicus
PUBLICATION LAG TIME: 4-6 months   STYLE SHEET: Yes
EARLY PUBLICATION OPTION: Yes   REVISED THESES: Yes
ACCEPTANCE RATE: Not given   STUDENT PAPERS: Yes
AUTHORSHIP RESTRICTIONS: No   REPRINT POLICY: None

SUBSCRIPTION ADDRESS: Human Sciences Press
Subscription Department
72 Fifth Avenue
New York, NY 10011

ANNUAL SUBSCRIPTION RATE: $15 individual, $35 institutional
INDEXED/ABSTRACTED IN: PA, EM, SS, SA, PHR

CIRCULATION: 5000   FREQUENCY: Quarterly

JOURNAL TITLE: SIMULATION

MANUSCRIPT ADDRESS: Managing Editor
Society for Computer Simulation
PO Box 2228
La Jolla, CA 92038

TYPE OF ARTICLES: Research articles, applications-oriented articles, theoretical articles

MAJOR CONTENT AREAS: Systems analysis, social theory, computer applications and simulation

TOPICS PREFERRED: Computer simulation and modeling

INAPPROPRIATE TOPICS: Not given

NUMBER OF MANUSCRIPT COPIES: 4   PAGE CHARGES: No
REVIEW PERIOD: 4-6 weeks STYLE REQUIREMENTS: APA and ASA
PUBLICATION LAG TIME: 3-9 months   STYLE SHEET: Yes
EARLY PUBLICATION OPTION: No   REVISED THESES: Acceptable
ACCEPTANCE RATE: 67%   STUDENT PAPERS: No
AUTHORSHIP RESTRICTIONS: No   REPRINT POLICY: 50

SUBSCRIPTION ADDRESS: Circulation Department
PO Box 2228
La Jolla, CA 92038

ANNUAL SUBSCRIPTION RATE: $25 individual, $38 institutional
INDEXED/ABSTRACTED IN: CIS, CC, DPD, EI, OR/MS, SA

CIRCULATION: 3000   FREQUENCY: Monthly

JOURNAL TITLE: SIMULATION AND GAMES

MANUSCRIPT ADDRESS: Garry Brewer
School of Organization and Management
Yale University
New Haven, CT 06520

TYPE OF ARTICLES: Research articles, theoretical articles, review articles, case studies, commentaries

MAJOR CONTENT AREAS: Simulations and games in social science

TOPICS PREFERRED: Not given

INAPPROPRIATE TOPICS: Not given

NUMBER OF MANUSCRIPT COPIES: 3   PAGE CHARGES: No
REVIEW PERIOD: Not given STYLE REQUIREMENTS: Not given
PUBLICATION LAG TIME: Not given   STYLE SHEET: Yes
EARLY PUBLICATION OPTION: No   REVISED THESES: Not given
ACCEPTANCE RATE: Not given   STUDENT PAPERS: No
AUTHORSHIP RESTRICTIONS: No   REPRINT POLICY: 24

SUBSCRIPTION ADDRESS: Sage Publications
275 S Beverly Drive
Beverly Hills, CA 90212

ANNUAL SUBSCRIPTION RATE: $14.40 individual, $24 institutional
INDEXED/ABSTRACTED IN: IPSA, SA, PA, HRA, SUSA, ABC PS, PAIS, CC, ERIC/TE, SPAA, SSCI, BRSSP, SSI, MMRI
CIRCULATION: Not given   FREQUENCY: Quarterly

JOURNAL TITLE: SMALL GROUP BEHAVIOR

MANUSCRIPT ADDRESS: William Fawcett Hill
Department of Behavioral Sciences
Cal. State Polytechnic University
Pomona, CA 91768

TYPE OF ARTICLES: Research articles, theoretical articles, review articles, case studies, commentaries

MAJOR CONTENT AREAS: Counseling, educational sociology, groups

TOPICS PREFERRED: Not given

INAPPROPRIATE TOPICS: Not given

NUMBER OF MANUSCRIPT COPIES: 2		PAGE CHARGES: No	
REVIEW PERIOD: Not given	STYLE REQUIREMENTS: Not given		
PUBLICATION LAG TIME: Not given	STYLE SHEET: Yes		
EARLY PUBLICATION OPTION: No	REVISED THESES: Not given		
ACCEPTANCE RATE: Not given	STUDENT PAPERS: No		
AUTHORSHIP RESTRICTIONS: No	REPRINT POLICY: 24		

SUBSCRIPTION ADDRESS: Sage Publications
275 S Beverly Drive
Beverly Hills, CA 90212

ANNUAL SUBSCRIPTION RATE: $13.50 individual, $22.50 institutional
INDEXED/ABSTRACTED IN: PA, ASW, HRA, SUSA, SPAA, EAA, SSCI, CC

CIRCULATION: Not given   FREQUENCY: Quarterly

JOURNAL TITLE: SOCIAL ACTION

MANUSCRIPT ADDRESS: Indian Social Institute
Lodi Road
New Delhi - 110003, India

TYPE OF ARTICLES: Research articles, case studies, theoretical articles

MAJOR CONTENT AREAS: Demography, educational sociology, ethnic groups, family planning, human organizations, industrial sociology, labor force/labor relations, occupations & careers, social movements, urban sociology

TOPICS PREFERRED: Not given

INAPPROPRIATE TOPICS: Not given

NUMBER OF MANUSCRIPT COPIES: 2		PAGE CHARGES: No	
REVIEW PERIOD: 1 month	STYLE REQUIREMENTS: ASA		
PUBLICATION LAG TIME: 6 months	STYLE SHEET: Not given		
EARLY PUBLICATION OPTION: Not given	REVISED THESES: No MA theses		
ACCEPTANCE RATE: 10%	STUDENT PAPERS: No		
AUTHORSHIP RESTRICTIONS: No	REPRINT POLICY: 25		

SUBSCRIPTION ADDRESS: Indian Social Institute
Lodi Road
New Delhi - 110003 , India

ANNUAL SUBSCRIPTION RATE: $6.50 individual, $10 institutional
INDEXED/ABSTRACTED IN: SEA, BRI, BAS

CIRCULATION: 2000   FREQUENCY: Quarterly

JOURNAL TITLE: SOCIAL AND ECONOMIC STUDIES

MANUSCRIPT ADDRESS: The Publications Editor
Institute of Social and Economic Research
University of the West Indies
Mona, Kingston 7, Jamaica

TYPE OF ARTICLES: Research articles, theoretical articles, review
articles, commentaries, unsolicited book reviews,
case studies

MAJOR CONTENT AREAS: Administrative behavior, bureaucracy, criminology,
economy and society, family formation, housing and
renewal, law, migration, political sociology, religion, social change, social mobility, stratification

TOPICS PREFERRED: Social, economic and political problems of under-
developed countries

INAPPROPRIATE TOPICS: Applications of standard methods to new data

NUMBER OF MANUSCRIPT COPIES: 3	PAGE CHARGES:	No
REVIEW PERIOD: 6 months	STYLE REQUIREMENTS:	Not given
PUBLICATION LAG TIME: 3 months	STYLE SHEET:	Yes
EARLY PUBLICATION OPTION: No	REVISED THESES:	Yes
ACCEPTANCE RATE: 10-15%	STUDENT PAPERS:	No
AUTHORSHIP RESTRICTIONS: No	REPRINT POLICY:	10

SUBSCRIPTION ADDRESS: The Subscription's Secretary
Inst. of Social and Economic Research
University of the West Indies
Mona, Kingston 7, Jamaica

ANNUAL SUBSCRIPTION RATE: $15 individual, $15 institutional

INDEXED/ABSTRACTED IN: SA

CIRCULATION: 2000   FREQUENCY: Quarterly

JOURNAL TITLE: SOCIAL BEHAVIOR AND PERSONALITY: AN
INTERNATIONAL JOURNAL

MANUSCRIPT ADDRESS: Dr. R.A.C. Stewart
Massey University
Palmerston North, New Zealand

TYPE OF ARTICLES: Research articles, theoretical articles

MAJOR CONTENT AREAS: Almost all areas of psychology

TOPICS PREFERRED: Social, personality

INAPPROPRIATE TOPICS: Not given

NUMBER OF MANUSCRIPT COPIES: Not given	PAGE CHARGES:	Not given
REVIEW PERIOD: 2 months	STYLE REQUIREMENTS:	APA
PUBLICATION LAG TIME: 3-4 months	STYLE SHEET:	Yes
EARLY PUBLICATION OPTION: No	REVISED THESES:	Not given
ACCEPTANCE RATE: Not given	STUDENT PAPERS:	Not given
AUTHORSHIP RESTRICTIONS: Not given	REPRINT POLICY:	300

SUBSCRIPTION ADDRESS: Editorial Services, Ltd.
PO Box 6443
Wellington, New Zealand

ANNUAL SUBSCRIPTION RATE: $NZ 8 individual, $NZ 12 institutional

INDEXED/ABSTRACTED IN: PA, CCSBS

CIRCULATION: 1000   FREQUENCY: Not given

JOURNAL TITLE: SOCIAL BIOLOGY

MANUSCRIPT ADDRESS: Room 5450, Social Science Building
1180 Observatory Drive
Madison, WI   53706

TYPE OF ARTICLES: Manuscript

MAJOR CONTENT AREAS: Population, anthropology, medical genetics

TOPICS PREFERRED: Population

INAPPROPRIATE TOPICS: Not given

NUMBER OF MANUSCRIPT COPIES: Not given   PAGE CHARGES: Not given
REVIEW PERIOD: 4-6 monthsSTYLE REQUIREMENTS: Chicago Manuscript
PUBLICATION LAG TIME: 4-6 months   STYLE SHEET: Yes
EARLY PUBLICATION OPTION: No   REVISED THESES: Not given
ACCEPTANCE RATE: 40%   STUDENT PAPERS: Not given
AUTHORSHIP RESTRICTIONS: Not given   REPRINT POLICY: Not given

SUBSCRIPTION ADDRESS: Room 5450, Social Science Building
1180 Observatory Drive
Madison, WI   53706

ANNUAL SUBSCRIPTION RATE: $20 individual, Not given institutional
INDEXED/ABSTRACTED IN: PA, AA, CCSBS, DSHA, IBSS, WSA

CIRCULATION: 1800   FREQUENCY: Not given

JOURNAL TITLE: SOCIAL CASEWORK

MANUSCRIPT ADDRESS: 44 E 23rd Street
New York, NY   10010

TYPE OF ARTICLES: Case studies, theoretical articles, social
work issues, minority/ethnic groups, practice
and social work education
MAJOR CONTENT AREAS: Adolescence, alcoholism & drug abuse, counseling,
ethnic groups, family planning, mental health &
illness, philanthropy, rehabilitation, sexual
behavior, social change, social conflict
TOPICS PREFERRED: Not given

INAPPROPRIATE TOPICS: Minor research studies, student papers, case
reports with no theoretical concepts

NUMBER OF MANUSCRIPT COPIES: 3   PAGE CHARGES: No
REVIEW PERIOD: 3-6 mos. STYLE REQUIREMENTS: Chicago Manuscript
PUBLICATION LAG TIME: Not given   STYLE SHEET: Yes
EARLY PUBLICATION OPTION: Yes   REVISED THESES: No
ACCEPTANCE RATE: 30%   STUDENT PAPERS: No
AUTHORSHIP RESTRICTIONS: No   REPRINT POLICY: None

SUBSCRIPTION ADDRESS: 44 E 23rd Street
New York, NY   10010

ANNUAL SUBSCRIPTION RATE: $12 individual, $18 institutional
INDEXED/ABSTRACTED IN: ASW, BRI, CC, HPG, HLI, LLBA, PA, SSCI, SSI, SA

CIRCULATION: 17,000   FREQUENCY: 10 times per year

JOURNAL TITLE: SOCIAL CHANGE IDEAS AND APPLICATIONS

MANUSCRIPT ADDRESS: Manuscript Editor
NTL Institute
PO Box 9155, Rosslyn Station
Arlington, VA 22209

TYPE OF ARTICLES: Research articles, theoretical articles, review articles, case studies, commentaries, unsolicited book reviews

MAJOR CONTENT AREAS: Social change

TOPICS PREFERRED: Not given

INAPPROPRIATE TOPICS: Not given

NUMBER OF MANUSCRIPT COPIES:	2	PAGE CHARGES:	Not given
REVIEW PERIOD:	Not given	STYLE REQUIREMENTS:	APA
PUBLICATION LAG TIME:	2 months	STYLE SHEET:	Yes
EARLY PUBLICATION OPTION:	No	REVISED THESES:	Not given
ACCEPTANCE RATE:	Not given	STUDENT PAPERS:	Not given
AUTHORSHIP RESTRICTIONS:	No	REPRINT POLICY:	10 journals

SUBSCRIPTION ADDRESS: Subscription Administrator
NTL Institute
PO Box 9155 Rosslyn Station
Arlington, VA 22209

ANNUAL SUBSCRIPTION RATE: $5 individual, $5 institutional
INDEXED/ABSTRACTED IN: Not given

CIRCULATION: 2000   FREQUENCY: Quarterly

JOURNAL TITLE: SOCIAL FORCES

MANUSCRIPT ADDRESS: Professor Everett K. Wilson, Editor
168 Hamilton Hall 070A
University of North Carolina
Chapel Hill, NC 27514

TYPE OF ARTICLES: Research articles, theoretical articles

MAJOR CONTENT AREAS: Sociology

TOPICS PREFERRED: Not given

INAPPROPRIATE TOPICS: Not given

NUMBER OF MANUSCRIPT COPIES:	3	PAGE CHARGES:	No
REVIEW PERIOD:	52 days	STYLE REQUIREMENTS:	ASA
PUBLICATION LAG TIME:	1 year	STYLE SHEET:	Yes
EARLY PUBLICATION OPTION:	No	REVISED THESES:	No
ACCEPTANCE RATE:	12-14%	STUDENT PAPERS:	No
AUTHORSHIP RESTRICTIONS:	No	REPRINT POLICY:	1 journal

SUBSCRIPTION ADDRESS: University of North Carolina Press
PO Box 2288
Chapel Hill, NC 27514

ANNUAL SUBSCRIPTION RATE: $10 individual, $12 institutional
INDEXED/ABSTRACTED IN: SA, PA, AA

CIRCULATION: 5000   FREQUENCY: Quarterly

JOURNAL TITLE: SOCIAL POLICY

MANUSCRIPT ADDRESS: Suite 500
184 Fifth Avenue
New York, NY 10010

TYPE OF ARTICLES: Research articles, theoretical articles,
commentaries, case studies, review articles,
unsolicited book reviews

MAJOR CONTENT AREAS: Aging and aged, mass communication, ecology,
general sociology, health and illness, indus-
trial sociology, medical sociology, political
sociology, social issues, urban sociology

TOPICS PREFERRED: Not given

INAPPROPRIATE TOPICS: Not given

NUMBER OF MANUSCRIPT COPIES: 2	PAGE CHARGES: No	
REVIEW PERIOD: 2 weeks	STYLE REQUIREMENTS: Chicago Manuscript	
PUBLICATION LAG TIME: 4-18 months	STYLE SHEET: Yes	
EARLY PUBLICATION OPTION: No	REVISED THESES: No	
ACCEPTANCE RATE: 35%	STUDENT PAPERS: No	
AUTHORSHIP RESTRICTIONS: No	REPRINT POLICY: 4 journals	

SUBSCRIPTION ADDRESS: Suite 500
184 Fifth Avenue
New York, NY 10010

ANNUAL SUBSCRIPTION RATE: $10 individual, $15 institutional
INDEXED/ABSTRACTED IN: SSI, MSRS, ABC:PSG,CC:BSES, SSCI

CIRCULATION: 10,000   FREQUENCY: 5 times per year

JOURNAL TITLE: SOCIAL PROBLEMS

MANUSCRIPT ADDRESS: Dr. Arlene Daniels, Editor
Sociology Department
Northwestern University
Evanston, IL 60201

TYPE OF ARTICLES: Research articles, theoretical articles, case
studies

MAJOR CONTENT AREAS: Not given

TOPICS PREFERRED: Micro analyses of social problems and macro
analyses of the political economy

INAPPROPRIATE TOPICS: Technical, methodological manuscripts

NUMBER OF MANUSCRIPT COPIES: 3	PAGE CHARGES: No	
REVIEW PERIOD: 12 weeks	STYLE REQUIREMENTS: ASA	
PUBLICATION LAG TIME: 3-9 months	STYLE SHEET: Yes	
EARLY PUBLICATION OPTION: No	REVISED THESES: Acceptable	
ACCEPTANCE RATE: 5-10%	STUDENT PAPERS: No	
AUTHORSHIP RESTRICTIONS: No	REPRINT POLICY: 5 journals	

SUBSCRIPTION ADDRESS: Society for the Study of Social Problems
114 Rockwell Hall
State University College at Buffalo
1300 Elmwood Avenue, Buffalo, NY 14222

ANNUAL SUBSCRIPTION RATE: $15 individual, $25 institutional
INDEXED/ABSTRACTED IN: SA, PA, ASW, APC, SEA, CMHR, DW

CIRCULATION: 4500   FREQUENCY: 5 times per year

JOURNAL TITLE: SOCIAL RESEARCH

MANUSCRIPT ADDRESS: New School for Social Research
65 Fifth Avenue, Room 341
New York, NY 10003

TYPE OF ARTICLES: Theoretical articles, research articles

MAJOR CONTENT AREAS: Administrative behavior, delinquency & crime,
family formation, general sociology, health &
illness, marriage & divorce, peace, sex roles,
social ideology, values, suicide

TOPICS PREFERRED: Not given

INAPPROPRIATE TOPICS: Experimental and empirical studies

NUMBER OF MANUSCRIPT COPIES: 2   PAGE CHARGES: No
REVIEW PERIOD: 6 weeks   STYLE REQUIREMENTS: Not given
PUBLICATION LAG TIME: 6-9 months   STYLE SHEET: Yes
EARLY PUBLICATION OPTION: Not given   REVISED THESES: No
ACCEPTANCE RATE: 5%   STUDENT PAPERS: No
AUTHORSHIP RESTRICTIONS: No   REPRINT POLICY: 50

SUBSCRIPTION ADDRESS: New School for Social Research
65 Fifth Avenue, Room 341
New York, NY 10003

ANNUAL SUBSCRIPTION RATE: $10 individual, $12 institutional
INDEXED/ABSTRACTED IN: UM, KRC, JA

CIRCULATION: 4000   FREQUENCY: Quarterly

JOURNAL TITLE: SOCIAL SCIENCE

MANUSCRIPT ADDRESS: Panos D. Bardis, Editor
University of Toledo
Toledo, OH 43606

TYPE OF ARTICLES: Research articles, theoretical articles, commentaries, case studies, review articles

MAJOR CONTENT AREAS: Not given

TOPICS PREFERRED: Not given

INAPPROPRIATE TOPICS: Not given

NUMBER OF MANUSCRIPT COPIES: 1   PAGE CHARGES: No
REVIEW PERIOD: 12 days   STYLE REQUIREMENTS: ASA
PUBLICATION LAG TIME: 6 months   STYLE SHEET: Yes
EARLY PUBLICATION OPTION: No   REVISED THESES: Acceptable
ACCEPTANCE RATE: 25%   STUDENT PAPERS: Yes
AUTHORSHIP RESTRICTIONS: No   REPRINT POLICY: 6 journals

SUBSCRIPTION ADDRESS: 1719 Ames
Winfield, KS 67156

ANNUAL SUBSCRIPTION RATE: $3 individual, $3 institutional
INDEXED/ABSTRACTED IN: HA, IPSA, SA

CIRCULATION: 8500   FREQUENCY: Quarterly

JOURNAL TITLE: THE SOCIAL SCIENCE JOURNAL

MANUSCRIPT ADDRESS: Social Science Building
Colorado State University
Fort Collins, CO 80523

TYPE OF ARTICLES: Research articles, theoretical articles,
case studies, commentaries, review articles

MAJOR CONTENT AREAS: Multidisciplinary social sciences

TOPICS PREFERRED: All social sciences

INAPPROPRIATE TOPICS: Unsolicited manuscripts, unsolicited book reviews

NUMBER OF MANUSCRIPT COPIES:	3	PAGE CHARGES:	No
REVIEW PERIOD:	3 months	STYLE REQUIREMENTS:	Chicago Manuscript
PUBLICATION LAG TIME:	6-12 months	STYLE SHEET:	Yes
EARLY PUBLICATION OPTION:	No	REVISED THESES:	Acceptable
ACCEPTANCE RATE:	20%	STUDENT PAPERS:	Yes
AUTHORSHIP RESTRICTIONS:	Yes	REPRINT POLICY:	None

SUBSCRIPTION ADDRESS: Social Science Building
Colorado State University
Fort Collins, CO 80523

ANNUAL SUBSCRIPTION RATE: $9 individual, $9 institutional
INDEXED/ABSTRACTED IN: Not given

CIRCULATION: 1600   FREQUENCY: Tri-yearly

JOURNAL TITLE: SOCIAL SCIENCE QUARTERLY

MANUSCRIPT ADDRESS: Professor Charles M. Bonjean, Editor
University of Texas at Austin
Austin, TX 78712

TYPE OF ARTICLES: Research articles, theoretical articles

MAJOR CONTENT AREAS: Bureaucracy, collective behavior, deviant
behavior, ethnic groups, migration, organizations,
political sociology, population, race relations,
sex roles, social change, social issues
TOPICS PREFERRED: Public policy, empirical research

INAPPROPRIATE TOPICS: Not given

NUMBER OF MANUSCRIPT COPIES:	4	PAGE CHARGES:	No
REVIEW PERIOD:	6 1/2 wks	STYLE REQUIREMENTS:	ASA
PUBLICATION LAG TIME:	6 months	STYLE SHEET:	Yes
EARLY PUBLICATION OPTION:	No	REVISED THESES:	Not given
ACCEPTANCE RATE:	10%	STUDENT PAPERS:	No
AUTHORSHIP RESTRICTIONS:	No	REPRINT POLICY:	None

SUBSCRIPTION ADDRESS: Journals Department
University of Texas Press
University of Texas at Austin,Box 7819
Austin, TX 78712
ANNUAL SUBSCRIPTION RATE: $12 individual, $15 institutional
INDEXED/ABSTRACTED IN: SSI, SA, ABC PS, PAIS, II, HA, IEJ

CIRCULATION: 3000   FREQUENCY: Quarterly

JOURNAL TITLE: SOCIAL SCIENCE RESEARCH

MANUSCRIPT ADDRESS: Department of Sociology
University of Massachusetts
Amherst, MA 01002

TYPE OF ARTICLES: Research articles, theoretical articles,
review articles

MAJOR CONTENT AREAS: Research methods and techniques

TOPICS PREFERRED: Applications of quantitative techniques to
substantive problems

INAPPROPRIATE TOPICS: Statistical methods

NUMBER OF MANUSCRIPT COPIES: 3	PAGE CHARGES: No
REVIEW PERIOD: 3 months	STYLE REQUIREMENTS: ASA
PUBLICATION LAG TIME: 12 months	STYLE SHEET: Yes
EARLY PUBLICATION OPTION: No	REVISED THESES: Acceptable
ACCEPTANCE RATE: 10-15%	STUDENT PAPERS: No
AUTHORSHIP RESTRICTIONS: No	REPRINT POLICY: 25

SUBSCRIPTION ADDRESS: Academic Press, Inc.
111 Fifth Avenue
New York, NY 10003

ANNUAL SUBSCRIPTION RATE: $18 individual, $36 institutional
INDEXED/ABSTRACTED IN: Not given

CIRCULATION: 900   FREQUENCY: Quarterly

JOURNAL TITLE: THE SOCIAL SERVICE REVIEW

MANUSCRIPT ADDRESS: 969 E 60th Street
Chicago, IL 60637

TYPE OF ARTICLES: Research articles, theoretical articles, review
articles, commentaries, case studies, unsolicited
book reviews
MAJOR CONTENT AREAS: Aging and aged, community development, deviant
behavior, human development, mental health &
illness, organizations, social planning, poverty,
inequality,and policy, social institutions
TOPICS PREFERRED: Social treatment and welfare

INAPPROPRIATE TOPICS: Not given

NUMBER OF MANUSCRIPT COPIES: 3	PAGE CHARGES: No
REVIEW PERIOD: 2-3 mos.	STYLE REQUIREMENTS: Chicago Manuscript
PUBLICATION LAG TIME: 6 months	STYLE SHEET: Yes
EARLY PUBLICATION OPTION: No	REVISED THESES: Yes
ACCEPTANCE RATE: 20%	STUDENT PAPERS: No
AUTHORSHIP RESTRICTIONS: No	REPRINT POLICY: 25

SUBSCRIPTION ADDRESS: University of Chicago Press
5801 Ellis Avenue
Chicago, IL 60637

ANNUAL SUBSCRIPTION RATE: $12 individual, $16 institutional
INDEXED/ABSTRACTED IN: ASW, SA

CIRCULATION: 6000   FREQUENCY: Quarterly

JOURNAL TITLE: SOCIAL STUDIES : IRISH JOURNAL OF SOCIOLOGY

MANUSCRIPT ADDRESS: Liam Ryan, Editor
St. Patrick's College, Maynooth
Co. Kildare, Ireland

TYPE OF ARTICLES: Not given

MAJOR CONTENT AREAS: Not given

TOPICS PREFERRED: Sociological analysis

INAPPROPRIATE TOPICS: Not given

NUMBER OF MANUSCRIPT COPIES: Not given	PAGE CHARGES:	Not given
REVIEW PERIOD: 1-3 mos.	STYLE REQUIREMENTS:	Not given
PUBLICATION LAG TIME: 2-6 months	STYLE SHEET:	Not given
EARLY PUBLICATION OPTION: Not given	REVISED THESES:	Not given
ACCEPTANCE RATE: 60%	STUDENT PAPERS:	Not given
AUTHORSHIP RESTRICTIONS: Not given	REPRINT POLICY:	12

SUBSCRIPTION ADDRESS: Liam Ryan, Editor
St. Patrick's College, Maynooth
Co. Kildare, Ireland

ANNUAL SUBSCRIPTION RATE: $9 individual, $9 institutional
INDEXED/ABSTRACTED IN: Not given

CIRCULATION: 3000   FREQUENCY: Bimonthly

JOURNAL TITLE: SOCIAL THEORY AND PRACTICE

MANUSCRIPT ADDRESS: Department of Philosophy
Florida State University
Tallahassee, FL 32306

TYPE OF ARTICLES: Theoretical articles, commentaries, review
articles, unsolicited book reviews

MAJOR CONTENT AREAS: Economy and society, political sociology, social
change, social conflict, social ideology, social
issues, social movements, social theory, values

TOPICS PREFERRED: Social and political philosophy

INAPPROPRIATE TOPICS: Not given

NUMBER OF MANUSCRIPT COPIES: 2	PAGE CHARGES:	No
REVIEW PERIOD: 1 month	STYLE REQUIREMENTS:	Chicago Manuscript
PUBLICATION LAG TIME: 2-4 months	STYLE SHEET:	No
EARLY PUBLICATION OPTION: No	REVISED THESES:	No
ACCEPTANCE RATE: 25%	STUDENT PAPERS:	No
AUTHORSHIP RESTRICTIONS: No	REPRINT POLICY:	None

SUBSCRIPTION ADDRESS: Department of Philosophy
Florida State University
Tallahassee, FL 32306

ANNUAL SUBSCRIPTION RATE: $10 individual, $21 institutional
INDEXED/ABSTRACTED IN: PI, SA, CIJE, ACP, ABC PS, RBP, SSCI, LLBA,
SSI
CIRCULATION: 650   FREQUENCY: Semiannually

JOURNAL TITLE: SOCIAL WORK

MANUSCRIPT ADDRESS: National Association of Social Workers
2 Park Avenue
New York, NY 10016

TYPE OF ARTICLES: Theoretical articles, commentaries, research
articles, case studies, review articles,
unsolicited book reviews

MAJOR CONTENT AREAS: Alcoholism & drug abuse, community development,
ethnic groups, marriage & divorce, social plann-
ing, race relations, sex roles, social interaction,
social movements, social theory, suicide

TOPICS PREFERRED: Social work practice, evaluate new techniques and
research, social problems, social work profession

INAPPROPRIATE TOPICS: Not given

NUMBER OF MANUSCRIPT COPIES: 3	PAGE CHARGES:	No
REVIEW PERIOD: 3 months	STYLE REQUIREMENTS:	Chicago Manuscript
PUBLICATION LAG TIME: 9 months	STYLE SHEET:	Yes
EARLY PUBLICATION OPTION: Yes	REVISED THESES:	No
ACCEPTANCE RATE: 15%	STUDENT PAPERS:	No
AUTHORSHIP RESTRICTIONS: No	REPRINT POLICY:	5 journals

SUBSCRIPTION ADDRESS: National Association of Social Workers
Publications Sales, 49 Sheridan Avenue
Albany, NY 12210

ANNUAL SUBSCRIPTION RATE: $20 individual, $20 institutional
INDEXED/ABSTRACTED IN: PA, SA, DSHA, CC, RL, SSI, ASW, ACP, CIJE

CIRCULATION: 75,200   FREQUENCY: Bimonthly

JOURNAL TITLE: SOCIETY FOR APPLIED ANTHROPOLOGY MONOGRAPH

MANUSCRIPT ADDRESS: Hyman Organization
Dept. of Soc/Anthro, West Virginia University
Morgantown, WV 26505

TYPE OF ARTICLES: Research articles, theoretical articles,
commentaries, case studies

MAJOR CONTENT AREAS: Applied social science

TOPICS PREFERRED: Applied social science

INAPPROPRIATE TOPICS: Programmatic statements, personal case histories
of research

NUMBER OF MANUSCRIPT COPIES: 4	PAGE CHARGES:	No
REVIEW PERIOD: 2-3 months	STYLE REQUIREMENTS:	AA
PUBLICATION LAG TIME: 1 year	STYLE SHEET:	Yes
EARLY PUBLICATION OPTION: Not given	REVISED THESES:	No
ACCEPTANCE RATE: 15%	STUDENT PAPERS:	No
AUTHORSHIP RESTRICTIONS: No	REPRINT POLICY:	Not given

SUBSCRIPTION ADDRESS: 1703 New Hampshire Avenue, NW
Washington, DC 20009

ANNUAL SUBSCRIPTION RATE: $17 individual, $25 institutional
INDEXED/ABSTRACTED IN: Not given

CIRCULATION: 4000   FREQUENCY: Quarterly

JOURNAL TITLE: SOCIETY MAGAZINE

MANUSCRIPT ADDRESS: Rutgers University
New Brunswick, NJ 08903

TYPE OF ARTICLES: Research articles, case studies, commentaries,
theoretical articles, unsolicited book reviews,
review articles
MAJOR CONTENT AREAS: Not given

TOPICS PREFERRED: Social science

INAPPROPRIATE TOPICS: Not given

NUMBER OF MANUSCRIPT COPIES: 3	PAGE CHARGES: Not given	
REVIEW PERIOD: 1-3 mos.	STYLE REQUIREMENTS: Chicago Manuscript	
PUBLICATION LAG TIME: 1-3 months	STYLE SHEET: Yes	
EARLY PUBLICATION OPTION: No	REVISED THESES: No	
ACCEPTANCE RATE: 30%	STUDENT PAPERS: No	
AUTHORSHIP RESTRICTIONS: No	REPRINT POLICY: 1 journal	

SUBSCRIPTION ADDRESS: Box A
Rutgers University
New Brunswick, NJ 08903

ANNUAL SUBSCRIPTION RATE: $15 individual, $18 institutional
INDEXED/ABSTRACTED IN: RGPL, CC, BSMS, MSRS, BRISSP, USPSD

CIRCULATION: 30,000   FREQUENCY: Bimonthly

JOURNAL TITLE: SOCIOLOGIA NEERLANDICA

MANUSCRIPT ADDRESS: Mauritsweg 26 a
Rotterdam 3002
Netherlands

TYPE OF ARTICLES: Research articles, theoretical articles, review
articles

MAJOR CONTENT AREAS: Anthropology, criminology, educational
sociology, industrial sociology, law, medical
sociology, migration, religion, rural sociology,
sex roles, sexual behavior, social theory
TOPICS PREFERRED: Not given

INAPPROPRIATE TOPICS: Not given

NUMBER OF MANUSCRIPT COPIES: 1	PAGE CHARGES: No	
REVIEW PERIOD: Not given	STYLE REQUIREMENTS: Not given	
PUBLICATION LAG TIME: 4 months	STYLE SHEET: Yes	
EARLY PUBLICATION OPTION: No	REVISED THESES: Yes	
ACCEPTANCE RATE: Not given	STUDENT PAPERS: No	
AUTHORSHIP RESTRICTIONS: No	REPRINT POLICY: 50	

SUBSCRIPTION ADDRESS: Elsevier Scientific Publishing Company
PO Box 211
Amsterdam, Netherlands

ANNUAL SUBSCRIPTION RATE: Not given - individual, $20.40 institutional
INDEXED/ABSTRACTED IN: Not given

CIRCULATION: 3000   FREQUENCY: Semiannually

JOURNAL TITLE: SOCIOLOGICAL ANALYSIS

MANUSCRIPT ADDRESS: Dr. Carroll J. Bourg
Department of Sociology
Fisk University
Nashville, TN 37203

TYPE OF ARTICLES: Research articles, theoretical articles,
review articles, case studies

MAJOR CONTENT AREAS: Religion

TOPICS PREFERRED: Religion

INAPPROPRIATE TOPICS: Not given

NUMBER OF MANUSCRIPT COPIES:	3	PAGE CHARGES:	No
REVIEW PERIOD:	6-8 weeks	STYLE REQUIREMENTS:	ASA
PUBLICATION LAG TIME:	8-14 months	STYLE SHEET:	Yes
EARLY PUBLICATION OPTION:	Yes	REVISED THESES:	Yes
ACCEPTANCE RATE:	18%	STUDENT PAPERS:	No
AUTHORSHIP RESTRICTIONS:	No	REPRINT POLICY:	10

SUBSCRIPTION ADDRESS: Dr. Robert McNamara
Department of Sociology
Loyola University
Chicago, IL

ANNUAL SUBSCRIPTION RATE: $15 individual, $15 institutional
INDEXED/ABSTRACTED IN: SA, LLA, IRPL, SSCI, CC/BSES

JOURNAL TITLE: SOCIOLOGICAL FOCUS

MANUSCRIPT ADDRESS: Department of Sociology
University of Akron
Akron, OH 44325

TYPE OF ARTICLES: Research articles, theoretical articles

MAJOR CONTENT AREAS: Demography, ecology, ethnic groups, law,
minorities, modernization, political sociology,
race relations, religion, social institutions,
social issues, social policy, stratification

TOPICS PREFERRED: Urban sociology and social policy analysis

INAPPROPRIATE TOPICS: Not given

NUMBER OF MANUSCRIPT COPIES:	3	PAGE CHARGES:	No
REVIEW PERIOD:	3 months	STYLE REQUIREMENTS:	ASA
PUBLICATION LAG TIME:	4-6 months	STYLE SHEET:	No
EARLY PUBLICATION OPTION:	No	REVISED THESES:	Acceptable
ACCEPTANCE RATE:	20%	STUDENT PAPERS:	Yes
AUTHORSHIP RESTRICTIONS:	No	REPRINT POLICY:	None

SUBSCRIPTION ADDRESS: Subscriptions Department
Department of Sociology
University of Akron
Akron, OH 44325

ANNUAL SUBSCRIPTION RATE: $10 individual, $15 institutional
INDEXED/ABSTRACTED IN: Not given

CIRCULATION: 1000   FREQUENCY: Quarterly

JOURNAL TITLE: SOCIOLOGICAL INQUIRY

MANUSCRIPT ADDRESS: Dr. Harry M. Johnson
326 Lincoln Hall
Urbana, IL 61801

TYPE OF ARTICLES: Research articles, theoretical articles,
commentaries, case studies

MAJOR CONTENT AREAS: Not given

TOPICS PREFERRED: Not given

INAPPROPRIATE TOPICS: Not given

NUMBER OF MANUSCRIPT COPIES: 3	PAGE CHARGES: No	
REVIEW PERIOD: 3-4 mos.	STYLE REQUIREMENTS: ASA	
PUBLICATION LAG TIME: 3-6 months	STYLE SHEET: Yes	
EARLY PUBLICATION OPTION: Not given	REVISED THESES: Yes	
ACCEPTANCE RATE: 5%	STUDENT PAPERS: Yes	
AUTHORSHIP RESTRICTIONS: No	REPRINT POLICY: None	

SUBSCRIPTION ADDRESS: Dr. Harry M. Johnson
326 Lincoln Hall
Urbana, IL 61801

ANNUAL SUBSCRIPTION RATE: $9 individual, $13 institutional
INDEXED/ABSTRACTED IN: Not given

CIRCULATION: 3000   FREQUENCY: Tri-yearly

JOURNAL TITLE: SOCIOLOGICAL METHODS & RESEARCH

MANUSCRIPT ADDRESS: Edgar F. Borgatta
Queen's College Department of Sociology
City University of New York
Flushing, NY 11367

TYPE OF ARTICLES: Research articles, theoretical articles, review
articles, case studies, commentaries

MAJOR CONTENT AREAS: General sociology, industrial sociology, political
sociology, rural sociology, social institutions,
social interaction, social policy, social structure,
social theory, society & institutions, sociometry

TOPICS PREFERRED: Not given

INAPPROPRIATE TOPICS: Not given

NUMBER OF MANUSCRIPT COPIES: 3	PAGE CHARGES: No	
REVIEW PERIOD: Not given	STYLE REQUIREMENTS: Not given	
PUBLICATION LAG TIME: Not given	STYLE SHEET: Yes	
EARLY PUBLICATION OPTION: No	REVISED THESES: Not given	
ACCEPTANCE RATE: Not given	STUDENT PAPERS: No	
AUTHORSHIP RESTRICTIONS: No	REPRINT POLICY: 24	

SUBSCRIPTION ADDRESS: Sage Publications
275 S Beverly Drive
Beverly Hills, CA 90212

ANNUAL SUBSCRIPTION RATE: $16.80 individual, $26 institutional
INDEXED/ABSTRACTED IN: SA, HRA, SEA, SUSA, SSCI, PAIS, CC

CIRCULATION: Not given   FREQUENCY: Quarterly

JOURNAL TITLE: SOCIOLOGICAL PRACTICE

MANUSCRIPT ADDRESS: Donald E. Gelfand
School of Social Work/Community Planning
525 W Redwood Street
Baltimore, MD 21201

TYPE OF ARTICLES: Research articles, theoretical articles, review articles, case studies, commentaries, unsolicited book reviews

MAJOR CONTENT AREAS: Medical sociology, mental health & illness

TOPICS PREFERRED: Sociological perspectives

INAPPROPRIATE TOPICS: Not given

NUMBER OF MANUSCRIPT COPIES: 3   PAGE CHARGES: Not given
REVIEW PERIOD: 12 weeks   STYLE REQUIREMENTS: ASA
PUBLICATION LAG TIME: Not given   STYLE SHEET: Yes
EARLY PUBLICATION OPTION: Yes   REVISED THESES: Yes
ACCEPTANCE RATE: Not given   STUDENT PAPERS: No
AUTHORSHIP RESTRICTIONS: No   REPRINT POLICY: 1 journal

SUBSCRIPTION ADDRESS: Human Sciences Press
72 Fifth Avenue
New York, NY 10011

ANNUAL SUBSCRIPTION RATE: $7.95 individual, $16 institutional
INDEXED/ABSTRACTED IN: HRA, SSCI, CC/SBS, SA

CIRCULATION: 500   FREQUENCY: Semiannually

JOURNAL TITLE: SOCIOLOGICAL QUARTERLY

MANUSCRIPT ADDRESS: Professor Jerry Gaston
Department of Sociology
Southern Illinois University
Carbondale, IL 62901

TYPE OF ARTICLES: Research articles, theoretical articles, review articles

MAJOR CONTENT AREAS: Not given

TOPICS PREFERRED: Not given

INAPPROPRIATE TOPICS: Not given

NUMBER OF MANUSCRIPT COPIES: 3   PAGE CHARGES: Yes
REVIEW PERIOD: 10 weeks   STYLE REQUIREMENTS: ASA
PUBLICATION LAG TIME: 10 months   STYLE SHEET: Yes
EARLY PUBLICATION OPTION: No   REVISED THESES: Acceptable
ACCEPTANCE RATE: 15%   STUDENT PAPERS: Yes
AUTHORSHIP RESTRICTIONS: No   REPRINT POLICY: 1 journal

SUBSCRIPTION ADDRESS: 1004 Elm Street
University of Missouri
Columbia, MO 65201

ANNUAL SUBSCRIPTION RATE: $12 individual, $15 institutional
INDEXED/ABSTRACTED IN: ASW, AHL, HA, SSI, PA, SSCI, SA

CIRCULATION: 2550   FREQUENCY: Quarterly

JOURNAL TITLE: SOCIOLOGICAL REVIEW

MANUSCRIPT ADDRESS: University of Keele
Keele Staffordshire ST5 5BG
England

TYPE OF ARTICLES: Research articles, theoretical articles, case
studies, commentaries, unsolicited book reviews,
review articles

MAJOR CONTENT AREAS: Anthropology, criminology, educational sociology,
law, mass media, organizations, political sociology,
rural sociology, sociology of science, sex roles,
social policy, social theory, urban sociology

TOPICS PREFERRED: Not given

INAPPROPRIATE TOPICS: Not given

NUMBER OF MANUSCRIPT COPIES:	2	PAGE CHARGES:	No
REVIEW PERIOD:	1-2 mos.	STYLE REQUIREMENTS:	Not given
PUBLICATION LAG TIME:	6 months	STYLE SHEET:	Yes
EARLY PUBLICATION OPTION:	No	REVISED THESES:	Yes
ACCEPTANCE RATE:	10%	STUDENT PAPERS:	No
AUTHORSHIP RESTRICTIONS:	No	REPRINT POLICY:	20

SUBSCRIPTION ADDRESS: University of Keele
Keele Staffordshire ST5 5BG
England

ANNUAL SUBSCRIPTION RATE: $15 individual, $20 institutional
INDEXED/ABSTRACTED IN: BRI, BRISSP, CC, GA, HA, SA, SEA

CIRCULATION: 2000   FREQUENCY: Quarterly

JOURNAL TITLE: SOCIOLOGICAL SYMPOSIUM

MANUSCRIPT ADDRESS: James K. Skipper, Jr. , Editor
Department of Sociology
Virginia Polytechnic Institute & State University
Blacksburg, VA 24061

TYPE OF ARTICLES: Research articles, theoretical articles, review
articles

MAJOR CONTENT AREAS: Behavioral sciences

TOPICS PREFERRED: Not given

INAPPROPRIATE TOPICS: Not given

NUMBER OF MANUSCRIPT COPIES:	3	PAGE CHARGES:	No
REVIEW PERIOD:	5-8 weeks	STYLE REQUIREMENTS:	ASA
PUBLICATION LAG TIME:	2-6 months	STYLE SHEET:	Yes
EARLY PUBLICATION OPTION:	No	REVISED THESES:	Acceptable
ACCEPTANCE RATE:	18%	STUDENT PAPERS:	No
AUTHORSHIP RESTRICTIONS:	No	REPRINT POLICY:	4 journals

SUBSCRIPTION ADDRESS: James K. Skipper, Jr. , Editor
Department of Sociology
Virginia Polytechnic Institute & State University
Blacksburg, VA 24061

ANNUAL SUBSCRIPTION RATE: $6 individual, $12 institutions
INDEXED/ABSTRACTED IN: SA, CC, BSMS, ASW

CIRCULATION: 1050   FREQUENCY: Quarterly

JOURNAL TITLE: SOCIOLOGIE ET SOCIETES

MANUSCRIPT ADDRESS: M. Jacques Dofny
Department of Sociology
University of Montréal, C.P. 6128 "A"
Montréal, Canada H3C 3J7

TYPE OF ARTICLES: Research articles, theoretical articles, commentaries

MAJOR CONTENT AREAS: Ethnic groups, health and illness, industrial sociology, labor force/labor relations, minorities, race relations, sociology of science, sex roles, social conflict, social structure

TOPICS PREFERRED: Not given

INAPPROPRIATE TOPICS: Not given

NUMBER OF MANUSCRIPT COPIES:	None	PAGE CHARGES: Yes
REVIEW PERIOD:	6 months	STYLE REQUIREMENTS: ASA
PUBLICATION LAG TIME:	6 months	STYLE SHEET: No
EARLY PUBLICATION OPTION:	Yes	REVISED THESES: No
ACCEPTANCE RATE:	Not given	STUDENT PAPERS: No
AUTHORSHIP RESTRICTIONS:	Yes	REPRINT POLICY: 50

SUBSCRIPTION ADDRESS: The University of Montréal Press
C.P. 6128 Succ. "A",
Montréal, Canada H3C 3J7

ANNUAL SUBSCRIPTION RATE: $10 individual, $10 institutional
INDEXED/ABSTRACTED IN: R/SA

CIRCULATION: 1500-2000   FREQUENCY: Semiannually

JOURNAL TITLE: SOCIOLOGY

MANUSCRIPT ADDRESS: The Editor
Department of Sociology and Social Administration
University of Durham, Elvet Riverside
Durham, England DH1 3JT

TYPE OF ARTICLES: Research articles, theoretical articles, review articles, case studies, commentaries, unsolicited book reviews

MAJOR CONTENT AREAS: Adolescence, bureaucracy, delinquency & crime, general sociology, industrial sociology, medical sociology, organizations, reference groups, religion, social change, social movements

TOPICS PREFERRED: Social stratification, sociology of education, industrial sociology

INAPPROPRIATE TOPICS: Psychoanalysis, social administration

NUMBER OF MANUSCRIPT COPIES:	2	PAGE CHARGES: No
REVIEW PERIOD:	2 months	STYLE REQUIREMENTS: Not given
PUBLICATION LAG TIME:	18 months	STYLE SHEET: Yes
EARLY PUBLICATION OPTION:	No	REVISED THESES: No
ACCEPTANCE RATE:	10%	STUDENT PAPERS: No
AUTHORSHIP RESTRICTIONS:	No	REPRINT POLICY: 25

SUBSCRIPTION ADDRESS: British Sociological Association
13 Endsleigh Street
London, England WI

ANNUAL SUBSCRIPTION RATE: $28 individual, $28 institutional
INDEXED/ABSTRACTED IN: Not given

CIRCULATION: 2000   FREQUENCY: Tri-yearly

JOURNAL TITLE: SOCIOLOGY AND SOCIAL RESEARCH : AN INTERNATIONAL
JOURNAL

MANUSCRIPT ADDRESS: The Managing Editor
University of Southern California
Los Angeles, CA 90007

TYPE OF ARTICLES: Research articles, research projects on
methodology

MAJOR CONTENT AREAS: Administrative behavior, bureaucracy, mass
communication, demography, ecology, ethnic groups,
family planning, health & illness, leadership,
marriage & divorce, sexual behavior

TOPICS PREFERRED: Not given

INAPPROPRIATE TOPICS: Essays, personal opinions

NUMBER OF MANUSCRIPT COPIES: 3
REVIEW PERIOD: 9-12 wks.
PUBLICATION LAG TIME: 3 months
EARLY PUBLICATION OPTION: Not given
ACCEPTANCE RATE: 12%
AUTHORSHIP RESTRICTIONS: No

PAGE CHARGES: No
STYLE REQUIREMENTS: ASA
STYLE SHEET: Yes
REVISED THESES: No
STUDENT PAPERS: Acceptable
REPRINT POLICY: None

SUBSCRIPTION ADDRESS: The Managing Editor
University of Southern California
Los Angeles, CA 90007

ANNUAL SUBSCRIPTION RATE: $13 individual, $18 institutional
INDEXED/ABSTRACTED IN: HA, IIP, SA, PA

CIRCULATION: 3000   FREQUENCY: Quarterly

JOURNAL TITLE: SOCIOLOGY OF EDUCATION

MANUSCRIPT ADDRESS: Department of Social Relations, Room 447
Johns Hopkins University
Baltimore, MD 21218

TYPE OF ARTICLES: Research articles, theoretical articles, review
articles, commentaries, case studies

MAJOR CONTENT AREAS: Educational sociology, human development,
socialization

TOPICS PREFERRED: Educational sociology

INAPPROPRIATE TOPICS: Case studies or non-research manuscripts

NUMBER OF MANUSCRIPT COPIES: 4
REVIEW PERIOD: 1-3 mos.
PUBLICATION LAG TIME: 3 months
EARLY PUBLICATION OPTION: No
ACCEPTANCE RATE: 10%
AUTHORSHIP RESTRICTIONS: No

PAGE CHARGES: No
STYLE REQUIREMENTS: ASA
STYLE SHEET: Yes
REVISED THESES: Acceptable
STUDENT PAPERS: No
REPRINT POLICY: None

SUBSCRIPTION ADDRESS: American Sociological Association
1722 N Street NW
Washington, DC 20036

ANNUAL SUBSCRIPTION RATE: $8 individual, $12 institutional
INDEXED/ABSTRACTED IN: Not given

CIRCULATION: 5000   FREQUENCY: Quarterly

JOURNAL TITLE: SOCIOLOGY OF WORK AND OCCUPATIONS: AN
INTERNATIONAL JOURNAL

MANUSCRIPT ADDRESS: Marie Haug
Department of Sociology
Case Western Reserve University
Cleveland, OH 44106

TYPE OF ARTICLES: Research articles, theoretical articles, review
articles, case studies, commentaries

MAJOR CONTENT AREAS: Occupations & careers, professions, sociology
of work

TOPICS PREFERRED: Not given

INAPPROPRIATE TOPICS: Not given

NUMBER OF MANUSCRIPT COPIES: 3	PAGE CHARGES:	No
REVIEW PERIOD: Not given	STYLE REQUIREMENTS:	Not given
PUBLICATION LAG TIME: Not given	STYLE SHEET:	Yes
EARLY PUBLICATION OPTION: No	REVISED THESES:	Not given
ACCEPTANCE RATE: Not given	STUDENT PAPERS:	No
AUTHORSHIP RESTRICTIONS: Not given	REPRINT POLICY:	24

SUBSCRIPTION ADDRESS: Sage Publications, Inc.
275 S Beverly Drive
Beverly Hills, CA 90212

ANNUAL SUBSCRIPTION RATE: $13.50 individual, $22.50 institutional
INDEXED/ABSTRACTED IN: Not given

CIRCULATION: Not given   FREQUENCY: Quarterly

JOURNAL TITLE: SOCIOMETRY

MANUSCRIPT ADDRESS: Howard Schuman, Editor
Department of Sociology
3012 LSA Building, University of Michigan
Ann Arbor, MI 48109

TYPE OF ARTICLES: Research articles, theoretical articles

MAJOR CONTENT AREAS: Reference groups, social interaction, socialization,
social psychology

TOPICS PREFERRED: Not given

INAPPROPRIATE TOPICS: Not given

NUMBER OF MANUSCRIPT COPIES: 4	PAGE CHARGES:	No
REVIEW PERIOD: 3 months	STYLE REQUIREMENTS:	ASA
PUBLICATION LAG TIME: 6-9 months	STYLE SHEET:	Yes
EARLY PUBLICATION OPTION: No	REVISED THESES:	No
ACCEPTANCE RATE: 10%	STUDENT PAPERS:	No
AUTHORSHIP RESTRICTIONS: No	REPRINT POLICY:	None

SUBSCRIPTION ADDRESS: American Sociological Association
1722 N Street, NW
Washington, DC 20036

ANNUAL SUBSCRIPTION RATE: $8 individual, $12 institutional
INDEXED/ABSTRACTED IN: Not given

CIRCULATION: 5000   FREQUENCY: Quarterly

JOURNAL TITLE: SOUNDINGS: AN INTERDISCIPLINARY JOURNAL

MANUSCRIPT ADDRESS: Vanderbilt University
Box 6309, Station B
Nashville, TN 37212

TYPE OF ARTICLES: Interdisciplinary essays concerned with values

MAJOR CONTENT AREAS: Death & dying, professions, religion, sex roles values

TOPICS PREFERRED: Not given

INAPPROPRIATE TOPICS: Not given

NUMBER OF MANUSCRIPT COPIES:	2	PAGE CHARGES:	No
REVIEW PERIOD:	2-3 mos.	STYLE REQUIREMENTS:	MLA
PUBLICATION LAG TIME:	6-9 months	STYLE SHEET:	Yes
EARLY PUBLICATION OPTION:	No	REVISED THESES:	No
ACCEPTANCE RATE:	10%	STUDENT PAPERS:	No
AUTHORSHIP RESTRICTIONS:	No	REPRINT POLICY:	50

SUBSCRIPTION ADDRESS: Vanderbilt University
Box 6309, Station B
Nashville, TN 37212

ANNUAL SUBSCRIPTION RATE: $10 individual, $13 institutional
INDEXED/ABSTRACTED IN: Not given

CIRCULATION: 1500 FREQUENCY: Quarterly

JOURNAL TITLE: SOUTH AFRICAN JOURNAL OF SOCIOLOGY

MANUSCRIPT ADDRESS: Pretoria University
Pretoria, Republic of South Africa

TYPE OF ARTICLES: Research articles, theoretical articles, case studies, commentaries, review articles, unsolicited book reviews
MAJOR CONTENT AREAS: Alcoholism & drug abuse, collective behavior, deviant behavior, ethnic groups, general sociology, mass media, race relations, social change, social conflict, social institutions, social issues
TOPICS PREFERRED: Race and ethnic relations, social change, social theory

INAPPROPRIATE TOPICS: Not given

NUMBER OF MANUSCRIPT COPIES:	1	PAGE CHARGES:	No
REVIEW PERIOD:	3 weeks	STYLE REQUIREMENTS:	ASA
PUBLICATION LAG TIME:	6 months	STYLE SHEET:	Yes
EARLY PUBLICATION OPTION:	No	REVISED THESES:	Yes
ACCEPTANCE RATE:	80%	STUDENT PAPERS:	No
AUTHORSHIP RESTRICTIONS:	No	REPRINT POLICY:	12

SUBSCRIPTION ADDRESS: Pretoria University
Pretoria, Republic of South Africa

ANNUAL SUBSCRIPTION RATE: $3 individual, $3 institutional
INDEXED/ABSTRACTED IN: SA

CIRCULATION: 500 FREQUENCY: Semiannually

JOURNAL TITLE: SOUTHEASTERN REVIEW

MANUSCRIPT ADDRESS: Department of Sociology
University of Virginia
Cabell Hall
Charlottesville, VA 22903

TYPE OF ARTICLES: Research articles, theoretical articles, review
articles, case studies, commentaries, unsolicited
book reviews

MAJOR CONTENT AREAS: Not given

TOPICS PREFERRED: Not given

INAPPROPRIATE TOPICS: Not given

NUMBER OF MANUSCRIPT COPIES:	2	PAGE CHARGES:	No
REVIEW PERIOD:	4 months	STYLE REQUIREMENTS:	ASA
PUBLICATION LAG TIME:	6-9 months	STYLE SHEET:	Yes
EARLY PUBLICATION OPTION:	Not given	REVISED THESES:	Yes
ACCEPTANCE RATE:	50%	STUDENT PAPERS:	Yes
AUTHORSHIP RESTRICTIONS:	No	REPRINT POLICY:	6

SUBSCRIPTION ADDRESS: Department of Sociology
University of Virginia
Cabell Hall
Charlottesville, VA 22903

ANNUAL SUBSCRIPTION RATE: $4 individual, $5 institutional

INDEXED/ABSTRACTED IN: SA

CIRCULATION: 200   FREQUENCY: Semiannually

JOURNAL TITLE: THE SOUTHERN SOCIOLOGIST

MANUSCRIPT ADDRESS: Dr. John A. Ballweg, Editor
College of Arts & Sciences
116 Williams Hall, VPI & State University
Blacksburg, VA 24061

TYPE OF ARTICLES: Research articles, case studies, commentaries

MAJOR CONTENT AREAS: Not given

TOPICS PREFERRED: Not given

INAPPROPRIATE TOPICS: Theoretical papers

NUMBER OF MANUSCRIPT COPIES:	3	PAGE CHARGES:	No
REVIEW PERIOD:	1-2 mos.	STYLE REQUIREMENTS:	ASA
PUBLICATION LAG TIME:	3-6 months	STYLE SHEET:	No
EARLY PUBLICATION OPTION:	No	REVISED THESES:	Yes
ACCEPTANCE RATE:	20%	STUDENT PAPERS:	No
AUTHORSHIP RESTRICTIONS:	No	REPRINT POLICY:	None

SUBSCRIPTION ADDRESS: 116 Williams Hall
VPI & State University
Blacksburg, VA 24061

ANNUAL SUBSCRIPTION RATE: $15 individual, $15 institutional

INDEXED/ABSTRACTED IN: Not given

CIRCULATION: 1700   FREQUENCY: Quarterly

JOURNAL TITLE: SOUTHERN SPEECH COMMUNICATION JOURNAL

MANUSCRIPT ADDRESS: Professor Ralph T. Eubanks, Editor
                       Faculty of Communication Arts
                       University of West Florida
                       Pensacola, FL 32504

TYPE OF ARTICLES: Research articles, theoretical articles, case
                     studies, commentaries

MAJOR CONTENT AREAS: Mass communication, mass media, theatre arts,
                        speech communication, speech pathology/ audiology,
                        oral interpretation, phonetics, speech science,
                        semantics, public relations

TOPICS PREFERRED: Rhetorical theory and criticism, mass communication,
                     interpersonal and small group communication, theatre
                     arts, oral interpretation

INAPPROPRIATE TOPICS: Popular culture, social ideology, social structure

NUMBER OF MANUSCRIPT COPIES:	3	PAGE CHARGES: No
REVIEW PERIOD:	8 weeks	STYLE REQUIREMENTS: MLA
PUBLICATION LAG TIME:	3-4 months	STYLE SHEET: Yes
EARLY PUBLICATION OPTION:	No	REVISED THESES: Yes
ACCEPTANCE RATE:	30%	STUDENT PAPERS: No
AUTHORSHIP RESTRICTIONS:	No	REPRINT POLICY: 2

SUBSCRIPTION ADDRESS: Professor G. Allan Yeomans
                         Department of Speech and Theatre
                         University of Tennessee
                         Knoxville, TN 37916

ANNUAL SUBSCRIPTION RATE: $10 individual, Not given - institutional
INDEXED/ABSTRACTED IN: HA, A:HL, (ERIC) CIJE

CIRCULATION: 2514   FREQUENCY: Quarterly

JOURNAL TITLE: SOVIET SOCIOLOGY

MANUSCRIPT ADDRESS: M.E. Sharpe, Inc.
                       901 N Broadway
                       White Plains, NY 10603

TYPE OF ARTICLES: Only soviet authors published in soviet sources
                     and receiving permission for foreign publication
                     from VAAP (Soviet Copyright Agency)

MAJOR CONTENT AREAS: Collective behavior, mass communication, ethnic
                        groups, migration, organizations, population, race
                        relations, religion, social change, stratification,
                        social theory

TOPICS PREFERRED: Soviet sociology

INAPPROPRIATE TOPICS: Not given

NUMBER OF MANUSCRIPT COPIES:	0	PAGE CHARGES: No
REVIEW PERIOD:	1 week	STYLE REQUIREMENTS: Chicago Manuscript
PUBLICATION LAG TIME:	Not given	STYLE SHEET: No
EARLY PUBLICATION OPTION:	No	REVISED THESES: No
ACCEPTANCE RATE:	Not given	STUDENT PAPERS: No
AUTHORSHIP RESTRICTIONS:	Yes	REPRINT POLICY: None

SUBSCRIPTION ADDRESS: M.E. Sharpe, Inc.
                         901 N Broadway
                         White Plains, NY 10603

ANNUAL SUBSCRIPTION RATE: $20 individual, $70 institutional
INDEXED/ABSTRACTED IN: HA

CIRCULATION: 300   FREQUENCY: Quarterly

JOURNAL TITLE: STUDIES IN COMPARATIVE INTERNATIONAL DEVELOPMENT

MANUSCRIPT ADDRESS: Rutgers University
New Brunswick, NJ 08903

TYPE OF ARTICLES: Research articles, theoretical articles, case
studies

MAJOR CONTENT AREAS: Bureaucracy, economy and society, family planning,
migration, social planning, poverty, inequality,
and policy, social issues, social mobility, social
movements, social policy, society and institutions
TOPICS PREFERRED: Problems of development in the Third World

INAPPROPRIATE TOPICS: Not given

NUMBER OF MANUSCRIPT COPIES:	2-3	PAGE CHARGES:	No
REVIEW PERIOD:	2 months	STYLE REQUIREMENTS:	Chicago Manuscript
PUBLICATION LAG TIME:	1 year	STYLE SHEET:	Yes
EARLY PUBLICATION OPTION:	Yes	REVISED THESES:	No
ACCEPTANCE RATE:	10%	STUDENT PAPERS:	No
AUTHORSHIP RESTRICTIONS:	No	REPRINT POLICY:	Not given

SUBSCRIPTION ADDRESS: Rutgers University
New Brunswick, NJ 08903

ANNUAL SUBSCRIPTION RATE: Not given
INDEXED/ABSTRACTED IN: Not given

CIRCULATION: 1500   FREQUENCY: Tri-yearly

JOURNAL TITLE: STUDIES IN FAMILY PLANNING

MANUSCRIPT ADDRESS: Population Council
One Dag Hammarskjold Plaza
New York, NY 10017

TYPE OF ARTICLES: Research articles, case studies, commentaries

MAJOR CONTENT AREAS: Administrative behavior, demography, family
formation, family planning, health and illness,
population

TOPICS PREFERRED: Not given

INAPPROPRIATE TOPICS: Not given

NUMBER OF MANUSCRIPT COPIES:	2	PAGE CHARGES:	No
REVIEW PERIOD:	6 weeks	STYLE REQUIREMENTS:	Not given
PUBLICATION LAG TIME:	6 months	STYLE SHEET:	Yes
EARLY PUBLICATION OPTION:	No	REVISED THESES:	No
ACCEPTANCE RATE:	50%	STUDENT PAPERS:	No
AUTHORSHIP RESTRICTIONS:	No	REPRINT POLICY:	20 journals

SUBSCRIPTION ADDRESS: Population Council
One Dag Hammarskjold Plaza
New York, NY 10017

ANNUAL SUBSCRIPTION RATE: No charge
INDEXED/ABSTRACTED IN: PI

CIRCULATION: 14,000   FREQUENCY: Monthly

JOURNAL TITLE: SUICIDE AND LIFE-THREATENING BEHAVIOR

MANUSCRIPT ADDRESS: Edwin S. Schneidman, Ph.D. , UCLA NPI
760 Westwood Plaza
Los Angeles, CA 90024

TYPE OF ARTICLES: Research articles, review articles, clinical
articles, theoretical articles

MAJOR CONTENT AREAS: All aspects of suicide and life-threatening
behavior

TOPICS PREFERRED: Suicide, death, life-threatening behaviors

INAPPROPRIATE TOPICS: Anecdotes about suicide, suicide prevention,
suicide prevention centers

NUMBER OF MANUSCRIPT COPIES: Not given	PAGE CHARGES: Not given	
REVIEW PERIOD: 1 month	STYLE REQUIREMENTS: APA	
PUBLICATION LAG TIME: 6-9 months	STYLE SHEET: Yes	
EARLY PUBLICATION OPTION: No	REVISED THESES: Not given	
ACCEPTANCE RATE: 50%	STUDENT PAPERS: Not given	
AUTHORSHIP RESTRICTIONS: Not given	REPRINT POLICY: Not given	

SUBSCRIPTION ADDRESS: Betsy S. Comstock, M.D., Dept. of Psychiatry
Baylor College of Medicine, 1200 Moursund Avenue
Houston, TX 72025

ANNUAL SUBSCRIPTION RATE: $7 individual, $20 institutional
INDEXED/ABSTRACTED IN: PA, CCSBS

CIRCULATION: 1000   FREQUENCY: Not given

JOURNAL TITLE: TEACHING SOCIOLOGY

MANUSCRIPT ADDRESS: Richard J. Gelles
Department of Sociology
University of Rhode Island
Kingston, RI 02881

TYPE OF ARTICLES: Research articles, theoretical articles,
review articles, case studies, commentaries

MAJOR CONTENT AREAS: Educational sociology, general sociology

TOPICS PREFERRED: Not given

INAPPROPRIATE TOPICS: Not given

NUMBER OF MANUSCRIPT COPIES: 3	PAGE CHARGES: No	
REVIEW PERIOD: Not given	STYLE REQUIREMENTS: Not given	
PUBLICATION LAG TIME: Not given	STYLE SHEET: Yes	
EARLY PUBLICATION OPTION: No	REVISED THESES: Not given	
ACCEPTANCE RATE: Not given	STUDENT PAPERS: No	
AUTHORSHIP RESTRICTIONS: No	REPRINT POLICY: 24	

SUBSCRIPTION ADDRESS: Sage Publications, Inc.
275 S Beverly Drive
Beverly Hills, CA 90212

ANNUAL SUBSCRIPTION RATE: $13.50 individual, $22.50 institutional
INDEXED/ABSTRACTED IN: SA, CIJE, CC, SSCI

CIRCULATION: Not given   FREQUENCY: Quarterly

JOURNAL TITLE: TECHNOLOGY AND CULTURE

MANUSCRIPT ADDRESS: Dr. M. Kranzberg, Editor
Department of Social Sciences
Georgia Tech
Atlanta, GA 30332

TYPE OF ARTICLES: Research articles, case studies, review articles,
theoretical articles, commentaries, unsolicited
book reviews, exhibit reviews, conference reports

MAJOR CONTENT AREAS: Anthropology, ecology, housing and renewal, industrial sociology, modernization, professions,
sociology of science, social ideology, social
institutions, social issues, social policy

TOPICS PREFERRED: History of technology

INAPPROPRIATE TOPICS: Technological benefits/disbenefits to society

NUMBER OF MANUSCRIPT COPIES: 2	PAGE CHARGES: No	
REVIEW PERIOD: 16-20 wks	STYLE REQUIREMENTS: Chicago Manuscript	
PUBLICATION LAG TIME: 6-9 months	STYLE SHEET: Yes	
EARLY PUBLICATION OPTION: No	REVISED THESES: Acceptable	
ACCEPTANCE RATE: 20%	STUDENT PAPERS: Acceptable	
AUTHORSHIP RESTRICTIONS: No	REPRINT POLICY: 25	

SUBSCRIPTION ADDRESS: University of Chicago Press
5801 Ellis Avenue
Chicago, IL 60637

ANNUAL SUBSCRIPTION RATE: $15 individual, $20 institutional
INDEXED/ABSTRACTED IN: HA, SA

CIRCULATION: 2200   FREQUENCY: Quarterly

JOURNAL TITLE: TECHNOLOGY ASSESSMENT

MANUSCRIPT ADDRESS: Marvin J. Cetron, Editor
Forecasting International
1500 Wilson Blvd.
Arlington, VA 22209

TYPE OF ARTICLES: Not given

MAJOR CONTENT AREAS: Not given

TOPICS PREFERRED: Acceptable approaches to the use and
abuse of technology

INAPPROPRIATE TOPICS: Not given

NUMBER OF MANUSCRIPT COPIES: Not given	PAGE CHARGES: Not given	
REVIEW PERIOD: 4 months	STYLE REQUIREMENTS: Not given	
PUBLICATION LAG TIME: 2 months	STYLE SHEET: Not given	
EARLY PUBLICATION OPTION: Not given	REVISED THESES: Not given	
ACCEPTANCE RATE: 50%	STUDENT PAPERS: Not given	
AUTHORSHIP RESTRICTIONS: Not given	REPRINT POLICY: 0	

SUBSCRIPTION ADDRESS: Marvin J. Cetron, Editor
Forecasting International
1500 Wilson Blvd.
Arlington, VA 22209

ANNUAL SUBSCRIPTION RATE: $16 individual, $53 institutional
INDEXED/ABSTRACTED IN: Not given

CIRCULATION: 1000   FREQUENCY: Quarterly

JOURNAL TITLE: THEORY AND DECISION

MANUSCRIPT ADDRESS: Professor W. Leinfellner
Department of Philosophy
University of Nebraska
Lincoln, NE 68508

TYPE OF ARTICLES: Theoretical articles, research articles, review
articles

MAJOR CONTENT AREAS: Social policy, social structure, systems analysis,
urban sociology, philosophy of sociology & social
sciences

TOPICS PREFERRED: Methodological issues in the philosophy of science

INAPPROPRIATE TOPICS: Papers on general themes in social/physical
sciences

NUMBER OF MANUSCRIPT COPIES: 3	PAGE CHARGES:	No
REVIEW PERIOD: 3-6 mos.	STYLE REQUIREMENTS:	Not given
PUBLICATION LAG TIME: 6-12 months	STYLE SHEET:	Yes
EARLY PUBLICATION OPTION: No	REVISED THESES:	Yes
ACCEPTANCE RATE: 10%	STUDENT PAPERS:	Yes
AUTHORSHIP RESTRICTIONS: No	REPRINT POLICY:	25

SUBSCRIPTION ADDRESS: D. Reidel, Publishers
PO Box 17
Dordrecht, Holland

ANNUAL SUBSCRIPTION RATE: $26 individual, $44 institutional
INDEXED/ABSTRACTED IN: Not given

CIRCULATION: 1000   FREQUENCY: Quarterly

JOURNAL TITLE: THEORY AND SOCIETY

MANUSCRIPT ADDRESS: Department of Sociology
Box 1113
Washington University
St. Louis, MO 63130

TYPE OF ARTICLES: Research articles, theoretical articles, review
articles, social-historical studies

MAJOR CONTENT AREAS: Bureaucracy, communes, general sociology,
sociology of knowledge, mass media, popular
culture, sociology of science, sex roles,sexual
behavior, social change, social issues

TOPICS PREFERRED: Social historical studies of social change-
especially political and cultural change, and
theoretically informed social history

INAPPROPRIATE TOPICS: Not given

NUMBER OF MANUSCRIPT COPIES: 3	PAGE CHARGES:	No
REVIEW PERIOD: 2 months	STYLE REQUIREMENTS:	Not given
PUBLICATION LAG TIME: 6 months	STYLE SHEET:	Yes
EARLY PUBLICATION OPTION: Yes	REVISED THESES:	Yes
ACCEPTANCE RATE: 10%	STUDENT PAPERS:	No
AUTHORSHIP RESTRICTIONS: No	REPRINT POLICY:	50

SUBSCRIPTION ADDRESS: Elsevier Scientific Publishing Co.,Inc.
52 Vanderbilt Avenue
New York, NY 10017

ANNUAL SUBSCRIPTION RATE: $15 individual, $32 institutional
INDEXED/ABSTRACTED IN: Not given

CIRCULATION: 5000   FREQUENCY: Bimonthly

JOURNAL TITLE: TOGETHER

MANUSCRIPT ADDRESS: Jack Nichols, Editor
200 Park Avenue, South Suite 1101
New York, NY 10003

TYPE OF ARTICLES: Lay reading/self help guidance in matters
relating to sexuality and relationships, research
articles, case studies, commentaries

MAJOR CONTENT AREAS: Adolescence, communes, counseling, deviant
behavior, family planning, health and illness,
marriage & divorce, public health, sex roles,
sexual behavior, social change, social issues

TOPICS PREFERRED: Sexuality and relationships

INAPPROPRIATE TOPICS: Not given

NUMBER OF MANUSCRIPT COPIES: Not given   PAGE CHARGES: No
REVIEW PERIOD: 1 month   STYLE REQUIREMENTS: New York Times
PUBLICATION LAG TIME: 5-10 months   STYLE SHEET: Yes
EARLY PUBLICATION OPTION: No   REVISED THESES: No
ACCEPTANCE RATE: 40%   STUDENT PAPERS: No
AUTHORSHIP RESTRICTIONS: No   REPRINT POLICY: 1

SUBSCRIPTION ADDRESS: 200 Park Avenue, South Suite 1101
New York, NY 10003

ANNUAL SUBSCRIPTION RATE: $10 individual, Not given - institutional
INDEXED/ABSTRACTED IN: Not given

CIRCULATION: 200,000   FREQUENCY: Monthly

JOURNAL TITLE: TOWN PLANNING REVIEW

MANUSCRIPT ADDRESS: Department of Civic Design
The University of Liverpool
PO Box 147
Liverpool, L69 3BX, England

TYPE OF ARTICLES: Research articles, theoretical articles, review
articles, case studies, commentaries

MAJOR CONTENT AREAS: Community development, demography, housing and
renewal, social planning, population, systems
analysis, transportation, urban sociology

TOPICS PREFERRED: Town and regional planning, landscape design, rural
planning, transport planning, social planning,
public policy

INAPPROPRIATE TOPICS: Geography research

NUMBER OF MANUSCRIPT COPIES: 2   PAGE CHARGES: No
REVIEW PERIOD: 3 months STYLE REQUIREMENTS: Not given
PUBLICATION LAG TIME: 6-9 months   STYLE SHEET: Yes
EARLY PUBLICATION OPTION: No   REVISED THESES: Acceptable
ACCEPTANCE RATE: 5-10%   STUDENT PAPERS: No
AUTHORSHIP RESTRICTIONS: No   REPRINT POLICY: 3 journals

SUBSCRIPTION ADDRESS: Periodicals Department
Liverpool University Press
123 Grove Street
Liverpool, L7 7AF, England

ANNUAL SUBSCRIPTION RATE: $30 individual, $30 institutional
INDEXED/ABSTRACTED IN: Not given

CIRCULATION: 1800   FREQUENCY: Quarterly

JOURNAL TITLE: TRANSACTION/SOCIETY

MANUSCRIPT ADDRESS: Irvin L. Horowitz, Editor
Rutgers University
New Brunswick, NJ 08903

TYPE OF ARTICLES: Research articles, case studies, review articles

MAJOR CONTENT AREAS: Collective behavior, ethnic groups, migration,
religion, sexual behavior, social issues, society
and institutions, urban sociology, sociology
of work

TOPICS PREFERRED: Not given

INAPPROPRIATE TOPICS: Not given

NUMBER OF MANUSCRIPT COPIES: 2   PAGE CHARGES: No
REVIEW PERIOD: 2-3 mos. STYLE REQUIREMENTS: Chicago Manuscript
PUBLICATION LAG TIME: 6 months   STYLE SHEET: Yes
EARLY PUBLICATION OPTION: Yes   REVISED THESES: No
ACCEPTANCE RATE: 10-15%   STUDENT PAPERS: No
AUTHORSHIP RESTRICTIONS: Yes   REPRINT POLICY: None

SUBSCRIPTION ADDRESS: Rutgers University
New Brunswick, NJ 08903

ANNUAL SUBSCRIPTION RATE: $12 individual, $15 institutional
INDEXED/ABSTRACTED IN: Not given

CIRCULATION: 45,000-50,000   FREQUENCY: Bimonthly

JOURNAL TITLE: UNIVERSITY OF CHICAGO SCHOOL REVIEW

MANUSCRIPT ADDRESS: Benjamin D. Wright, Editor
Dept. of Education, University of Chicago
5801 Ellis Avenue
Chicago, IL 60637
TYPE OF ARTICLES: Research articles, theoretical articles, and
philosophical inquiry

MAJOR CONTENT AREAS: Not given

TOPICS PREFERRED: Education and social change

INAPPROPRIATE TOPICS: Not given

NUMBER OF MANUSCRIPT COPIES: Not given   PAGE CHARGES: Not given
REVIEW PERIOD: 1-3 months STYLE REQUIREMENTS: Not given
PUBLICATION LAG TIME: 3-12 months   STYLE SHEET: Not given
EARLY PUBLICATION OPTION: Not given   REVISED THESES: Not given
ACCEPTANCE RATE: 5%   STUDENT PAPERS: Not given
AUTHORSHIP RESTRICTIONS: Not given   REPRINT POLICY: 0

SUBSCRIPTION ADDRESS: Benjamin D. Wright, Editor
Dept. of Education, University of Chicago
5801 Ellis Avenue
Chicago, IL 60637
ANNUAL SUBSCRIPTION RATE: $10 individual, $14 institutional
INDEXED/ABSTRACTED IN: Not given

CIRCULATION: 4200   FREQUENCY: Quarterly

JOURNAL TITLE: URBAN AFFAIRS QUARTERLY

MANUSCRIPT ADDRESS: Louis Masotti
Center for Urban Affairs
Northwestern University
Evanston, IL 60201

TYPE OF ARTICLES: Research articles, theoretical articles,
review articles, case studies, commentaries

MAJOR CONTENT AREAS: Community development, demography, housing and
renewal, transportation, urban sociology

TOPICS PREFERRED: Not given

INAPPROPRIATE TOPICS: Not given

NUMBER OF MANUSCRIPT COPIES:	3	PAGE CHARGES: No
REVIEW PERIOD:	Not given	STYLE REQUIREMENTS: Not given
PUBLICATION LAG TIME:	Not given	STYLE SHEET: Yes
EARLY PUBLICATION OPTION:	No	REVISED THESES: Not given
ACCEPTANCE RATE:	Not given	STUDENT PAPERS: No
AUTHORSHIP RESTRICTIONS:	No	REPRINT POLICY: 24

SUBSCRIPTION ADDRESS: Sage Publications
275 S Beverly Drive
Beverly Hills, CA 90212

ANNUAL SUBSCRIPTION RATE: $14.40 individual, $24 institutional
INDEXED/ABSTRACTED IN: SUSA, HRA, SA, ASW, ABC PS, SEA, UAA, SPAA, IPSA,
CC, PAIS, EI, SSCI, SSI

CIRCULATION: Not given   FREQUENCY: Quarterly

JOURNAL TITLE: URBAN AND SOCIAL CHANGE REVIEW

MANUSCRIPT ADDRESS: Managing Editor
McGuinn Hall
Boston College
Chestnut Hill, MA 02167

TYPE OF ARTICLES: Review articles, theoretical articles, research
articles, unsolicited book reviews

MAJOR CONTENT AREAS: Aging and aged, family planning, social planning,
public health, social change, social issues,
social movements, social policy, social theory,
community development, alcoholism & drug abuse

TOPICS PREFERRED: Social welfare planning and program development

INAPPROPRIATE TOPICS: Sociological perspectives

NUMBER OF MANUSCRIPT COPIES:	2	PAGE CHARGES: No
REVIEW PERIOD:	1-3 mos.	STYLE REQUIREMENTS: Chicago Manuscript
PUBLICATION LAG TIME:	1-3 months	STYLE SHEET: Yes
EARLY PUBLICATION OPTION:	No	REVISED THESES: No
ACCEPTANCE RATE:	10%	STUDENT PAPERS: Yes
AUTHORSHIP RESTRICTIONS:	No	REPRINT POLICY: 5

SUBSCRIPTION ADDRESS: Subscription Manager
McGuinn Hall
Boston College
Chestnut Hill, MA 02167

ANNUAL SUBSCRIPTION RATE: $5 individual, $8 institutional
INDEXED/ABSTRACTED IN: Not given

CIRCULATION: 5000-6000   FREQUENCY: Biannually

JOURNAL TITLE: URBAN ANTHROPOLOGY

MANUSCRIPT ADDRESS: Dr. Jack R. Rollwagen
Department of Anthropology
SUNY College at Brockport
Brockport, NY 14420

TYPE OF ARTICLES: Research articles, theoretical articles, case studies

MAJOR CONTENT AREAS: Anthropology, community development, ethnic groups, migration, minorities, modernization, poverty, inequality, and policy, race relations, social change, social institutions, social issues

TOPICS PREFERRED: Urban anthropology

INAPPROPRIATE TOPICS: Not given

NUMBER OF MANUSCRIPT COPIES:	3	PAGE CHARGES: No
REVIEW PERIOD:	2 months	STYLE REQUIREMENTS: AA
PUBLICATION LAG TIME:	6 months	STYLE SHEET: Yes
EARLY PUBLICATION OPTION:	Yes	REVISED THESES: Acceptable
ACCEPTANCE RATE:	30-40%	STUDENT PAPERS: Acceptable
AUTHORSHIP RESTRICTIONS:	No	REPRINT POLICY: None

SUBSCRIPTION ADDRESS: Plenum Publishing Corporation
227 West 17th Street
New York, NY 10011

ANNUAL SUBSCRIPTION RATE: Not given - individual, $50 institutional
INDEXED/ABSTRACTED IN: AA, SUSA, GA, CC, SSCI

CIRCULATION: 500   FREQUENCY: Quarterly

JOURNAL TITLE: URBAN EDUCATION

MANUSCRIPT ADDRESS: Warren Button
Educational Studies
State University of New York
Buffalo, NY 14260

TYPE OF ARTICLES: Research articles, theoretical articles, review articles, case studies, commentaries

MAJOR CONTENT AREAS: Educational sociology, urban sociology

TOPICS PREFERRED: Not given

INAPPROPRIATE TOPICS: Not given

NUMBER OF MANUSCRIPT COPIES:	2	PAGE CHARGES: No
REVIEW PERIOD:	Not given	STYLE REQUIREMENTS: Not given
PUBLICATION LAG TIME:	Not given	STYLE SHEET: Yes
EARLY PUBLICATION OPTION:	No	REVISED THESES: Not given
ACCEPTANCE RATE:	Not given	STUDENT PAPERS: No
AUTHORSHIP RESTRICTIONS:	No	REPRINT POLICY: 24

SUBSCRIPTION ADDRESS: Sage Publications
275 S Beverly Drive
Beverly Hills, CA 90212

ANNUAL SUBSCRIPTION RATE: $13.50 individual, $22.50 institutional
INDEXED/ABSTRACTED IN: HRA, SUSA, EAA, UAA, SEA, ERIC/TE, CIJE, BII, CC, SSCI

CIRCULATION: Not given   FREQUENCY: Quarterly

JOURNAL TITLE: URBAN LIFE AND CULTURE

MANUSCRIPT ADDRESS: Peter Manning
Department of Sociology
Michigan State University
East Lansing, MI

TYPE OF ARTICLES: Research articles, theoretical articles, review
articles, case studies, commentaries

MAJOR CONTENT AREAS: Social interaction, urban sociology

TOPICS PREFERRED: Not given

INAPPROPRIATE TOPICS: Not given

NUMBER OF MANUSCRIPT COPIES:	3	PAGE CHARGES:	No
REVIEW PERIOD:	Not given	STYLE REQUIREMENTS:	Not given
PUBLICATION LAG TIME:	Not given	STYLE SHEET:	Yes
EARLY PUBLICATION OPTION:	No	REVISED THESES:	Not given
ACCEPTANCE RATE:	Not given	STUDENT PAPERS:	No
AUTHORSHIP RESTRICTIONS:	No	REPRINT POLICY:	24

SUBSCRIPTION ADDRESS: Sage Publications, Inc.
275 S Beverly Drive
Beverly Hills, CA 90212

ANNUAL SUBSCRIPTION RATE: $13.50 individual, $22.50 institutional
INDEXED/ABSTRACTED IN: APC, SA, HRA, SUSA, CIJE, SSCI, PAIS, CC

CIRCULATION: Not given   FREQUENCY: Quarterly

JOURNAL TITLE: WAR ON HUNGER

MANUSCRIPT ADDRESS: Office of Public Affairs, AID, Room 4886
State Department Building
Washington, DC 20523

TYPE OF ARTICLES: Research articles, case studies, review articles

MAJOR CONTENT AREAS: Economy and society, family formation, family
planning, human development, population, poverty,
inequality, and policy, public health, rural
sociology, social change, social conflict
TOPICS PREFERRED: World health, hunger & disease

INAPPROPRIATE TOPICS: Not given

NUMBER OF MANUSCRIPT COPIES:	3	PAGE CHARGES:	No
REVIEW PERIOD:	1 month	STYLE REQUIREMENTS:	Not given
PUBLICATION LAG TIME:	1-3 months	STYLE SHEET:	Yes
EARLY PUBLICATION OPTION:	Yes	REVISED THESES:	No
ACCEPTANCE RATE:	25%	STUDENT PAPERS:	Acceptable
AUTHORSHIP RESTRICTIONS:	No	REPRINT POLICY:	Unlimited

SUBSCRIPTION ADDRESS: Office of Public Affairs, AID, Room 4886
State Department Building
Washington, DC 20523

ANNUAL SUBSCRIPTION RATE: No charge
INDEXED/ABSTRACTED IN: U.S. Government Publication List

CIRCULATION: 40,000   FREQUENCY: Monthly

JOURNAL TITLE: WAR/PEACE REPORT

MANUSCRIPT ADDRESS: Richard Hudson, Editor
Gordon & Breach Science Publishers
218 East 18th Street
New York, NY 10003
TYPE OF ARTICLES: Not given

MAJOR CONTENT AREAS: Not given

TOPICS PREFERRED: Fact and opinion on progress toward a world
of peace and justice

INAPPROPRIATE TOPICS: Not given

NUMBER OF MANUSCRIPT COPIES:	Not given	PAGE CHARGES:	Not given
REVIEW PERIOD:	2 weeks	STYLE REQUIREMENTS:	Not given
PUBLICATION LAG TIME:	2-3 months	STYLE SHEET:	Not given
EARLY PUBLICATION OPTION:	Not given	REVISED THESES:	Not given
ACCEPTANCE RATE:	10%	STUDENT PAPERS:	Not given
AUTHORSHIP RESTRICTIONS:	Not given	REPRINT POLICY:	0

SUBSCRIPTION ADDRESS: Richard Hudson, Editor
Gordon & Breach Science Publishers
218 East 18th Street
New York, NY 10003
ANNUAL SUBSCRIPTION RATE: $9.50 individual, $19.50 institutional
INDEXED/ABSTRACTED IN: Not given

CIRCULATION: 6000   FREQUENCY: Bimonthly

JOURNAL TITLE: THE WEST AFRICAN JOURNAL OF SOCIOLOGY AND
POLITICAL SCIENCE
MANUSCRIPT ADDRESS: Justin Labinjoh
Faculty of the Social Sciences
University of Ibadan Sociology Department
Ibadan, Nigeria
TYPE OF ARTICLES: Research articles, theoretical articles, case
studies, review articles, commentaries,
unsolicited book reviews
MAJOR CONTENT AREAS: Bureaucracy, collective behavior, communes, indus-
trial sociology, organizations, political
sociology, popular culture, sociology of science,
social change
TOPICS PREFERRED: Developmental studies

INAPPROPRIATE TOPICS: Not given

NUMBER OF MANUSCRIPT COPIES:	3	PAGE CHARGES:	No
REVIEW PERIOD:	3 months	STYLE REQUIREMENTS:	Chicago Manuscript
PUBLICATION LAG TIME:	9 months	STYLE SHEET:	No
EARLY PUBLICATION OPTION:	Yes	REVISED THESES:	Yes
ACCEPTANCE RATE:	10%	STUDENT PAPERS:	Yes
AUTHORSHIP RESTRICTIONS:	No	REPRINT POLICY:	25

SUBSCRIPTION ADDRESS: University of Exeter
Exeter, England

ANNUAL SUBSCRIPTION RATE: $15 individual, $30 institutional
INDEXED/ABSTRACTED IN: Not given

CIRCULATION: 2000   FREQUENCY: Quarterly

JOURNAL TITLE: WISCONSIN SOCIOLOGIST

MANUSCRIPT ADDRESS: George K. Floro, Editor
Department of Sociology
University of Wisconsin - Eau Claire
Eau Claire, WI 54701

TYPE OF ARTICLES: Research articles, theoretical articles, case
studies, commentaries, review articles, unsolicited
book reviews

MAJOR CONTENT AREAS: Not given

TOPICS PREFERRED: Not given

INAPPROPRIATE TOPICS: Not given

NUMBER OF MANUSCRIPT COPIES: 3	PAGE CHARGES:	No
REVIEW PERIOD: 2 months	STYLE REQUIREMENTS:	ASA
PUBLICATION LAG TIME: 6 months	STYLE SHEET:	No
EARLY PUBLICATION OPTION: Not given	REVISED THESES:	No
ACCEPTANCE RATE: 33%	STUDENT PAPERS:	No
AUTHORSHIP RESTRICTIONS: No	REPRINT POLICY:	1 journal

SUBSCRIPTION ADDRESS: George K. Floro, Editor
Department of Sociology
University of Wisconsin - Eau Claire
Eau Claire, WI 54701

ANNUAL SUBSCRIPTION RATE: $4 individual, $6 institutional

INDEXED/ABSTRACTED IN: SA

CIRCULATION: 350   FREQUENCY: Tri-yearly

JOURNAL TITLE: WOMEN'S STUDIES: AN INTERDISCIPLINARY JOURNAL

MANUSCRIPT ADDRESS: Wendy Martin, Editor
Queens College
City University of New York
Flushing, NY 11367

TYPE OF ARTICLES: Research articles, literary criticism, review
articles,

MAJOR CONTENT AREAS: Anthropology, family formation, marriage & divorce,
medical sociology, reference groups, sex roles,
sexual behavior, social change, social conflict,
social ideology, social structure, social theory

TOPICS PREFERRED: Not given

INAPPROPRIATE TOPICS: Sex role differences, male domination

NUMBER OF MANUSCRIPT COPIES: 3	PAGE CHARGES:	No
REVIEW PERIOD: 6 months	STYLE REQUIREMENTS:	MLA
PUBLICATION LAG TIME: 2 1/2 years	STYLE SHEET:	No
EARLY PUBLICATION OPTION: No	REVISED THESES:	No
ACCEPTANCE RATE: 10%	STUDENT PAPERS:	No
AUTHORSHIP RESTRICTIONS: No	REPRINT POLICY:	1

SUBSCRIPTION ADDRESS: Gordon & Breach Science Publishers
42 William IV Street
London W.C. 2 England

ANNUAL SUBSCRIPTION RATE: $14.50 individual, $14.50 institutional

INDEXED/ABSTRACTED IN: Not given

CIRCULATION: 2000   FREQUENCY: Tri-yearly

JOURNAL TITLE: WORKLIFE

MANUSCRIPT ADDRESS: U.S. Department of Labor
601 D Street, NW - Room 10414
Washington, DC 20213

TYPE OF ARTICLES: Research articles, case studies, theoretical
articles

MAJOR CONTENT AREAS: Alcoholism & drug abuse, counseling, ethnic groups,
human development, labor force/labor relations,
migration, rehabilitation, social institutions,
social issues, sociology of work
TOPICS PREFERRED: Employment and training for jobs

INAPPROPRIATE TOPICS: Not given

NUMBER OF MANUSCRIPT COPIES:	1	PAGE CHARGES:	No
REVIEW PERIOD:	6 weeks	STYLE REQUIREMENTS:	U.S. Government
PUBLICATION LAG TIME:	12 weeks	STYLE SHEET:	Yes
EARLY PUBLICATION OPTION:	No	REVISED THESES:	No
ACCEPTANCE RATE:	50%	STUDENT PAPERS:	No
AUTHORSHIP RESTRICTIONS:	No	REPRINT POLICY:	None

SUBSCRIPTION ADDRESS: Superintendent of Documents
U.S. Government Printing Office
Washington, DC 20402

ANNUAL SUBSCRIPTION RATE: $15.30 individual, $15.30 institutional
INDEXED/ABSTRACTED IN: Not given

CIRCULATION: 26,000   FREQUENCY: Monthly

JOURNAL TITLE: WORLD POLITICS

MANUSCRIPT ADDRESS: 112 Corwin Hall
Princeton University
Princeton, NJ 08540

TYPE OF ARTICLES: Theoretical articles, research articles, review
articles, case studies, commentaries, unsolicited
book reviews

MAJOR CONTENT AREAS: Administrative behavior, bureaucracy, mass
communication, economy and society, family
planning, law, modernization, political sociology,
social change, social policy, systems analysis
TOPICS PREFERRED: Not given

INAPPROPRIATE TOPICS: Not given

NUMBER OF MANUSCRIPT COPIES:	2	PAGE CHARGES:	No
REVIEW PERIOD:	1-3 mos.	STYLE REQUIREMENTS:	Not given
PUBLICATION LAG TIME:	6-12 months	STYLE SHEET:	Yes
EARLY PUBLICATION OPTION:	No	REVISED THESES:	No
ACCEPTANCE RATE:	15%	STUDENT PAPERS:	Acceptable
AUTHORSHIP RESTRICTIONS:	No	REPRINT POLICY:	100

SUBSCRIPTION ADDRESS: Princeton University Press
Princeton, NJ 08540

ANNUAL SUBSCRIPTION RATE: $10 individual, $20 institutional
INDEXED/ABSTRACTED IN: ABC PS , BRI, CRIS, PAIS, SSI, USPSD, BRD, HA,
IPSA
CIRCULATION: 4,500   FREQUENCY: Quarterly

JOURNAL TITLE: YOUNG CHILDREN

MANUSCRIPT ADDRESS: NAEYC
1834 Connecticut Avenue, NW
Washington, DC 20009

TYPE OF ARTICLES: Practical articles, review articles, research
articles, theoretical articles

MAJOR CONTENT AREAS: Educational sociology, ethnic groups, human
development

TOPICS PREFERRED: Early childhood education, child development,
teacher education

INAPPROPRIATE TOPICS: Not given

NUMBER OF MANUSCRIPT COPIES: 3	PAGE CHARGES:	No
REVIEW PERIOD: 10-12 wks	STYLE REQUIREMENTS:	Chicago Manuscript
PUBLICATION LAG TIME: Not given	STYLE SHEET:	Yes
EARLY PUBLICATION OPTION: No	REVISED THESES:	Acceptable
ACCEPTANCE RATE: 10%	STUDENT PAPERS:	No
AUTHORSHIP RESTRICTIONS: No	REPRINT POLICY:	2 journals

SUBSCRIPTION ADDRESS: NAEYC
1834 Connecticut Avenue, NW
Washington, DC 20009

ANNUAL SUBSCRIPTION RATE: $12 individual, $12 institutional
INDEXED/ABSTRACTED IN: EI, PA/CDA, RA, M-MRI, ED

CIRCULATION: 31,000   FREQUENCY: Bimonthly

JOURNAL TITLE: YOUTH AND SOCIETY

MANUSCRIPT ADDRESS: David Gottlieb
College of Social Sciences
University of Houston
Houston, TX 77004
TYPE OF ARTICLES: Research articles, theoretical articles

MAJOR CONTENT AREAS: Educational sociology

TOPICS PREFERRED: Not given

INAPPROPRIATE TOPICS: Not given

NUMBER OF MANUSCRIPT COPIES: 3	PAGE CHARGES:	No
REVIEW PERIOD: Not given	STYLE REQUIREMENTS:	Not given
PUBLICATION LAG TIME: Not given	STYLE SHEET:	Yes
EARLY PUBLICATION OPTION: No	REVISED THESES:	Not given
ACCEPTANCE RATE: Not given	STUDENT PAPERS:	No
AUTHORSHIP RESTRICTIONS: No	REPRINT POLICY:	24

SUBSCRIPTION ADDRESS: Sage Publications
275 S Beverly Drive
Beverly Hills, CA 90212

ANNUAL SUBSCRIPTION RATE: $13.50 individual, $22.50 institutional
INDEXED/ABSTRACTED IN: ASW, SA, SEA, HA, A:HL, HRA, SUSA, SSCI, CC

CIRCULATION: Not given   FREQUENCY: Quarterly

JOURNAL TITLE: ADMINISTRATION IN SOCIAL WORK

MANUSCRIPT ADDRESS: Simon Slavin, Editor
School of Social Administration
Temple University
Philadelphia, Pennsylvania   19122
TYPE OF ARTICLES: Research, review, theoretical, case studies

MAJOR CONTENT AREAS: Administrative behavior; bureaucracy; human organizations; labor relations; leadership; minorities;
occupations & careers; social planning; social change;
social issues; social policy; society & institutions
TOPICS PREFERRED: Those pertaining to social agency management

INAPPROPRIATE TOPICS: Not given

NUMBER OF MANUSCRIPT COPIES: 3   PAGE CHARGES: None
REVIEW PERIOD: 2 months   STYLE REQUIREMENTS: APA
PUBLICATION LAG TIME: 6-12 months   STYLE SHEET: Yes
EARLY PUBLICATION OPTION: No   REVISED THESES: Yes
ACCEPTANCE RATE: Not yet known   STUDENT PAPERS: Yes
AUTHORSHIP RESTRICTIONS: None   REPRINT POLICY: 10 free

SUBSCRIPTION ADDRESS: The Haworth Press
149 Fifth Avenue
New York, New York   10010

ANNUAL SUBSCRIPTION RATE: $22 individuals; $34 institutions
INDEXED/ABSTRACTED IN: Abstracts for Social Workers; Sociological
Abstracts; Hospital Literature Index; Current Contents
CIRCULATION: 3,500   FREQUENCY: Quarterly

JOURNAL TITLE: ALTERNATIVES: Marriage, Family & Changing Lifestyles

MANUSCRIPT ADDRESS: Roger Libby, Ph.D., Editor
Dept. of Sociology & Anthropology
University of New Hampshire
Durham, New Hampshire   03824
TYPE OF ARTICLES: Research, theoretical, review articles,
commentaries

MAJOR CONTENT AREAS: Marriage & divorce; communes; deviant behavior; family
formation; sexual behavior; sex roles; reference groups;
family planning; counseling; human development; popular
culture; social structure; social theory; systems analysis
TOPICS PREFERRED: Those dealing with the integration between changing sex
roles, psychosexual orientation and sexual expression
through alternative lifestyles
INAPPROPRIATE TOPICS: Descriptive studies of cohabitation or child-free marriages
with no theoretical framework

NUMBER OF MANUSCRIPT COPIES: 3   PAGE CHARGES: No
REVIEW PERIOD: 1-2 months STYLE REQUIREMENTS: ASA
PUBLICATION LAG TIME: 5-6 months   STYLE SHEET: Yes
EARLY PUBLICATION OPTION: Yes   REVISED THESES: If appropriate
ACCEPTANCE RATE: 10-20%   STUDENT PAPERS: Yes
AUTHORSHIP RESTRICTIONS: None   REPRINT POLICY: 25

SUBSCRIPTION ADDRESS: Sage Publications
275 S. Beverly Drive
Beverly Hills, California   90212

ANNUAL SUBSCRIPTION RATE: $13.50 individuals; $27.00 institutions
INDEXED/ABSTRACTED IN: Not yet known (new journal)

CIRCULATION: Not yet known   FREQUENCY: Quarterly

JOURNAL TITLE: AMERICAN QUARTERLY

MANUSCRIPT ADDRESS: Box 1, Logan Hall CN
University of Pennsylvania
Philadelphia, Pennsylvania   19174

TYPE OF ARTICLES: Research, historical, unsolicited book reviews

MAJOR CONTENT AREAS: History & systems; American culture

TOPICS PREFERRED: Interdisciplinary articles analyzing
American society, past and present

INAPPROPRIATE TOPICS: Topics that are too narror or pertain only
to one discipline

NUMBER OF MANUSCRIPT COPIES: Not given
REVIEW PERIOD: 3 months
PUBLICATION LAG TIME: 6 months
EARLY PUBLICATION OPTION: No
ACCEPTANCE RATE: 5%
AUTHORSHIP RESTRICTIONS: None

PAGE CHARGES: None
STYLE REQUIREMENTS: MLA
STYLE SHEET: Yes
REVISED THESES: Not given
STUDENT PAPERS: Not given
REPRINT POLICY: 25 free

SUBSCRIPTION ADDRESS: American Studies Association
4025 Chestnut Street
Philadelphia, Pennsylvania   19174

ANNUAL SUBSCRIPTION RATE: $15
INDEXED/ABSTRACTED IN: ASW, AES, HA, MLA, SSHI, SSCI, WSA

CIRCULATION: 5,500   FREQUENCY: Not given

JOURNAL TITLE: BRITISH JOURNAL OF SOCIAL WORK

MANUSCRIPT ADDRESS: Prof. P. Parsloe, Univ. of Aberdeen
Dept of Social Work - King's College
Old Aberdeen AB9 2UB   Scotland

TYPE OF ARTICLES: Research, review, theoretical, practice-oriented

MAJOR CONTENT AREAS: Social work and social services

TOPICS PREFERRED: Discussions of social work practice

INAPPROPRIATE TOPICS: Ph.D. theses of no relevance to social work

NUMBER OF MANUSCRIPT COPIES: 3
REVIEW PERIOD: 4-6 weeks
PUBLICATION LAG TIME: Variable
EARLY PUBLICATION OPTION: No
ACCEPTANCE RATE: 25%
AUTHORSHIP RESTRICTIONS: None

PAGE CHARGES: None
STYLE REQUIREMENTS: Own style
STYLE SHEET: Yes
REVISED THESES: Not given
STUDENT PAPERS: Not given
REPRINT POLICY: 25 free

SUBSCRIPTION ADDRESS: British Association of Social Workers
16 Kent Street
Birmingham B5 6RD   England

ANNUAL SUBSCRIPTION RATE: $30
INDEXED/ABSTRACTED IN: PA, ASW, CC, SSCI

CIRCULATION: 3,000   FREQUENCY: Quarterly

JOURNAL TITLE: CHILDREN TODAY

MANUSCRIPT ADDRESS: Office of Child Development
P.O. Box 1182
Washington, DC 20013

TYPE OF ARTICLES: Research, review, theoretical, program descriptions,
commentaries

MAJOR CONTENT AREAS: Educational sociology, material related to
child development and services for children

TOPICS PREFERRED: Those describing innovative programs designed to
improve the health, education, and welfare of children
and families

INAPPROPRIATE TOPICS: Case studies involving too few subjects

NUMBER OF MANUSCRIPT COPIES: Not given	PAGE CHARGES: None
REVIEW PERIOD: 2-4 months	STYLE REQUIREMENTS: MLA
PUBLICATION LAG TIME: 2-8 months	STYLE SHEET: Yes
EARLY PUBLICATION OPTION: No	REVISED THESES: Not given
ACCEPTANCE RATE: 10%	STUDENT PAPERS: Not given
AUTHORSHIP RESTRICTIONS: None	REPRINT POLICY: 25 copies of issue

SUBSCRIPTION ADDRESS: Superintendent of Documents
U.S. Government Printing Office
Washington, DC 20402

ANNUAL SUBSCRIPTION RATE: $6.10
INDEXED/ABSTRACTED IN: PA, ASW, EI, others

CIRCULATION: 29,000   FREQUENCY: Not given

JOURNAL TITLE: CONTEMPORARY DRUG PROBLEMS

MANUSCRIPT ADDRESS: Editor, CDP
111 Broadway
New York, N.Y. 10006

TYPE OF ARTICLES: Research, theoretical

MAJOR CONTENT AREAS: Social and legal aspects of drug abuse

TOPICS PREFERRED: Drug use and abuse; trends, treatment, social
policy and drug abuse

INAPPROPRIATE TOPICS: Statistical surveys

NUMBER OF MANUSCRIPT COPIES: 2	PAGE CHARGES: Not given
REVIEW PERIOD: 45 days	STYLE REQUIREMENTS: Own style
PUBLICATION LAG TIME: 4 months	STYLE SHEET: Yes
EARLY PUBLICATION OPTION: No	REVISED THESES: Not given
ACCEPTANCE RATE: 10-15%	STUDENT PAPERS: Not given
AUTHORSHIP RESTRICTIONS: None	REPRINT POLICY: Not given

SUBSCRIPTION ADDRESS: 95 Morton Street
New York, N.Y. 10014

ANNUAL SUBSCRIPTION RATE: $20 individuals; $24 institutions
INDEXED/ABSTRACTED IN: EM, CC, ASW

CIRCULATION: 3,000   FREQUENCY: Quarterly

JOURNAL TITLE: DEVELOPMENTAL PSYCHOLOGY

MANUSCRIPT ADDRESS: Richard D. Odom, Editor
Dept. of Psychology
Vanderbilt University
Nashville, Tennessee   37240

TYPE OF ARTICLES: Research, review, brief reports

MAJOR CONTENT AREAS: Developmental psychology

TOPICS PREFERRED: Research papers clearly delineating developmental
concepts and implications

INAPPROPRIATE TOPICS: None

NUMBER OF MANUSCRIPT COPIES: 3	PAGE CHARGES: None	
REVIEW PERIOD: Varies	STYLE REQUIREMENTS: APA	
PUBLICATION LAG TIME: 8-9 months	STYLE SHEET: None	
EARLY PUBLICATION OPTION: No	REVISED THESES: Not given	
ACCEPTANCE RATE: 18%	STUDENT PAPERS: Not given	
AUTHORSHIP RESTRICTIONS: None	REPRINT POLICY: 20 free	

SUBSCRIPTION ADDRESS: American Psychological Association
1200 17th Street NW
Washington, DC 20036

ANNUAL SUBSCRIPTION RATE: $30
INDEXED/ABSTRACTED IN: PA, others

CIRCULATION: 5,000   FREQUENCY: Not given

JOURNAL TITLE: ETHOS

MANUSCRIPT ADDRESS: Dept of Anthropology
UCLA
Los Angeles, California   90024

TYPE OF ARTICLES: Research, theoretical

MAJOR CONTENT AREAS: Cross-cultural psychology and psychiatry

TOPICS PREFERRED: Research demonstrating the relationship between
cultural patterns and individual behavior

INAPPROPRIATE TOPICS: None

NUMBER OF MANUSCRIPT COPIES: Not given	PAGE CHARGES: None	
REVIEW PERIOD: 2 months	STYLE REQUIREMENTS: AAA	
PUBLICATION LAG TIME: Not given	STYLE SHEET: Yes	
EARLY PUBLICATION OPTION: No	REVISED THESES: Not given	
ACCEPTANCE RATE: 40%	STUDENT PAPERS: Not given	
AUTHORSHIP RESTRICTIONS: None	REPRINT POLICY: 25 free	

SUBSCRIPTION ADDRESS: Univ of California Press
Univ of California at Berkeley
Berkeley, California   94720

ANNUAL SUBSCRIPTION RATE: $12 individuals; $16 institutional
INDEXED/ABSTRACTED IN: Not given

CIRCULATION: 600   FREQUENCY: Not given

JOURNAL TITLE: HIGH SCHOOL BEHAVIORAL SCIENCE

MANUSCRIPT ADDRESS: Dr. Robert Mendelsohn, Editor
IAPS, Adelphi University
Garden City, N.Y. 11530

TYPE OF ARTICLES: Research, review, theoretical, book review,
descriptions of high school programs

MAJOR CONTENT AREAS: Behavioral science teaching at the pre-college
level

TOPICS PREFERRED: High school sociology curricula

INAPPROPRIATE TOPICS: Social science topics inapplicable to the
pre-college level

NUMBER OF MANUSCRIPT COPIES: 2   PAGE CHARGES: None
REVIEW PERIOD: 3-4 monthsSTYLE REQUIREMENTS: APA
PUBLICATION LAG TIME: 6-8 months   STYLE SHEET: Yes
EARLY PUBLICATION OPTION: No   REVISED THESES: Not given
ACCEPTANCE RATE: 65%   STUDENT PAPERS: Not given
AUTHORSHIP RESTRICTIONS: None   REPRINT POLICY: 1 free

SUBSCRIPTION ADDRESS: Human Sciences Press
72 Fifth Avenue
New York, N.Y. 10011

ANNUAL SUBSCRIPTION RATE: $6.95 individuals; $15 institutions
INDEXED/ABSTRACTED IN: PA, CIJE

CIRCULATION: 1,000   FREQUENCY: Biannual

JOURNAL TITLE: HUMAN STUDIES

MANUSCRIPT ADDRESS: George Psathas, Editor
Department of Sociology
Boston University
Boston, Massachusetts 02215
TYPE OF ARTICLES: Theoretical, research, case studies, review
articles, unsolicited book reviews, commentaries

MAJOR CONTENT AREAS: General sociology, sociology of knowledge,
sociology of science, social theory, social
philosophy, ethno-methodology, studies based on or
oriented to phenomenological or existential approaches
TOPICS PREFERRED: Phenomenological and existential approaches in
the social sciences--particularly ethno-methodology

INAPPROPRIATE TOPICS: Not given

NUMBER OF MANUSCRIPT COPIES: 3   PAGE CHARGES: No
REVIEW PERIOD: 3 months STYLE REQUIREMENTS: ASA
PUBLICATION LAG TIME: 1 year   STYLE SHEET: Yes
EARLY PUBLICATION OPTION: No   REVISED THESES: Yes
ACCEPTANCE RATE: 50%   STUDENT PAPERS: No
AUTHORSHIP RESTRICTIONS: None   REPRINT POLICY: None

SUBSCRIPTION ADDRESS: Ablex Publishing
355 Chestnut Street
Norwood, New Jersey 07648

ANNUAL SUBSCRIPTION RATE: Individuals: $15.00; Institutions: not given
INDEXED/ABSTRACTED IN: Not yet known

CIRCULATION: 500   FREQUENCY: Quarterly

8888

8888888888

JOURNAL TITLE: INTERNATIONAL JOURNAL OF CRIMINOLOGY & PENOLOGY

MANUSCRIPT ADDRESS: Prof. W.H. Nagel
4 Oegstgeest
Warmondermy 4, The Netherlands

TYPE OF ARTICLES: Theoretical, review

MAJOR CONTENT AREAS: Criminology and penology

TOPICS PREFERRED: Theoretical and comparative issues

INAPPROPRIATE TOPICS: None

NUMBER OF MANUSCRIPT COPIES: 3 — PAGE CHARGES: None
REVIEW PERIOD: Not given — STYLE REQUIREMENTS: Not given
PUBLICATION LAG TIME: Not given — STYLE SHEET: Yes
EARLY PUBLICATION OPTION: No — REVISED THESES: Not given
ACCEPTANCE RATE: 35% — STUDENT PAPERS: Not given
AUTHORSHIP RESTRICTIONS: Not given — REPRINT POLICY: 50 free

SUBSCRIPTION ADDRESS: Academic Press, Inc.
111 Fifth Avenue
New York, N.Y. 10003

ANNUAL SUBSCRIPTION RATE: $24.50
INDEXED/ABSTRACTED IN: ACP, CC

CIRCULATION: 550 — FREQUENCY: Not given

JOURNAL TITLE: INTERNATIONAL JOURNAL OF FAMILY THERAPY

MANUSCRIPT ADDRESS: Gerald Zuk, Ph.D., Editor
Eastern Pennsylvania Psychiatric Institute
Henry Avenue at Abbottsford Road
Philadelphia, Pennsylvania 19129
TYPE OF ARTICLES: Research, theoretical, case studies, review,
commentaries, unsolicited book reviews

MAJOR CONTENT AREAS: Marriage & family, family planning, family
formation, sexual behavior, divorce, adolescence,
aging, religion & values, human development,
mental health
TOPICS PREFERRED: Family therapy. All family-focused topics are
relevant, provided they have relevance for clinical
practice or prevention
INAPPROPRIATE TOPICS: Not given

NUMBER OF MANUSCRIPT COPIES: 3 — PAGE CHARGES: Not yet known
REVIEW PERIOD: 60-90 days — STYLE REQUIREMENTS: APA
PUBLICATION LAG TIME: not yet known — STYLE SHEET: No
EARLY PUBLICATION OPTION: No — REVISED THESES: Yes
ACCEPTANCE RATE: not yet known — STUDENT PAPERS: No
AUTHORSHIP RESTRICTIONS: None — REPRINT POLICY: Not yet known

SUBSCRIPTION ADDRESS: Human Sciences Press
72 Fifth Avenue
New York, N.Y. 10011

ANNUAL SUBSCRIPTION RATE: Not yet known (new journal)
INDEXED/ABSTRACTED IN: Not yet known

CIRCULATION: Not yet known — FREQUENCY: Quarterly

JOURNAL TITLE: JOURNAL OF SPECIAL EDUCATION

MANUSCRIPT ADDRESS: 3515 Woodhaven Road
Philadelphia, Pennsylvania   19154

TYPE OF ARTICLES: Research, review, theoretical, commentaries

MAJOR CONTENT AREAS: Educational sociology, mental retardation

TOPICS PREFERRED: Carefully documented articles from all
social science disciplines that pertain to
special education

INAPPROPRIATE TOPICS: Case studies with inappropriate or undersized
samples

NUMBER OF MANUSCRIPT COPIES:	2	PAGE CHARGES:	None
REVIEW PERIOD:	3 months	STYLE REQUIREMENTS:	APA
PUBLICATION LAG TIME:	12 months	STYLE SHEET:	Yes
EARLY PUBLICATION OPTION:	None	REVISED THESES:	Not given
ACCEPTANCE RATE:	5-10%	STUDENT PAPERS:	Not given
AUTHORSHIP RESTRICTIONS:	None	REPRINT POLICY:	20 free

SUBSCRIPTION ADDRESS: Grune & Stratton, Inc.
111 Fifth Avenue
New York, N.Y. 10003

ANNUAL SUBSCRIPTION RATE: $18.50
INDEXED/ABSTRACTED IN: PA, CC, others

CIRCULATION: 3,500   FREQUENCY: Quarterly

JOURNAL TITLE: JOURNAL OF SOCIAL SERVICE RESEARCH

MANUSCRIPT ADDRESS: S.K. Khinduka, Chairman, Editorial Board
George Warren Brown School of Social Work
St. Louis, Missouri   63130

TYPE OF ARTICLES: Research

MAJOR CONTENT AREAS: All areas pertaining to research and the
social services

TOPICS PREFERRED: Same as above

INAPPROPRIATE TOPICS: Those of poor quality

NUMBER OF MANUSCRIPT COPIES:	3	PAGE CHARGES:	None
REVIEW PERIOD:	2-3 months	STYLE REQUIREMENTS:	APA
PUBLICATION LAG TIME:	7-12 months	STYLE SHEET:	Yes
EARLY PUBLICATION OPTION:	No	REVISED THESES:	Yes
ACCEPTANCE RATE:	20%	STUDENT PAPERS:	Yes
AUTHORSHIP RESTRICTIONS:	None	REPRINT POLICY:	10 free

SUBSCRIPTION ADDRESS: The Haworth Press
149 Fifth Avenue
New York, N.Y. 10010

ANNUAL SUBSCRIPTION RATE: $20 individuals; $35 institutions
INDEXED/ABSTRACTED IN: Not yet known (new journal)

CIRCULATION: Not yet known   FREQUENCY: Quarterly

JOURNAL TITLE: MANKIND QUARTERLY

MANUSCRIPT ADDRESS: 1 Darnaway Street
Edinburgh EH3 6DW   Scotland

TYPE OF ARTICLES: Research

MAJOR CONTENT AREAS: Ethnology, anthropology, demography, race relations

TOPICS PREFERRED: Same as above

INAPPROPRIATE TOPICS: None

NUMBER OF MANUSCRIPT COPIES: 3	PAGE CHARGES:	None
REVIEW PERIOD: 2-3 weeks	STYLE REQUIREMENTS:	Own style
PUBLICATION LAG TIME: 1-2 years	STYLE SHEET:	Yes
EARLY PUBLICATION OPTION: No	REVISED THESES:	Not given
ACCEPTANCE RATE: 90%	STUDENT PAPERS:	Not given
AUTHORSHIP RESTRICTIONS: None	REPRINT POLICY:	12 free

SUBSCRIPTION ADDRESS: 1 Darnaway Street
Edinburgh EH3 9DW   Scotland

ANNUAL SUBSCRIPTION RATE: $12
INDEXED/ABSTRACTED IN: Not given

CIRCULATION: 1,500   FREQUENCY: Not given

JOURNAL TITLE: QUALITATIVE SOCIOLOGY

MANUSCRIPT ADDRESS: Editor, "Qualitative Sociology"
University of Baltimore Dept of Sociology
Charles at Mount Royal
Baltimore, Maryland   21201
TYPE OF ARTICLES: all are considered

MAJOR CONTENT AREAS: almost all areas of sociology

TOPICS PREFERRED: not given

INAPPROPRIATE TOPICS: not given

NUMBER OF MANUSCRIPT COPIES: 4	PAGE CHARGES:	No
REVIEW PERIOD: 3 months	STYLE REQUIREMENTS:	ASA
PUBLICATION LAG TIME: 8 months	STYLE SHEET:	No
EARLY PUBLICATION OPTION: No	REVISED THESES:	Not given
ACCEPTANCE RATE: 7%	STUDENT PAPERS:	Not given
AUTHORSHIP RESTRICTIONS: None	REPRINT POLICY:	6 plus 2 journals

SUBSCRIPTION ADDRESS: Same as editorial address

ANNUAL SUBSCRIPTION RATE: $14 individuals; $18 institutions
INDEXED/ABSTRACTED IN: SA

CIRCULATION: 1,500   FREQUENCY: Triennial

JOURNAL TITLE: SIGNS: Journal of Women in Culture & Society

MANUSCRIPT ADDRESS: 307 Barnard Hall
Barnard College
New York, N.Y.   10027

TYPE OF ARTICLES: Research, review, theoretical

MAJOR CONTENT AREAS: Family formation, health & illness, human
development, marriage & divorce, mental health,
occupations & careers, popular culture, reference groups,
sex roles, sexual behavior, social change, socialization
TOPICS PREFERRED: All areas as applied to women; those contributing
to theory and offering an interdisciplinary methodology

INAPPROPRIATE TOPICS: Narrow research reports; sex differences in college
students along a narrow dimension

NUMBER OF MANUSCRIPT COPIES: 3	PAGE CHARGES:	None
REVIEW PERIOD: 4-6 months	STYLE REQUIREMENTS:	Chicago
PUBLICATION LAG TIME: 12-18 months	STYLE SHEET:	Yes
EARLY PUBLICATION OPTION: Yes	REVISED THESES:	Not given
ACCEPTANCE RATE: 3-5%	STUDENT PAPERS:	Not given
AUTHORSHIP RESTRICTIONS: None	REPRINT POLICY:	50 free

SUBSCRIPTION ADDRESS: University of Chicago Press
11030 Langley Avenue
Chicago, Illinois   60628

ANNUAL SUBSCRIPTION RATE: $12 individuals; $16 institutions
INDEXED/ABSTRACTED IN: Not yet known

CIRCULATION: 8,000   FREQUENCY: Quarterly

JOURNAL TITLE: SOCIAL WORK IN HEALTH CARE

MANUSCRIPT ADDRESS: Sylvia S. Clarke, ACSW
Director, Social Work Department
The Roosevelt Hospital
New York, N.Y. 10019
TYPE OF ARTICLES: Research, review, case studies, theoretical,
commentaries

MAJOR CONTENT AREAS: Health & illness; adolescence; aging; medical
sociology; alcoholism & drug abuse; mental health &
illness

TOPICS PREFERRED: Those relevant to social work practice in
health settings

INAPPROPRIATE TOPICS: None

NUMBER OF MANUSCRIPT COPIES: 3	PAGE CHARGES:	None
REVIEW PERIOD: 2-12 weeks	STYLE REQUIREMENTS:	APA
PUBLICATION LAG TIME: 6-10 months	STYLE SHEET:	Yes
EARLY PUBLICATION OPTION: None	REVISED THESES:	Yes
ACCEPTANCE RATE: 30%	STUDENT PAPERS:	Yes
AUTHORSHIP RESTRICTIONS: None	REPRINT POLICY:	10 free

SUBSCRIPTION ADDRESS: The Haworth Press
149 Fifth Avenue
New York, N.Y. 10010

ANNUAL SUBSCRIPTION RATE: $20 individuals; $36 institutions
INDEXED/ABSTRACTED IN: Abstracts for Social Workers; Index Medicus;
Hospital Literature Index; Psychological Abstracts; SA
CIRCULATION: 3,000   FREQUENCY: Quarterly

JOURNAL TITLE: SOCIOLOGICAL FORUM

MANUSCRIPT ADDRESS: Russell H. Meier, Editor
Northeast Louisiana University
Monroe, Louisiana   71209

TYPE OF ARTICLES: Research, theoretical, case studies,
commentaries, short research reports

MAJOR CONTENT AREAS: all aspects of sociology

TOPICS PREFERRED: no preference

INAPPROPRIATE TOPICS: none

NUMBER OF MANUSCRIPT COPIES: 4
REVIEW PERIOD: 3 months
PUBLICATION LAG TIME: 6 months
EARLY PUBLICATION OPTION: No
ACCEPTANCE RATE: 20%
AUTHORSHIP RESTRICTIONS: No

PAGE CHARGES: no
STYLE REQUIREMENTS: ASA
STYLE SHEET: Yes
REVISED THESES: Yes
STUDENT PAPERS: No
REPRINT POLICY: 5 journal issues

SUBSCRIPTION ADDRESS: Transactions Periodicals
Rutgers-The State University
New Brunswick, New Jersey   08903

ANNUAL SUBSCRIPTION RATE: $12 individuals; $15 institutions
INDEXED/ABSTRACTED IN: not yet known (new journal)

CIRCULATION: 700   FREQUENCY: Semi-annual

SUBJECT , TITLE, AND KEYWORD INDEX

This Index will refer the reader to the page numbers on which journals are listed. Journals are listed by title, subject, and key words within their title.

In addition, if a journal's editor indicated a clear preference for certain types of manuscripts, these "manuscript preference subject areas" are also included as indexing terms. The reader will therefore be able to search for appropriate journals for article submission according to the general subject areas in which his or her article falls.